KITNE GHAZI AAYE
KITNE GHAZI GAYE

KITNE GHAZI AAYE
KITNE GHAZI GAYE

My Life Story

Lt Gen. K.J.S. *'Tiny'* Dhillon (Retd)

PENGUIN

VEER

An imprint of Penguin Random House

PENGUIN VEER

USA | Canada | UK | Ireland | Australia
New Zealand | India | South Africa | China

Penguin Veer is part of the Penguin Random House group of companies
whose addresses can be found at global.penguinrandomhouse.com

Published by Penguin Random House India Pvt. Ltd
4th Floor, Capital Tower 1, MG Road,
Gurugram 122 002, Haryana, India

Penguin
Random House
India

First published in Penguin Veer by Penguin Random House India 2023

Copyright © Lt Gen. K.J.S. Dhillon (Retd) 2023

Photographs courtesy of Lt Gen. K.J.S. Dhillon (Retd),
Brigadier Trigunesh Mukherjee (Retd) and Chinar Media Archives

ISBN 9780670097050

Typeset in Adobe Caslon Pro by MAP Systems, Bengaluru, India
Printed at Thomson Press India Ltd, New Delhi

www.penguin.co.in

I dedicate this book to four generations of four wonderful women in my life: my grandmother, mother, wife and daughter; and our son.

I bow my head in reverence to the memory of, and moral values and teachings imparted by my maternal grandmother (Naniji), without whose care and fighting spirit I may never have become what I am today. Thank you, 'Bijee'.

I also pay obeisance to the unmatched strength and courage of my mother, who inspired me throughout my personal and professional life. My mother may not have been physically present in my life, but the memory of her prowess has steered me through the toughest challenges and, time and again, honed me as a son, husband, father, soldier of the Indian Army and, above all, an Indian who was always taught to walk tall and fight hard for his motherland.

My wife, Nita, has especially been a pillar of strength and a constant companion over the last thirty-five years of our married life, supporting me through the most challenging times in this journey. Thank you, Nita, for being there, through the good and not-so-good times. You were my unshakeable pillar when everything around me was wavering.

And our daughter has been my biggest positive critic, from the way I dress to my choice of music to my (mis)pronunciation.

Last, but not least, I want to thank the bedrock of the family, our son, a quiet witness to all the momentous happenings in my life, who very rarely says anything, but when he does, his laconic comment, 'mast hai', conveys everything.

Contents

CONTENTS

1

Inspired by the Fighting Spirit of a Fearless Mother

Kitne Ghazi Aaye, Kitne Ghazi Gaye . . .

'*Kitne Ghazi Aaye, Kitne Ghazi Gaye*', this seminal phrase was first used during the press conference at Badami Bagh Cantonment[1], headquarters of the Indian Army's 15 Corps, on 19 February 2019, post the elimination of the Pakistani terrorist Kamran alias Ghazi of the proscribed terrorist group Jaish-e-Mohammed. The phrase has become synonymous with the valour of the Indian Armed Forces that have relentlessly combated—and continue to do so every day—many anti-India elements like the above-mentioned Pakistani terrorist, who masterminded the

---

1 Please refer to https://www.aninews.in/news/national/general-news/as-hizbul-gets-new-chief-top-general-tweets-kitne-ghazi-aaye-kitne-ghazi-gaye20200510235754/. In addition, please refer to https://www.newindianexpress.com/nation/2022/jan/31/operation-maa-author-in-kashmir-lieutenant-general-kjs-dhillon-hangs-up-his-boots-2413559.html (accessed on 29 June 2022)

dastardly IED (improvised explosive device) attack on a convoy of Central Reserve Police Force (CRPF) personnel in Pulwama, Kashmir, on the fateful day of 14 February 2019. Ghazi, like many before him, was annihilated by the security forces within 100 hours of the barbarous incident engineered by him. But at a more synergistic level, this phrase succinctly articulates the trajectory of my life: a life lived in the constant shadow of uncertainty, with fearlessness and faith in the professional integrity of my soldiers and officers being the only imperative for survival.

Shermaar Maa

I am told that the genesis of my boldness stemmed from my mother's womb, a mother whom I lost at the young age of three years, but who has intrinsically shaped my character, subconsciously guiding me in every endeavour throughout my chequered life as a soldier, husband, father and, above all, an Indian. She was always present in her absence. In early 1964, when my civil engineer father received a foreign deputation to Nepal immediately after his first posting in Lutyens' Delhi, little would he have imagined what lay in store for him and his family. One of his morning strolls with my mother in the chilly Nepalese winter on 19 December 1964 ended in a lethal encounter with a wild animal, which ravaged my unsuspecting parents, inflicting heavy wounds on my father who was almost mauled to death by the beast. My father still carries the scars and paw marks of that misadventure on his wrist, ankle and neck. Even as he was helplessly looking death in the eye, the real hero of the incident was my mother, who, standing tall at 5' 8", despite being grievously injured herself but unfazed by the savagery of the beast, managed to gather her wits and flung her shawl around its neck, wringing it mercilessly till she knocked the breath out of the animal. She thus saved her husband from certain death through her sheer pluck and courage. Both my parents were grievously injured, but while my father survived his wounds, life was not so kind to my mother. As she lay fighting for life in the hospital in a remote hamlet of Nepal, she was administered an injection that had travelled more than 100 km, all the way from Gorakhpur in Uttar Pradesh, in a flask that became contaminated due to storage under suboptimal temperature. My mother succumbed to the dual impact of her injuries and an infection on 20 January 1965, but her courage has lived on, earning her the moniker of 'Shermaar' or lion-slayer. The day Ghazi was neutralized for perpetrating an assault on the protectors of our motherland thus inadvertently took me back to the day years ago when my mother too had faced a similar brutal attack. The memory of her courage lives on, constantly inspiring me to face the collective threat of all the Ghazis who have come and gone.

My mother, 'Jindaan', with my father, circa 1957

Kitne Jaggi Aaye, Kitne Jaggi Gaye . . .

The roots of the phrase '*Kitne Ghazi Aaye, Kitne Ghazi Gaye*' lay in an incident of my childhood, the evocative memories of which take me back to my maternal uncle's place in my home state of Punjab,

3

where I spent all my formative years under the guardianship of my Naniji (my maternal grandmother), or 'Bijee' as we all called her. One evening, my cousin and I, aged seven and nine years, respectively, after winning an intense game of marbles against a local lad called Jaggi, were ecstatic at defeating him but he refused to give us the marbles and was spoiling for a fight. Unwilling to get into any fracas with Jaggi, the bully, my cousin suggested that we should let the matter rest and quietly return home. However, I became adamant about retrieving the marbles, which were rightfully ours, egging my cousin on with the bluster, *'Kitne Jaggi aaye aur kitne Jaggi gaye'*. Eventually, we were victorious and left with both our 'property' and pride intact. Like the incantation of Wordsworthian memory, it was perhaps this incident that subconsciously emerged from the recesses of my mind decades later in Pulwama, again impelling me not to retreat in the face of bullying, no matter how fearful or challenging the situation may be.

'Bijee', my grandmother (Naniji) Sardarni Labh Kaur

Childhood . . . Made Me a Man Ahead of My Time

There was more grief and drama in store in my eventful childhood. After my mother's demise, my father, having remarried, decided to stay on in Nepal and had two younger sons later, whereas my elder brother and I moved to live with Bijee and our maternal uncles in rural Punjab, visiting Nepal mostly during our school vacations. While the elder uncle was in the Army, the younger one joined the Border Security Force (BSF), and I used to watch both of them with awe and admiration as they donned their uniforms, which also sowed the seeds of my secret ambition to wear such a uniform one day. This desire was further reinforced as another tragedy shook my life yet again on 16 February 1974, merely nine years after the first one, when my elder brother, Jasbir Singh Dhillon, 'Lalli Veer' as I used to call him respectfully, met with a fatal road accident as the scooter he was riding was hit by a truck. A 1969-make Seiko 5 watch that he was wearing on that fateful day fell off his hand during the evacuation to the hospital. This watch was found by an honest rickshaw-puller who brought it to our house the next day and handed it to me. I am wearing this watch till date and have always kept it in working condition even after fifty-odd years as a memento. Having lost both my mother and only sibling to violent deaths, I soon realized that the days of my carefree boyhood were over and I had to garner all my guts and gumption to fend for myself for the rest of my life. Notwithstanding the extreme love, affection and care of my Nani, maternal uncles and father, with the passage of time and encounters with the real world, this feeling crystallized into an intense solitude and self-dependence, and I found myself well and truly on my own, with no 'immediate' family to fall back upon As I grew older and more aware of life's realities, there seemed no letter place than the Army to shape the tragedies of my earlier years into the tenacity of a 'pucca' soldier. The grit and determination to be utterly honest to my job while serving the nation without fear have characterized my entire career in the Army, with my seniors too at times admonishing me for taking too many risks. But that is who

I am, and that is how my tale will unfold through the narrative of my experiences and escapades in the rest of the book.

My mother with my elder brother, Lalli Veer, circa 1958

My elder brother, Jasbir Singh Dhillon, aka Lalli Veer, circa 1974

With my elder brother and younger brother, Sukhbir, circa 1973

With my brothers, circa 1969

With my elder brother, circa 197

My grandmother carrying my one-and-a-half-month-old
elder brother, Lalli Veer, along with my mother and father in
Delhi on 29 September 1957

An Adolescence Laced with Blithe Mischief

Although my early childhood was mired in tragedy and loss,
reminiscences of the subsequent years of my youth spent in the
comfort of my grandmother's lap and home are filled with numerous
naughty anecdotes. The first incident that comes to mind is one of an
innocent deception that I, along with a few young cousins, practised
on my Nani. She was a very religious person, and it is due to this
reason she was a staunch vegetarian. However, our band of boys loved
to eat *kukkad* (chicken dish) and were always on the lookout for an
opportunity to cook and consume it slyly in the absence of my Nani,
as cooking it in her presence was an absolute 'no-no'. We looked
forward to her weekly outings to attend the satsangs every Sunday,
when she would be away for a full three hours. This was our period of
'carnivorous consumption', as it were, when we would gather all the
raw material for the dish, cook, eat and clean up, leaving no trace of
the chicken in the kitchen. And on the few occasions when there was
a mistiming, and we watched her early return from our perch atop the
terrace, would have to abort our culinary adventure midway and
discard the half-cooked dish to destroy all evidence before Nani could

get a whiff of what was cooking behind her back. Those culinary skills came in very handy during my National Defence Academy (NDA) and Indian Military Academy (IMA) training camps later and even as a married man on certain occasions.

I recall another incident when my younger uncle (Mamaji or my Mom's brother), a BSF officer, was engaged to a lecturer in a local girls' college. While he was posted in Kashmir, his fiancée would often come home to meet Bijee. One day, she decided to take Bijee for a movie along with her friends, and when I insisted that I too wanted to accompany them, I was sternly told that I had to stay home. Full of resentment at this affront, I decided to get back at the women by planning something nasty. I uprooted all the colourful plants from Bijee's carefully curated flower bed and re-planted them superfluously in the soil. When the movie party returned, they did not immediately see anything fishy, but a couple of days later, when the plants started dying one by one, Bijee got suspicious and asked me what was going on. I replied with a straight face that this would happen again if she went for a movie without me next time. Do I need to further elaborate on the events that followed?

My maternal uncle (Mamaji), Guravtar Singh Sandhu,
my inspiration, circa 1972

With one of my uncles, Kulwant Singh, circa 1974

The Road to NDA

The impish mischief that was the hallmark of my stay at Bijee's house gradually coalesced into a profound desire to channelize my inner aggression into a positive force, and joining the Armed Forces clearly seemed the way to go. The opportunity presented itself when I moved from Bijee's residence in a small town to a hostel in the relatively bigger town of Ferozepur. One of my classmates, Haresh Jang Bahadur, who had an Army family background with four of his elder brothers having joined the NDA, and who was keen to follow in the footsteps of his elder siblings, always motivated all the boys in the class to appear for the NDA examination. In fact, he was so committed to the idea that he fetched the NDA entrance forms from the local recruiting office and even proceeded to fill them up himself on behalf of all the other class fellows.

We decided to pander to his obsession and were even ready to go to Patiala to appear for the exams as our town did not have an examination centre. However, the more important incentive for visiting Patiala was that it would give us a chance to watch the latest Hindi films that reached our hometown much later. So, with a comprehensive 'entertainment plus examination' plan in place, we headed for Patiala, and the itinerary went something like this: examination from 9 a.m. to 12 noon, followed by a sprint to the movie hall to catch the 12.30 p.m. to 3.30 p.m. show. On the day of the final examination, we had to leave the movie halfway and run to the bus stand to catch the last bus at 3 p.m. from Patiala to Ferozepur. A few months later, I headed to Nepal to visit my parents and two younger brothers for a brief vacation, and the NDA adventure was consigned to the backburner for the moment.

Fate, however, had other plans. As I was travelling in a bus to reach Ludhiana Railway Station for boarding the train to Lucknow and thereafter Gorakhpur and then Nepal, I borrowed the front page of a newspaper from the passenger sitting next to me in the bus to while away the time. My glance fell on a boxed notification on the front page announcing that the results of the NDA examination were available on an inside page. I hesitatingly requested for that particular page of the newspaper, curiously opened it and was dumbstruck to find my name on the list of successful candidates who had to report to the Services Selection Board (SSB), the next stage of selection. This unknown gentleman was the first-ever person to congratulate me and wish me well for what was to set the tone for the most enjoyable journey of my life. I could not help thinking that it was destiny that guided me to undertake that bus journey, and destiny again that suddenly produced that particular newspaper for me to see the results. It was obviously ordained that I would join the Indian Army, which is why everything fell into place in this incredible fashion; otherwise, I would never have made the effort to find out the NDA results.

Wooing My Father

Having cleared my SSB and medical examination, and finally making it into the merit list of successful candidates, another challenge was waiting for me—my father's absolute refusal to allow me to join the Army. I returned to Nepal to try and convince him to change his decision but he was adamant that I become a civil engineer. He also pointed out that the salary I would earn in the Army would not even match what he was paying his support staff helping in what was now a flourishing transport business. But being my mother's son, I too obstinately stood my ground, insisting that I was joining the Army not for the pay but for the pride and prestige it would entail. With neither of us budging from our decisions, I decided to use my *Brahmastra* (weapon capable of destroying creation and vanquishing all beings), that is, support from Bijee, who I knew would definitely stand by me.

I thus brought Bijee from Punjab to Nepal, and she urged my father (her son-in-law) to let me indulge this whim, and she even emotionally blackmailed my Dad by saying that she did not want to face the allegation from society that the boy could not be successful in life and fulfil his dreams as he was brought up by his maternal grandmother, away from his father. She also prudently suggested that my father could eventually persuade me to use the option of 'discharge by purchase', or obtaining a discharge from the military by making a stipulated payment, a procedure that is colloquially known as buying oneself out of service. In my heart of hearts, I knew that once I entered the NDA, I would never exit the Army, let alone attempt to buy myself out of it. But this olive branch seemed the best firefighting solution for the moment, and my father reluctantly allowed me to join the NDA. This tug-of-war between leaving and staying at the NDA continued between father and son for a full year during the first two terms of the NDA till it finally came to an end as a lost cause for one and a long hard journey ahead for the other. My Naniji, father, mother and youngest brother came for my NDA passing-out parade in December 1982. This helped in smoothening things between us a little, as my father finally seemed to have accepted my decision. After the NDA passing-out parade, my parents could not come to me at the place of my posting for fifteen long years till the time when my Dad visited me in Bhutan in 1997, where I was posted as a major. However, by this time, his initial days' opposition was replaced by a deep admiration and respect for the Army way of life and the bonhomie among every member of the team at that station, which he was witnessing in person there. His words of praise, admitting that I had actually 'made the right decision', have always stayed with me, eventually redeeming my choice of profession in the eyes of my father.

In a way, the Army also changed the trajectory of our family life, as, like me, my younger brothers too decided not to join my father's business and instead opted for professional careers—the elder one is a doctor settled in the US, and the younger one is a computer engineer in New Zealand. Bitterly complaining that if none of his three sons was ready to take the mantle from him, he had no reason to continue his work in a foreign land. My father thus wound up the business, selling all his trucks and buses to his drivers, who gradually paid back all the dues in convenient instalments. Thereafter, my parents packed their bags and moved back to Punjab, where they bought a house, and have been living a quiet retired life for the last thirty years.

All these extraordinary developments in my life have taught me to respect the ways of god and humbly accept what destiny has ordained. *Que sera sera*—what will be will be, and the future is not ours to see.

Having said that, life also taught me that at times it may be correct to stand up for the cause you feel is right. As Sri Guru Gobind Singh Ji, the tenth Sikh guru, mentioned in *Zafarnama*, the epistle of victory, addressed to the Mughal ruler Aurangzeb, '*Chu kar az hama heelte dar guzasht, Halal ast burdan ba shamsheer dast*', meaning 'Having exhausted all strategies/efforts to redress a wrong or resolve an issue, raising a sword is a pious and just decision'. In my case, asking Bijee to fight for my cause was probably that moment in my life but in the later years of my Army career, there came numerous occasions where this early lesson of life changed the course of things to come.

A 'High-Spirited' Drink

Notwithstanding our initial disagreement over my decision to join the Army, I have had some incredible moments with my Dad, and one incident that I would like to recount here is relatable to any *fauji* (army man) when he goes home. It is a highly anticipated event for both the soldier and his family, who look forward to meeting each other, often after a long time. While these meetings or reunions may not be called celebrations per se, the occasions are certainly special, as they entail a welcome meal or drink, or ardent meetings with neighbours, when we all sit together and reminisce about our experiences, as everyone back home is always curious to hear about Army life. In my case, every time I go home, my father looks forward to enjoying a drink with me, like an enthusiastic mixologist, preparing the ground for the jovial evening by keeping ready a pair of sparkling crystal glasses and an assortment of spirits.

One day, I was just passing through Punjab and stopped over at home for lunch. As I entered the house, I told my father, 'Dad, let's have a glass of vodka.' Since he generally does not drink during the day and prefers his Scotch in the evening, he responded, 'No, I'll take my usual drink. You go ahead and have your vodka.' I started mixing the drink with full vigour, adding an assortment of ingredients, including vodka, a dash of cocktail bitters, a little bit of ginger, a few fresh mint leaves, some sliced pickled onions and even a few green chillies. To top it all, I added some fresh lime and a few more spices, ending up with a really rich cocktail. Intrigued by this interesting recipe, my dad kept watching me add one ingredient after another to the drink and finally, unable to quell his emotions, he fulminated, with his typical Punjabi sarcasm, '*Beta, hunn ehde vich thoda jeha desi gheo paa ke tadka vi laga hi lai* (Why don't you also add a bit of *desi ghee* for roast and seasoning)!' Replying to his wry Punjabi humour, I had to explain to him that adding all these unique ingredients to the drink spices it up, not only making it tangier but also absorbing the bitterness of the vodka by suppressing it with the flavour of fresh vegetables. He did not seem very convinced though!

In the following chapters, I will take readers on an intimate journey through my Army life, peppering it with anecdotes and remembrances as we go along.

2

Destined to Become an Army Man

Early Association with 4th Battalion The Rajputana Rifles

Life in the Army is full of challenges, and for an officer, taking timely and correct decisions under adverse and life-threatening conditions is the ultimate responsibility that can make the difference between certain death and assured victory for the nation, the Army, his regiment and unit, his men and himself. Let me assure you here that no live-combat situation can ever be aptly described in any military pamphlet or taught in any military training classroom. The anecdotes I am narrating here reflect how various events at different points in my life have imparted strength of character, making me physically, mentally and emotionally imperturbable.

In retrospect, I realize that these diverse incidents, though seemingly unconnected to each other, were actually parts of a larger blueprint, woven together as microcosmic elements in the macrocosm of my life. One such interesting phase in my childhood occurred when I was studying in school at Ferozepur before joining the NDA in January 1980, and both my maternal uncles were also posted there. Providentially, the Army unit into which I was eventually commissioned, Fourth Battalion The Rajputana Rifles (4 RAJRIF), was also stationed in Ferozepur around this time. I enjoyed playing basketball but our school did not have a proper basketball ground. So, for our practice sessions, all the members of our school team used to visit the expansive basketball ground of 4 RAJRIF, which also had an outstanding basketball team of its own, including a few players who had represented the team at the services and national levels. As schoolkids, we used to have what were popularly known as friendly matches with the 4 RAJRIF team, and irrespective of whether we won or lost the match, we were always treated to steaming hot samosas and freshly made jalebis procured from the unit's wet canteen, which, needless to say, were always on the house for us. Hence, interestingly, the genesis of my career-long association with 4 RAJRIF began while I was still in school in the mid- to late-1970s, long before I was formally commissioned into the Army and joined the elite battalion on 17 December 1983. Interestingly, 4 RAJRIF was also famously called the 'Fleet Street Battalion' during the Second World War. The reference was to Fleet Street in London, where the offices of all the major newspapers were located during the Second World War, and since during the War, 4 RAJRIF was so often in the news because of its successful wartime operations, it earned the epithet 'Fleet Street Battalion'. And it was in this famous battalion that I began my Army career. Here, too, destiny seemed to be mediating, driving me close to my eventual destination in the Army during my formative years so that I could imbibe the fighting spirit and core values that characterize 4 RAJRIF long before my formal association with the unit. I must mention here that the samosas and jalebis, which we feasted on after our matches with the 4 RAJRIF team, continue to remain my favourite snacks till date in addition to choorma, a North Indian delicacy made of sugar and desi ghee, and lots of love, which is eagerly sought after by the troops of Rajputana Rifles, who mainly hail from Rajasthan and Haryana.

School Lessons Coalesce into Life Lessons

My school years in Ferozepur were, in fact, momentous years of my childhood, imparting life lessons and the 'never-say-die' spirit in the face of certain failures, in addition to academic learning. One such humorous incident occurred when I had messed up one of my examinations in the tenth standard and had been hauled up by Mr Juneja, the newly appointed principal, who had recently joined from a very reputed school in Delhi. I was asked by the principal to bring either my parents or local guardian to school for a suitable admonishment. Petrified, I sought the help of one Gurdeep Singh Sandhu, who was working in the office of my uncle as a mid-level executive. Incidentally, my uncle, Guravtar Singh Sandhu, shared the same initials as Gurdeep Singh Sandhu, which convinced me that it would be easy to pass him off as G.S. Sandhu in front of the new principal who had not met my uncle previously. Agreeing to accompany me to the school as my local guardian, he carried me pillion on his bicycle, ready to confront the principal's ire.

Everything was going as planned and the principal was quite congenial with my 'local guardian' till Murphy's Law played its part just when we were about to leave the principal's office. Gurdeep Singh got carried away, pompously stating that I was a good student and had even got a scholarship in my class the previous year. Nonplussed, the principal summoned my class teacher, Mr Manohar Lal Kakkar, to inquire as to how things could have gone so seriously wrong that a scholarship holder ended up with a poor performance. Mr Kakkar knew me well as I had been in the same school for the last three years, and his appearance on the scene would not bode well for me. Thus, realizing that the matter was getting out of hand due to my local guardian's overzealousness, both of us quietly slipped away.

This incident also indirectly conveys the message that it is not imperative for one to always perform well in all examinations in life or to get disheartened by an occasional poor performance, as these exams are stepping stones towards a larger pedagogical goal, the goal of proving one's mettle in real life. The second lesson I learnt from this episode involving Gurdeep Singh Sandhu was that while planning for an uncertain or first-time operation, the end state must always be well thought through and all contingencies that may arise must be considered, as I also learnt later in my military career that no plan survives the first contact with the enemy.

The Vacuum of a Mother's Affection

As I have mentioned earlier, my mother's death so early in my life left me with an inherent sense of deprivation that plagued me subconsciously, especially during my years of adolescence and immediately after being commissioned into the Army as a young officer. This feeling left me distinctly distressed on a particular occasion when the unit had moved to a peace station after an extremely difficult field tenure. I wanted to own a Bullet motorcycle and had even struck a deal with a family friend for his bike but could not buy it. When I pondered upon this denial in solitude, I could not help but feel that had my mother been alive, she would not have let her son go through such a situation. My childhood angst perhaps shaped my character, making me accept the fact that everything in life may not be available to me on a platter and I would have to toil for it. This incident, however, did not hamper my determination to own a Bullet (or *Bultt*, as it is colloquially called in Punjabi and I too prefer that). I approached my school classmate and NDA coursemate, then Lieutenant Harminder Singh Bhullar (aka Jimmy Bhullar, my closest friend till date), who immediately bought a second-hand bike at an amazing price because Bullet motorcycles were banned in Punjab in the mid-1980s and were thus available at good bargains. He even transported the *Bultt* by the Railways to Udaipur. In the absence of mobiles or online tracking systems, I would visit the Udaipur Railway Station every day to check if my 'First Love' or '*Bultt Meri Jaan*' had arrived. My determination to work hard towards acquiring whatever I wanted was also reflected in my choice of profession, which was an analogy for self-dependence and inner strength.

The feeling of a vacuum due to the lack of a mother's affection emerged very strongly when I was Corps Commander in Kashmir and was the kernel behind my idea of 'Operation Maa'. This initiative, which will be discussed in detail in a later chapter, was a watershed in counter-terrorism operations in Kashmir, as our attempt to enlist mothers' help in preventing their sons from becoming terrorists was unexpectedly successful, potentially deterring many young men from picking up arms against the nation. The core thought behind this operation was that 'no mother should be without a child and no child should be without a mother'.

My first 'Bultt', 1985

My Bultt today

Overcoming Childhood Fears

Like most children, I too was initially afraid of the dark, but even this fear was overcome through a very interesting situation during my teen years. My grandmother owned a buffalo but since her house was located a little away from habitation, at a distance of about 1 km from the nearest locality, leaving the buffalo outside the house at night posed a big risk of cattle theft, and we could not afford to lose this asset. Hence, the buffalo had to be paraded every night to a relative's house in the nearby locality and brought back the next morning. And being the youngest in the family at the time, this duty of marching the buffalo up and down invariably fell on my shoulders. The long walk with the animal during the night acclimatized me to the strange sounds and silences of the outback, which held me in good stead years later as an Army man, who could not afford to be ruled by fear of any kind. I am purposely narrating these incidents to help the young Army aspirants realize and understand that the mental build-up to joining the defence forces does not commence with the passing of a written examination or getting through an SSB or on physically joining the NDA/IMA/any other pre-commissioning training academy but is the sum total of all of life's teachings and experiences that shape the character of a soldier. And my advice to all who ask for tips for clearing the SSB is 'Just be yourself'.

The toughness of a soldier is manifested in both his work and play, and I too nurtured a love of sports and played inter-school basketball and kabaddi at various levels throughout my academic years. This, however, landed me in serious trouble once in the tenth standard when I injured my knee badly during a kabaddi game. Fearing that if I showed my injury to anyone at home, I would not be allowed to go for the practice sessions, I neglected the injury. I did not seek any medical attention and carried on all my activities normally, including cycling to school, until one day, I could no longer hide or ignore the festering wound. Noticing me limping, my Naniji started probing and we both found that gangrene had set in. With memories of my mother's death due to infection still fresh in her mind, she was reduced to tears and rushed me to a doctor, who was also shocked to see the laceration, which had become quite ugly by then and took a long time to heal. I guess the ability to withstand physical pain and overcoming unknown fears and mental stress at such a young age proved to be an asset on several occasions in the course of my perilous sojourns and counter-terrorism operations. During one such operation in Kashmir in 1999, I sustained an injury on my shin bone but did not report it and carried on until the end of the operation, till we had successfully eliminated the cordoned terrorists. Although they say that 'the Army teaches you to be tough', in my case, I suppose one could say that life had taught me to be tough even before joining the Army.

Death Be Not Proud

As with pain and injury, my encounters with death too cropped up unbidden on various occasions in my life. In his famous sonnet 'Death Be Not Proud', the renowned seventeenth-century English metaphysical poet John Donne describes death as a mighty and dreadful force. However, the most important caveat here is that no matter how tough you may be, nothing prepares you to take death in your stride, and death has stalked me and my dear ones throughout my life.

After the death of my mother and brother, the next person close to me who left this world too soon was my first cousin, my Mamaji's younger son, Major Harinder Pal Singh Sandhu, with whom I had spent many happy days of fun and frolic in Bijee's house. We had grown up together, playing not only marbles but countless other games like hockey, cricket and French cricket (a concocted version of the game, played between only two players, where the legs of the batsman act as wickets and the bowling is done from a rather close distance). He had also been my partner in crime as we took on the bully Jaggi when he was trying to swindle our marbles.

He was commissioned into the 6th Battalion, the Brigade of Guards, two years after me and subsequently served in the Rashtriya Rifles unit deployed in South Kashmir. On the fateful day of 23 December 1993, he made the supreme sacrifice while attempting to rescue his commanding officer whose vehicle was ambushed by terrorists close to his post near Bijbehara. I am certain the soldierly spirit of 'never say die' was in his mind when he rushed to the site of the encounter. He was awarded the Shaurya Chakra (posthumously) by the Honourable President of India for his act of gallantry, which was received by his wife. His untimely death at the age of thirty years, leaving behind two small children, a three-year-old daughter and a four-month-old son, apart from his young wife, was yet another personal loss and shock that was difficult to overcome. I still remember my last meeting with him, when I was posted in the Jammu sector. He had come on a short leave to see his newly born son and stayed the night with me on his return before rejoining duty at the Jammu transit camp prior to returning to his unit in Kashmir. The emptiness and intense pain that the passing of a loved one unleashes on you is magnified by the physical presence of inanimate objects in the same setting, which remain, but the human being associated with them is no longer around, such as the still-unfolded bedsheet on the bed in my house on which my cousin had slept a few nights before his fatal encounter with terrorists; a bedsheet that would no longer be used by him lying on a bed that he would never occupy again! His wife, a very brave lady, brought up her children in an exceptional manner and ensured the best quality education and subsequent professional training. The boy is a commercial pilot and the girl is working with an international airline.

All these tragedies in my life, involving the deaths of people close to me at work or at home, undoubtedly affected me immensely emotionally but definitely made me more committed to my duty as also physically and mentally stronger. These tormenting personal losses also underscored the impermanence of the journey through the transitory experience called 'life'. This realization is particularly stark in the Army, where the very next instant could lead to a deadly assault or a fatal encounter with the enemy or terrorists.

In fact, I have had many close encounters with death during my entire service career, fighting terrorists in Kashmir or the North-east of India, wherein coming face-to-face with live bullets could have killed me every single time. These omnipresent threats to my life, or the lives of my colleagues or subordinates, and actual death at times, have thus been almost a routine for me. But the grief deep inside me for the people I have lost in my personal or professional journey cannot be negated, and a part of me too has died each time there has been a fatal loss.

Here, I must reiterate that a soldier killing the adversary, including terrorists or enemy soldiers, as part of his duty also re-emphasizes the reality of death, for it was just a stroke of luck that the gods of death this time were kind to his side rather than theirs. The first and only fatal casualty that occurred in my command during my service until I took over as Chinar Corps Commander in January 2019 with seven tenures in counter-insurgency/counter-terrorism operations in the North-east or Jammu and Kashmir was that of Lance Naik Patey Tassuk, Bar to Sena Medal (Gallantry)—that is, winner of Sena Medals for two separate gallant acts. He was also from the Brigade of Guards, and at the time of his fatal encounter with terrorists, was serving in the Rashtriya Rifles Battalion deployed in North Kashmir where I was commanding a Rashtriya Rifles Sector as a brigadier. He hailed from Arunachal Pradesh and had a natural hunter instinct wherein he could actually sense the presence of a terrorist in a group merely by observing his style of walking or limb movements. The bravery of Lance Naik Patey Tassuk, and how the commanders cater to the welfare of the families of the bravehearts who make the supreme sacrifice for the nation, is narrated in greater detail later in this book.

The Hindi song 'Zindagi to bewafa hai, ek din thukrayegi, maut mehbooba hai, apne saath lekar jaayegi' (Life is treacherous and will one day betray you. Death, on the other hand, is your real lover as it will eventually take you along), from the movie Muqaddar ka Sikandar, is the most apt description of this harsh reality, and nowhere is it more applicable than in the life of a soldier, who flirts with death almost on a daily basis, be it to fight a foe, or hunt a hidden target, or just attempt to survive in the most hostile terrains and weather conditions he has to endure.

Death, for a soldier, is always a constant companion, but most of us never acknowledge it while in service as the concept of '*Paltan ki Izzat aur Desh ki Izzat*' (honour of the battalion and the nation) is the most dominant thought in our minds at the time. I, as an individual or more importantly as a soldier, am no different, as, since the age of three, death has been almost like a backdrop in my life and career, though I have never allowed it to emerge in the forefront.

In the forthcoming chapter, I will take my readers back to the very beginning, the onset of my Army life, the training and the numerous lessons and values I imbibed upon being commissioned as an officer of the Indian Army.

With my elder maternal uncle's (Mamaji) children, from left to right: Devinder (retd as Colonel), Tejinder (married to a Colonel), Harinder (Major, Shaurya Chakra [posthumously]), circa 1975

3

How It All Began: Cradle for Leadership

As I had mentioned before, my classmate in Ferozepur, Haresh Jang Bahadur, was responsible for my entry into the NDA, the cradle for leadership, as he motivated the entire class to apply for the NDA examination. After passing the examination, the result of which I had randomly seen in a newspaper during a bus journey, I returned to my Mamaji's home in Ferozepur to get ready for the next stage of the entry process, the SSB interview. I, along with another successful candidate and my long-time friend and classmate, Harminder Singh Bhullar, whom we affectionately call Jimmy Bhullar, enrolled in the Minerva Academy in Chandigarh to prepare for the interview. After successfully appearing for the interview, and also clearing the medical exam, both of which were held in Bhopal, I awaited the announcement of the merit list with tense anticipation until I received the call letter asking me to report for the training.

Before joining NDA, December 1979

A Tale of Two Trunks at Kalyan and Pune Railway Station

My momentous journey as a member of the Indian Army began on the evening of 2 January 1980, when Jimmy Bhullar and I boarded the Punjab Mail train from Ferozepur to Pune, carrying all our stuff in unique customized trunks (flattish and broad) that are specifically made for Army travel as they can be conveniently pushed under a train berth or a bed in a barracks and can easily be fitted into awkward grooves and niches. The voyage began with an interesting incident at Kalyan station where we had to switch trains for Pune. Since we were carrying a lot of luggage crammed to the brim in the two trunks, the ticket checker ordered us to pay a fine of Rs 80 for our overweight trunks, a royal sum in those days. Alarmed at this hurdle even before reaching our destination, we meekly told the ticket checker that the total cash both of us were carrying collectively was less than this amount, and we were in no position to pay the huge fine. So, the gentleman that he was, he took pity on two budding young soldiers of the nation and helped us by suggesting that we could do an inter-trunk transfer of the excess weight in one box, making the other one fine-free, while some excess items could be shoved into a shoulder bag (*jhola*) that was available at the railway station itself (he also told us where it was being sold). This exercise helped us balance the weight distribution in the trunks, thereby substantially reducing the fine. Needless to say, this early lesson also helped me in managing the weight of my luggage during my numerous travels by air or train later in life. The term 'manage' is frequently used in NDA/IMA and the Army, literally meaning 'Beg, Borrow or Steal' (metaphorically speaking) to turn an adverse situation to our advantage. We learnt our lessons well at Kalyan Railway Station on the morning of 4 January 1980, prior to even entering the hallowed gates of the NDA. Later in the evening, we arrived at Pune Railway Station.

Since we had reached Pune a day before the scheduled commencement of training on 5 January 1980, and having saved some precious cash at Kalyan Railway Station, we made elaborate plans to stay in a hotel for a day and binge-watch some of the latest movies, which was our favourite pastime. However, this was not to be as the subedar saab from NDA who was present at the railway station immediately recognized our trunks, bundled us along with our luggage into an Army 3-ton vehicle waiting outside, and took us to Ghorpuri, Pune, where the first-term training of NDA used to be conducted. This dashed our dreams of watching films, which would now be possible only when we would be granted 'Liberty', that is, permission to go to the city on a Sunday once or twice during the entire training term of six months.

Academy No. : 14156
Name: KANWALJEET SINGH DHILLON
Service: ARMY
SQN: A
Course: 63

14156 A 63 NDA Course—
my identity since
4 January 1980

Academy No. : 14157
Name: HARMINDER SINGH BHULLAR
Service: ARMY
SQN: F
Course: 63

14157 F 63 NDA Course—
Harminder Singh Bhullar aka
Jimmy Bhullar

The First Transgression

Our Army training was divided into two parts, with the first term of six months slated to take place in Ghorpuri in Pune, and the balance five terms in the main NDA campus at Khadakwasla. Just two months into the training, on the occasion of Holi, our group of about twelve cadets aged just around seventeen–eighteen years procured a bottle of local liquor to celebrate the festival, overriding the stipulation of prohibition of drinking throughout the training period at NDA. We merrily consumed the entire bottle (just imagine, one bottle of 750 ml among twelve!) and the repercussions were immediate as the empty bottle was discovered by the divisional officer (captain) the next day. As the offence was severe, we were marched up to the office of the Deputy Commandant, Commodore Vijay Singh Shekhawat, who subsequently rose to become the Admiral and Chief of the Naval Staff. Being the senior-most among all the transgressors, I was right at the front of the renegade group comprising twelve cadets. We were pretty sure that the punishment would be relegation, which implies losing one term at the NDA or becoming junior by six months, and being compelled to train with the next batch, which is a rather unpleasant experience.

As I stood crestfallen in his office, and the charge of 'consuming liquor' was read out, Commodore V.S. Shekhawat asked me crisply, looking directly into my eyes, 'Did you drink?' My innocent and honest reply was, 'Yes, sir'. The next question was even more stern and crisp, 'Why?' As per the drill square teachings, one is supposed to look directly into the eyes of the person one is talking to. I could see the smouldering lava in the eyes of the deputy commandant and knew exactly what lay in store for me and my eleven compatriots waiting outside for their respective turns to be marched in. My options to answer that blunt one-word question were 'Sorry, sir' or the rather longish but truthful explanation, 'Sir, I did not know that drinking on Holi is an offence as everyone in my family drinks on the day of Holi as a part of the celebrations'. I chose the latter and waited for the obvious outcome. However, my response must have struck an amicable chord with Commodore Shekhawat, as he smilingly replied, 'In my family too, drinking on Holi is a regular tradition.' With these words, he told me to 'March out', and to my utter amazement, spared the relegation, but we were awarded fourteen days' restrictions (certain physical drill and no 'Liberty' for the duration) instead. We all continued with our original course but it was a lesson well learnt, and we refrained from doing anything delinquent ever again, stringently adhering to all the rules and regulations. We were also careful never to drink again until the day when the platoon commander in the IMA, Captain Bharat Singh Sangwan, invited us to his home for a glass of beer as per the tradition, just a few days prior to our commissioning on 17 December 1983.

The 'Puri' that Never Was

'Liberty' is a concession given a few months after the commencement of NDA training when the cadet passes the drill square test, a test to check his proficiency in drill movements. Aptly named, 'Liberty' actually implies liberation or getting permission to make a short visit to Pune town on Sunday from 10 a.m. to 6 p.m., and is eagerly looked forward to by all cadets, since prior to this, they are not allowed to leave the NDA campus at all. Both Jimmy Bhullar and I were desperately awaiting the announcement of 'Liberty', as, belonging to a small town in Punjab, we had not seen much of the outside world until then, and Pune seemed like a veritable El Dorado for us. Armed with our meagre pocket money of about Rs 10, we set forth towards Pune town, wondering how we would manage to finance a bus ticket, a movie and lunch/snacks with this paltry amount.

In the town, Jimmy and I were drawn towards a street vendor selling bhelpuri at an affordable price of Re 1, and the word 'puri' immediately brought visions of hot deep-fried bread back home in Punjab, a very welcome wholesome snack to launch our first 'Liberty' experience. Little did we realize that bhelpuri, a Maharashtrian street food, has nothing to do with the puffed puri. After having consumed the 'initial' serving of what we presumed was an appetizer, we kept waiting in vain for the vendor to serve us delectable puris and he kept waiting for us to make the payment after he had served the dish of puffed rice mixed with spices and vegetables. Eventually, we paid up and walked out dejected at being deprived of our 'puris'. Hence, our first 'Liberty' ended with a lesson in the diversity of Indian cultures and cuisines, and an empty stomach, as our budget had collapsed, preventing us from buying any more food. I must, however, issue a disclaimer here that bhelpuri remains one of my favourite snacks till date.

The 'Mis'-treatment of My Injured Finger

The training at the NDA also offered me the chance to indulge my passion for sports, as the NDA affords an opportunity to every cadet to play all games, including golf, squash and tennis, in addition to the traditional 'troop games'. During one such inter-squadron football match in the second term of my training, I was the goalkeeper. At the NDA, such matches work on the principle of 'winner takes all' and are imbued with the intensity of a proxy war and 'do or die' situations for the two squadrons playing each other, as losing the game leads to complete loss of respect in the squadron for the losing team. In this particular match on 30 October 1980, inclement weather had left the playground very slippery. Thus, in trying to save a goal, I skidded on the slushy ground, hitting my hand on the goalpost while trying to cushion my fall, and ended up dislocating the index finger of my right hand so badly that my bones popped out of the finger.

This was followed by a hilarious incident, as after injuring my finger, I walked up to a fellow team member, who was playing as the fullback on our side, and tried to tell him about the accident. When he saw the gruesome sight of my finger bones smeared with blood and dangling out of the skin, he fainted, and everyone ran towards him in panic. An ambulance was immediately summoned; he was put on a stretcher and rushed to the hospital, whereas I, the person who was actually injured, was left standing on the ground, wondering what to do! Then I walked to the divisional officer present on the field, Lieutenant Anil Save, telling him that I too had suffered an injury. At first, he looked at my hand in utter disbelief, and then gathered his wits to take me to the Khadakwasla military hospital on his motorcycle.

Thereafter, in view of the seriousness of my injury, after being administered initial first aid at Khadakwasla, I was transferred to the military hospital at Kirkee late at night, where the duty surgeon and anaesthetist were called urgently to carry out a midnight surgery on my finger. The next day, as per the senior surgeon, the late-night surgery had ostensibly not been done properly, so I was taken to the operation theatre again for the second surgery, with the senior surgeon opening up the finger and doing the operation again. When I came back to the ward, the duty surgeon, who had performed the first surgery, came on his rounds and seeing my finger, he irately suggested that the surgery had again missed the mark, and he would have to operate on it again, that is, the third surgery was being planned for me. In the meantime, a nursing assistant in the ward, a know-all smart Sikh youth hailing from Punjab, offered me the most practical advice under the circumstances. He said, 'Sir, *yeh log aapka aise hi kholna jodna karte rahenge, isliye aap yahan se nikal lo* (Sir, these people will keep opening and closing your finger. It would be best if you leave).' So, I grabbed my bag and belongings and ran from the Kirkee hospital to return to Khadakwasla. My fear was that I would be taken to task for fleeing the hospital without informing anyone or collecting my discharge slip. However, I was spared and no disciplinary action was taken even as the treatment was renewed and finally, my injury was attended to. Phew!

This not-so-aptly stitched index finger of my right hand remains 'crooked' to date but it was also instrumental in creating a picture-perfect historic pose during a press conference that became synonymous with the phrase, '*Kitne Ghazi Aaye, Kitne Ghazi Gaye*', and also adorns the cover of this book. A lot has been written and said about this picture of my crooked finger on social media, which probably would not have garnered as much attention had my finger been normal and straight! Interestingly, this picture also aptly justifies the famous Hindi idiom, '*Ghee seedhi ungli se na nikle toh ungli tedhi karni padti hai*', meaning that straightforwardness should be applied only for those who are straight but a crooked attitude is needed to deal with the crooked.

While clearly highlighting the extent to which discipline is followed in the Army, at times even to the extent of overriding the need for urgent medical care, this 'passing the parcel' incident of my injured finger also underscores the ability to withstand mental and physical agony in an uncertain environment (or 'fog of war', a term that I learnt later in my career) and forbearance ingrained early in life, enabling me to endure intense pain with little fuming and fussing.

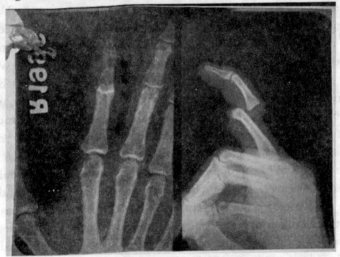

X-ray of the injured index finger

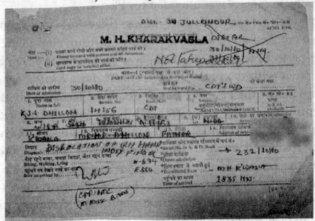

Hospital Admission Form—'Not taken on Diet' remark is probably because of my unauthorized returning to NDA

No Escape from the Burden of Books

All along, I have recounted how keen I was to join the Army and how much I was inspired by my uncles and others to don the uniform of the Armed Forces, driven by a desire to serve the nation as a soldier. However, a well-kept secret, especially from my family members, was that one of the biggest motivating factors for me to join the Forces was the opportunity it would give me to avoid studies, which I suspect was also the primary reason why many of my classmates in Ferozepur filled in the NDA entrance examination forms. However, this illusion was soon shattered when I realized that the training at the NDA and the subsequent career in the Army service was not all about brawn but entailed a significant involvement of the brain as well.

I remember very vividly, on the very second day of our joining the NDA, all the cadets in our batch were instructed to visit a store, where the havildar issued us a whole lot of heavy books on physics, chemistry and mathematics (PCM). As the books were thrust upon us, we looked at each other in dismay, our expressions conveying our inner feelings—we had come here to escape studies, not to be caught up in an even more rigorous quagmire of academic burdens. Seeing our dilemma, the havildar came to our rescue, nonchalantly offering the following advice, 'Don't worry, these books are not actually meant to be read. Just take them, cover them diligently, and keep them safely in your cupboards.' What a relief—these words were really like balm to the soul!

The relief was, however, short-lived and much to our chagrin, we subsequently found that we had to study as many as thirty subjects during the NDA training. It was bad enough that even as a humanities student, I had to delve into the highly technical PCM subjects, but the ordeal was magnified by the roster of specialized subjects, many of which I had never imagined would be part of an academic curriculum, including soldering, moulding, welding, carpentry, engineering drawing and lathe work, among others. It is another matter that the intensely competitive environment in the NDA motivated me to become an avid learner from a reluctant student, and I went on to not only complete my NDA degree with an impressive performance but also acquired an MPhil and later even a PhD degree.

However, I took some time to recover from the initial shock of seeing the extensive syllabus and those weighty books, which was reflected in my extremely low cumulative grade point average (CGPA) of 2.0 (the barest minimum) in the first term. Admonishing myself for this poor performance, I decided to pull up my socks and got down to doing some serious studies. This resolve bore fruit and I passed the final term with a much more respectable CGPA of 6.8. This once again reinforced my belief that poor performance in one particular exam or semester does not decide your fate. Life is a long journey and persistent hard work is the only key to success, with each failure teaching us precious lessons of life. Here, I must reiterate that the real learning for me came not from books but from the advice and mentoring of junior commissioned officers (JCOs) and jawans of the Indian Army, especially in my regiment, Rajputana Rifles, partly in an organized manner but mostly during highly competitive and keenly contested sports events or under fire during field tenures in not-so-organized a manner.

After completing the first six months of training in the Mike squadron at Ghorpuri, I was assigned to the Alpha squadron in the main NDA, which would be my home for the remaining two and a half years of training at the NDA. This association with a particular squadron is also one of the most appealing aspects of one's service tenure, as it ascribes a unique identity to each cadet, which translates into a lifelong relationship with the squadron and with its other members.

Food for the Body and Soul

I also found that a fresh student from school, merely seventeen-odd years of age, is like shapeless clay that the NDA training skilfully moulds into a distinctively strong yet suave individual, tough on the outside but with a soft core inside that engenders empathy and the highest degree of endurance in unexpected and unfathomable situations. This is due to the fact that the NDA training is conditioned to train one to not only become physically and mentally strong but also excel in academics while simultaneously focusing on behavioural aspects and social etiquette.

During the training, however, one of the biggest focal points of attention is food—though there was plentiful food to go around at all times in terms of both quantity and quality, somehow we had a perpetually insatiable appetite. This could be because being very young and at a formative age, and also, perhaps largely due to the fact that we were subjected to intense physical activity, we used to feel ravenous most of the time. Another reason could also be the excellent food served in the NDA mess—in fact, I have not had such delicious and wholesome food anywhere else during the course of my career or personal life as that served at the NDA mess. The portions our gluttonous group consumed routinely included about twenty-five toasts for breakfast, smeared in butter. However, along with milk, butter was rationed at about 26–28 grams per head, as a result of which we often ate our toasts by dipping them in milk, tea or coffee, and even water as a last resort, and even after that, our refrain would be, 'Yaar, aaj lunch mein kya hai? (Buddy, what's the menu for lunch today?)' The time allotted for finishing this humongous breakfast was limited and was immediately followed by academic classes delivered mostly by civilian instructors, some of whom had been teaching in the NDA for more than three decades and knew about the cadets' lives much better than the latter themselves. We had to gulp down whatever food we could and rush to avoid being punished for reporting late for class. Since wasting food or not being able to consume the allocated quantity was sacrilege for a cadet, what could not go into our mouths during the stipulated time would find its way into our pockets, and we often arrived in class with bread slices peeking out of the pockets of our khaki dress shorts.

One of my most endearing memories of the NDA food was that of devouring endless quantities of chana bhaturas, which were part of the special menu served in the NDA mess on Sundays. The spicy chana also travelled to our rooms, where we secretly stored an empty tin container of Rath Vanaspati, a popular vegetable oil that had a huge market in those days, along with oodles of pure homemade desi ghee that my grandmother packed for me when I returned from home after vacation. The Rath Vanaspati container also served as a frying pan, and the ghee was added to it to temper the chana with additional spices, making the dish more aromatic—life could not have been more heavenly for our group of about five cadets including my long-time mate, Jimmy Bhullar, with all of us greedily slurping the chana gravy dripping with fat and roasted in a puree of tomatoes, onions, green chillies and garlic. Bless the cooks at the NDA for providing such delectable food to the perpetually starving cadets. Cooking in the cadets' cabins was not authorized but we ignored this diktat and continued the practice of seasoning the chana—here my childhood habit of standing watch when chicken was being cooked in Bijee's absence (as narrated in a previous chapter) came in handy. The instructors at the NDA must have been aware of our cooking escapades but allowed us some liberties on Sundays, the only day of relaxation in an otherwise extremely hectic week of training.

The training period at the NDA was also marked by several other anecdotes and humorous incidents, recounted in the next chapter.

NDA Alpha 63 Army cadets with our weapons
training instructor

NDA Cross Country was the most fiercely contested
inter-squadron event

NDA outdoor camps were the most enjoyable but gruelling events.
Sitting (from left): Self, Jimmy Bhullar, Tarundeep.
Standing (from left): Paramjit, Kandhola, Shamsher

4

The Joys of Being a Cadet in the NDA and Gentleman Cadet in the IMA

Esprit de Corps

Another takeaway from the NDA training is the sense of stringent discipline, *esprit de corps*, and collegiality that cadets learn during the hands-on training, which are not taught per se but are imparted as a non-negotiable way of life to each cadet. The most effective way by which a potential Army man learns team spirit is through the rigorous policy of 'collective reward and collective treatment for improvement' (which was technically a punishment, though I am reluctant to call it so). Even a minor transgression or act of omission by just one member of the team would end in collective treatment for improvement for the entire class/course in the squadron, and similarly, an outstanding achievement by an individual coursemate was acknowledged by applauding the whole batch.

There were thus occasions when due to an act of minor indiscipline or boisterous behaviour by one cadet in class, even as ostensibly harmless as shouting in the classroom, the entire class would find itself running up to Sinhagad, a 2000-year-old historic fort, on a Sunday morning. This collective improvement treatment was compounded by the fact that it came in lieu of 'Liberty', consequently preventing us from visiting Pune city for the much-anticipated weekly day out. Initially, enduring this treatment was cruelty personified as it deprived us of our weekly privilege, but akin to the Stockholm syndrome, we soon developed an intimate bond with this physically challenging activity, as it signified some of the most memorable moments of our training where we made friends for life during the back and forth run up to the fort. Some of the cadets who ran up to Sinhagad with me are still great friends, and we call each other the 'Sinhagad' types. Even today, my wife and children know these officers as such. By the way, we also have other 'types' of lifelong friends such as the 'school', 'squadron', 'class' and 'hiking' types, but the closest friends are the 'punishment' types!

Another sure-fire but less appealing way of building fraternity among the cadets was the regulation that all the cadets had to bathe in the buff in a common big open washroom with no walls or partitions between each other. This was intended to eliminate any self-consciousness or shyness among the cadets so as to prepare them for any eventuality or unsavoury situation in real life demanding collective action without any reservation.

NDA Sixth Term 1982

The Significance of Punishment

Punishment is actually a critical tool of military training, for it effectively equips the trainees to deal with the tough times that lie ahead, and to be able to withstand the adversities and hardships that they will invariably experience in real life. At times, punishment may also be meted out to a cadet even if he isn't guilty of any wrongdoing, with the objective of preparing him to subsequently cope with and unquestioningly accept physical distress and unjustified 'nonsense', as it were, because a soldier should expect to face a lot of such unfriendly behaviour from the enemy or terrorists or whoever he is likely to face off against in battle or any combat situation.

Here, I recall an instance when after the injury to my finger in the game of football, I was cooling my heels on the sides while the other cadets were performing their physical exercises. Seeing me standing idle, a physical training instructor on duty asked me the reason for my non-participation in the physical training, so I showed him my injured finger. His blasé response was, 'So what if your finger is injured, your legs seem fine. Why don't you do some sit-ups instead?' This incident again reiterates how the Army constantly incites cadets to become rugged and resilient, regardless of all odds, enabling them to face any situation with equanimity and without cracking under pressure. As an aside, it may be mentioned here that unable to sustain the gruelling ordeal, some cadets abandon the training midway and return home. This thought, however, never entered my mind, as I had a point to prove to my family and was thus determined to never buckle under any pressure, either from home or at the training ground.

The various occasions of unjustified punishment also symbolize the best of 'humour in uniform'. One such hilarious instance of punishment that came my way related to the stipulation whereby each cadet had to carry an identity slip in his pocket, bearing his name, number, squadron and term details, so that each time a transgression occurred, the identity slip of the cadet concerned was confiscated and used for delivering the punishment decided by the adjutant during a muster, generally held after the academic classes and prior to lunch. One day, unaware of the offence I had committed, I was summoned to the office of the adjutant, Major S.S. Dhillon, with whom I share my last name, a very diligent officer from the Maratha Light Infantry Regiment of Infantry. There as I noticed my identity slip, it became clear that another cadet, who was the guilty party on this occasion, had, by a 'smart act' (deliberate mischief committed by one cadet to put another one on the block) mentioned my number on his identity slip, which made me the fall guy for punishment. Intriguingly, the offence against my name was 'long hair', as all cadets were supposed to have an 'Army cut' or really short hair. Seeing me, a Sikh cadet being accused of this incongruous punishment when I was exempted from haircuts, the adjutant smiled and asked, 'So, namesake, what brings you here?' Being very sure that I would be let off because the charge would not hold, I replied confidently, 'Sir, I have been charged for keeping long hair.' Instead, the adjutant replied in a non-committal manner, 'Yes, you do keep long hair, so seven days extra drill.' As I marched off, I could hear a tongue-in-cheek invocation from Lord Tennyson's famous poem, *The Charge of the Light Brigade*, advising, 'Theirs not to make reply, Theirs not to reason why, Theirs but to do and die'!

NDA Special

Another interesting part of the NDA training is the break that a cadet gets after completing each term, and we always looked forward with great anticipation to travelling home for the break in the 'NDA Special', the 'cadets-only military train' that carried us from Kirkee Railway Station near Pune to Delhi. The two days each during the to and fro journey from the NDA to home and back that we spent in the train at the time of our term-end break were absolute bliss, symbolizing a break not only from the training but also from the strict discipline imposed at the NDA, though the return journey was understandably subdued as it literally implied a return to the tough training routine tempered by the desire to reunite with our coursemates and more interestingly, to meet the new batch of juniors.

Every journey in the NDA Special came with an additional set of 'privileges' for the senior-term cadets, ranging from no longer being required to wear a pyjama or shirt under the gown to getting one's coffee on priority to more visible perks like not having to cross the satchels across our chests and simply being allowed to hang them on our shoulder. These small bonuses brought such immense happiness that they were akin to a fortune those days.

DLTGH is the acronym for 'Days Left to Go Home' that every ex-NDA would remember throughout his life as '00' would mean movement towards Kirkee Railway Station to board the military special. Some squadrons had a board in the central lobby on which DLTGH would be scribbled every morning by a cadet from the junior-most term. The day one could be the lucky one meant being in high spirits the whole of that day.

Dinner Nights

The notion of Dinner Night, which was conceptualized by the British, is an integral component of the NDA training, comprising detailed lessons and demonstrations on table etiquette. The cadets are expected to exhibit this etiquette and put their training on table manners to good use during Dinner Night when a special three- or four-course meal is served in the academy mess and is partaken of by both cadets and their instructors, all of whom have to report to the NDA mess in a pre-specified uniform.

It was in the course of one such Dinner Night during my third term that one cadet, a term senior to me, decided to sit next to the instructor to impress him. Ironically, this very proximity to the instructor had a negative outcome for him—he was struggling to eat the chicken dish with his cutlery whereas those of us who were seated at a safe distance from the instructor were heartily enjoying the chicken, surreptitiously also abandoning the fork and knife and using our hands to dig into it.

At one point, the cadet's not-so-perfect handling of the dish with his fork and knife embarrassingly caused the drumstick to fly off his plate and land in the middle of the table. Unable to conceal our mirth at this display of acrobatics by an inanimate chicken, we visibly smirked at his discomfiture but soon had to pay the price for mocking a senior. He got back on us for our 'insubordination' by subjecting us to a concomitant punishment—we were made to roll under the very same dining table across which his chicken piece had been flying a little while back!

In retrospect, all these incidents make us realize the immense value of the training at the NDA, which is equivalent to the most complete and comprehensive education that a youngster can ever imbibe—in fact, every single activity at the NDA is designed to hone us into becoming better individuals to be able to face the good and, more importantly, the not-so-good times with unflinching fortitude. These core attributes of brotherhood and camaraderie are nowhere more evident than during a war or a combat situation where soldiers automatically fight as units with utter disregard for individual preservation or safety, and we end up making friends, nay brothers, for life. The most abiding friendships I have forged are with my co-trainees at the NDA, who, even today, are among my best buddies, often even closer than relatives, as they have been part of my life for over four decades.

Never Leave Your Bicycle Behind

Each cadet was issued a bicycle to help him navigate the expansive NDA campus for the entire duration of the training. This mode of transport, however, came with its own strings attached, and more often than not, the bicycle was riding the trainee rather than the other way round. While riding the bicycle, we had to follow a rigorous set of rules, including the stipulation that we could never ride the bike alone and had to mandatorily move around only in a squad of six or minimum four, or that riding into certain areas was absolutely taboo. Whenever there was a tyre puncture or we were caught flouting any of these regulations, the comeuppance was to lift the bike and run while carrying it on our shoulders—the stricture was that the bicycle was now an inherent part of our life on the campus and we could never abandon it, come what may!

These incidents of bearing the burden of the bicycle created a lot of angst among us at the time but their import came home to us later when we learnt that shouldering the weight of the bicycle was actually a precursor for not leaving anything or anyone behind on the battlefield during a war or during a counter-terrorism operation—the numerous scenes of soldiers running with injured or dead colleagues on their shoulders on a battlefront that we have witnessed in movies have been part of Army routine and are living examples of the burdens that we were taught to bear on our shoulders through the simple regulation evoked by a popular nursery rhyme: 'Everywhere the cadet went, the bike was sure to go'. 'Leaving no one behind' is a commonly followed maxim in most armies of the world, but is more pronounced in the Indian Army where it is virtually a religion, as we never leave anyone behind, not even our dead. In fact, I believe that the NDA bicycles became an intrinsic part of our bodies, as they were always carried wherever we went.

Fashion Parade with a Difference

Another element of training at the NDA and IMA is the *Patti Parade*. The parade involves a senior appointment cadet standing at a central point with a stopwatch in hand, ordering the junior cadets to run to their cabins, don a particular dress or uniform, and run back to the ground within a stipulated time, which invariably ranged between two and three minutes. Every dress change was followed by an order to change into another dress or uniform, which could be Drill Order, PT Dress, Mufti (comprising trousers, shirt, jacket and tie) or the Field Service Marching Order (FSMO), that is, full battle fatigues with a backpack containing all the specified items, including additional pairs of socks, jersey, undergarments and a very interesting kit item called 'Housewife', which is essentially a small pouch containing sewing accessories like a thimble, needles and a few olive green and white coloured threads and buttons, among other things.

The patti parade would continue till complete satisfaction on the part of the senior was achieved. By itself, this was a tough task but it was even more arduous for me, as Sikh cadets were not given any extra time for putting on their turbans, and since each change of dress entailed wearing a different coloured turban (navy blue for mufti, grey for drill and rifle green for FSMO). At that time, I did feel that it was grossly unfair to expect a Sikh cadet to complete the exercise in the same time as stipulated for my short-haired counterparts; however, in hindsight, I realized the logic behind this supposed injustice, that is, any crisis on the battlefield would not discriminate between a Sikh and non-Sikh soldier, or for that matter, soldiers of any religious faith, and both would have to face the same odds with the same time available for action or reaction. This was perhaps the first lesson in the equality of all soldiers, irrespective of their religious or financial backgrounds, among the most important aspects that characterize the Indian defence forces. Here onwards, the officer would only be known by his squadron, course, regiment, battalion or the 'Bultt' (Punjabi accent to say 'Bullet', the name of a popular motorcycle by Royal Enfield) that he may ride proudly. One particular rig that was rather popular with some seniors and that I can never forget was 'Phantom order', dedicated to the legendary ghost who walks from Bangalla. The Phantom order meant wearing only swimming trunks and a rain cape as a free-flowing robe over your shoulders.

I must, however, point out a caveat here. Although these patti parades effectively trained us to dress to the nines in seconds, this perfection also posed a major disadvantage on another frontier—the *pati* (husband) had to face off against the *patni* (wife) for breathing down her neck after completing his dressing routine in record time during social and other occasions. This military advantage definitely became a home disadvantage in real life and the cause of many unwarranted familial tensions!

Onward March to the Indian Military Academy

The three-year training at the NDA culminated in December 1982 with the award of a graduate degree from Jawaharlal Nehru University (JNU). These three years spent undergoing

NDA, circa 1980   NDA, December 1980

the toughest forms of physical and mental training in the world literally transformed us from boys into men, men of steel, and we were now ready for the next, even tougher phase of training at the Indian Military Academy (IMA), from which we would emerge as officers of the Indian Army, ready to take on the world to protect our nation. The IMA chapter in our lives began in January 1983, when our colleagues selected to join the Air Force and Navy left us to join their respective service academies while we moved to the Indian Military Academy in Dehradun. This next phase of our military training at IMA is detailed in the following paragraphs.

Mussoorie Nights

One of the most fascinating (which it seems in retrospect, though at the time, it was quite onerous) episodes of training at IMA was captioned 'Mussoorie Nights'. As in the NDA, Mussoorie Nights too was a sort of collective 'treatment' (I will not call it a punishment) doled out to the entire course even if the transgression was committed by a single individual. At times, this treatment was carried out purely to make us mentally stronger as part of the unwritten training curriculum. Mussoorie is a beautiful tourist destination, nestled atop a hill very close to Dehradun, visible both by day and night from the IMA. This treatment was usually meted out during the chilly winter nights of Dehradun where the temperature dips as low as sub-zero at times. The treatment entailed stripping in the shivering cold and standing bare feet facing the effervescent night lights of Mussoorie visible in the distance, with the duration of the punishment decided in accordance with the severity of the offence, the *marzi* (wish) of the senior, and of course, the discipline displayed during the treatment. Like all other treatments or punishments, this was also designed to toughen the gentlemen cadets (GCs) and habituate them to all kinds of weather that they may encounter during their high-altitude field postings, especially in the Jammu region, Kashmir, Ladakh, Siachen, Himachal Pradesh, Uttarakhand, Sikkim and Arunachal Pradesh, which fall in the cold regions.

First Official Drink

Another ritual typical to the Army is the manner in which the completion of training at the IMA is announced, which sort of cements the relationship between the GC and his calling as an Army officer. As part of this ritual, just a week before the conclusion of the IMA training, the cadet's platoon commander, an officer of the rank of captain, officially invites the trainees to his house and offers them a glass of beer. Technically, this is the first time that the cadet is allowed to consume any alcoholic drink on the academy campus during the course of the training. In my case, this occasion, coming a week before my official commissioning on 17 December 1983, was extra special as it rekindled memories of the Holi festival three years ago when we had been caught drinking on campus during the first term of our training at NDA.

As I drank my beer, I started feeling high not because of being intoxicated but because it was hard to believe that I was now going to be an Army officer who could handle things on his own! Like many other aspects of Army life, this evoked an indescribable feeling, combining the sentiment of freedom bestowed on me as an adult with an overwhelming sense of responsibility and adherence to duty for a man who had successfully completed his training in the Indian Army, which is widely believed to be one of the toughest training grounds in the world. The words, 'Come and have a drink,' uttered by Captain Bharat Singh Sangwan of the Madras Regiment, my platoon commander in the Zojila Company of IMA, are thus still ingrained in my memory as a special incantation for doing all that I had aspired to when I had filled up the NDA form at school in Ferozepur. The nostalgia was palpable!

5

Escapades and Memorable Times in the Rajputana Rifles

Rajputana Rifles—Home Away From Home

Here, it is apt to recount the sequence of events that led me to join the Rajputana Rifles, which was virtually my home during my entire tenure in the Army. This occurred around the time I had completed the second term of my training at the IMA and proceeded on a four-day leave to Delhi. At this time, instead of going home to my parents in Nepal, I stayed with a close friend, six months senior to me at the NDA, Second Lieutenant Manwant Singh Johar, who had been commissioned as an officer in June 1983 and joined the 16th Battalion of the Rajputana Rifles. He was undergoing regimental orientation training at the Rajputana Rifles Regimental Centre at Delhi Cantonment. Every regiment of the Indian Army has a regimental centre where the jawans of that particular regiment are trained, and the jawans of the Rajputana Rifles are trained at the regimental centre in Delhi.

After completing the training at the IMA and before joining his unit, every officer has to mandatorily visit the regimental centre for two weeks for initiation into the regimental history, details about the backgrounds and habits of the jawans, and other facets of the regiment. Significantly, the jawans assigned for training to a particular infantry regimental centre usually belong to the same recruitment area, as for instance, a majority of the jawans in the Rajputana Rifles regiment are Rajputs and Jats belonging to Rajasthan, Haryana, Madhya Pradesh and Uttar Pradesh. A few battalions of the Rajputana Rifles also have some members of other castes and this is true for most of the infantry regiments of the Indian Army, such as the Sikh, Dogra, Jat, Bihar, Kumaon, Maratha Light Infantry and Sikh Light Infantry regiments. The fixed class composition of troops in a company or battalion is actually a binding factor having major motivational and operational implications. For instance, before embarking on an operation with the Rajput caste company of the Rajputana Rifles, as the company commander, all I had to say to motivate the jawans in the sub-unit was, '*Rajputon ki shaan rakhni hai, unka naam hamesha uppar rehna chahiye*' (Must keep the honour of the Rajputs intact and their name must remain untarnished), and the job of pumping up the morale and motivation was well and truly done. The practice of fixed class troops' composition in the infantry regiments has existed since the British times, who for pragmatic and other reasons, undertook homogeneous grouping of the fighting military units as their members shared a common language, eating habits and cultures.

Another incident related to my commissioning in the Rajputana Rifles concerns my love for the game of basketball, which has been my favourite sport. The GCs in IMA would indulge in a daily game of basketball at around 4 p.m. in the respective company courts, but I would always arrive much earlier, immediately after lunch, say around 2.30 p.m., and start practising all by myself in the basketball court. During one such practice session in the heat of a September afternoon in 1983, Brigadier P.S. Verma, the head of training at the IMA, who was commissioned in the Fourth Battalion of the Rajputana Rifles, and who had fought the 1971 war with the battalion and later commanded 8 RAJRIF, noticed me playing there alone at that odd hour when cadets are supposed to rest. He stopped for a few minutes and watched me running around and aiming for the basket and then asked me why I was playing alone during my rest hour, and also why I had only one basketball for practice, which made me expend extra energy and time in retrieving the ball after the netting of each basket. Worried that this unscheduled game on my part could mean that I was not adhering to the stipulated training schedule, I hesitatingly replied that there was only one basketball in the platoon. Without any further conversation, he just asked my name and left. In the IMA, an instructor asking your name is reason enough to believe that you are in trouble!

The next morning, after I returned from the morning PT classes and even before I could go for my breakfast, I was summoned by Major D.J. Singh, our company commander, a cavalry officer, who asked me what had happened the previous day on the basketball court. I immediately realized the gravity of the situation when he told me that he had been asked to meet Brigadier Verma in his office along with me. Fearing the worst, I was remonstrating myself as to why I had said that there is only one basketball in the platoon, while the possibility of missing breakfast was another major thing playing on my mind. However, my second apprehension was taken care of as Major D.J. Singh, the gentleman that he is, told me, 'Go have your breakfast and meet me in front of Chetwode Hall in ten minutes.' Ten minutes in the academy is equivalent to a lifetime, and I forgot everything about the march up to the brigadier and concentrated fully on my breakfast, managed to do full justice to it, and still made it to Chetwode Hall well within time.

As soon as we reached Brigadier Verma's office, he handed us six brand-new basketballs, while instructing Major D.J. Singh to ensure that the GCs had access to adequate sports equipment for practice. He also asked me if I had made up my mind about my prospective unit, and whether I was interested in joining the Rajputana Rifles.

Instantly recalling the fascination with which I had observed the training at the Rajputana Rifles Regimental Centre while I had been a guest of Second Lieutenant Manwant Singh Johar there, I nodded enthusiastically and expressed my keenness to join the regiment. Another motivating factor for me to volunteer to join Rajputana Rifles (RAJRIF) was my then weapons training instructor Havildar Moti Singh, a six-foot-tall Rajput from the Rajputana Rifles with a well-maintained handlebar moustache, leopard-like swiftness and that omnipresent soldierly pride in everything he did, from wearing his well-starched cotton uniform to handling the rifle like a toy in his big hands. With RAJRIF as one of my choices within the infantry, I was eventually commissioned into the 4th Battalion of the Rajputana Rifles, with Havildar Moti Singh, Second Lieutenant Manwant Singh Johar and Brigadier Pritam S. Verma playing crucial roles as tools of destiny in my tryst with the Rajputana Rifles.

I got commissioned into a more than 163-year-old battalion at that time, that is, 4th Battalion, the Rajputana Rifles, the oldest rifles regiment of the Indian Army, on 17 December 1983. Generally, the visiting parents of GCs do the honours of pipping—a ceremony wherein a lone star is placed on both shoulder flaps of the olive green uniform that is going to be your second skin for the rest of your professional life—the newly commissioned officers. Since my parents did not come for my passing-out parade, I was pipped by none other than the ever-so-suave and one of the finest professionals from the cavalry, Major D.J. Singh, my company commander and mentor in the IMA. My first salute as a commissioned officer was also to Major D.J. Singh, who after returning my salute smartly, firmly patted my shoulder, covering and gripping the recently placed black metal star—Rajputana Rifles officers and JCOs wear black metal stars on their uniform as also all the other rifle regiments of the Indian Army and Jammu and Kashmir Light Infantry (JAKLI)—and I can never forget his steely words, 'Wear your ranks with honour and pride, which is bestowed on only the very selected few and ensure you make a difference in whatever you do in the service of the nation. Your nation, army, regiment and paltan is the pride that you will live and die for.'

17 December 1983, Indian Military Academy, Dehradun;
Major D.J. Singh pipping the first black star on my shoulders

Hereon begins my life and career in the Army, as an officer in the much-decorated and much-lauded oldest rifles regiment of the Indian Army, the Rajputana Rifles, which accounted for many memorable times and episodes in my life.

With Subedar Major and Honorary
Captain Amar Singh Saab—as
commanding officer, 2005

As commanding officer ready
to lead a ceremonial parade,
January 2005

'Sugar and Spice' Welcome

After being commissioned from the IMA on 17 December 1983 and following a two-week mandatory leave post commissioning, I arrived at the Rajputana Rifles Regimental Centre, Delhi Cantonment, with starry eyes but uncertain about what lay ahead. Because of the conspicuous NDA box that was accompanying me, I was easily recognized and greeted at the gate with a very crisp and elegant salute by an extremely well-turned-out RAJRIF Regimental Police (RP) soldier sporting a typical curled-up Rajasthani moustache. He helped me with my box but did not lift the barrier boom at the entrance gate. Trying to conceal my surprise at this unusual welcome, I bent down in an effort to squeeze through the barrier but was politely stopped by the RP sentry, who in his typical Rajasthani accent said, '*Saab*, gate *khulega magar* welcome tax *lagega* (Sir, the gates will open after the welcome tax is paid).' I soon learnt that a new entrant to the regiment has to offer 5 kilograms of jalebis to the Regimental Centre RP section in keeping with the Indian ritual of '*munh meetha karna*' (eat something sweet in celebration) before every auspicious occasion. Thereafter, I was ceremoniously welcomed into the Rajputana Rifles with a bite of fresh jalebis and the regimental pipe band escorting me to the officers' mess. Overwhelmed by this pomp and show, indeed by the entire turn of events, my twenty-one-year-old self could feel a distinct lump in my throat and apprehension about the future, as I tried to hold my composure while following the band.

The walk of barely 60 metres up to the mess lawns seemed like an eternity, compounded by the sense of responsibility that swamped my mind. On the way, I noticed a very smartly turned-out forty-something officer donning a rifle green jacket on the front lawns of the mess, sipping his hot cup of coffee on the cold January morning. I wished him and after the customary greetings and handshake, with my hand still in his, he asked me in a typical fauji and stern voice, 'So son, which unit?' As I replied '4 RAJRIF, sir', I could feel the handshake turning even firmer as though conveying to me that I was now in safe hands. I later learnt that he was Colonel Raj Singh, a 4 RAJRIF officer, who had been decorated with the

Vir Chakra during the 1971 operations, and who, because of his legendary strategic and military attributes, was popularly known as Colonel Raj Singh 'McArthur'. The close bond engendered as a result of being part of 4 RAJRIF was manifested in his authoritative call to the waiter, '*Saab ke liye* beer *lao* (Get a beer for the officer).' In this way, my regimental orientation started on a twin sweet and malty note, laying the foundation for the good times that lay ahead in the journey of my military life.

Two weeks of orientation training at the regimental centre made me fully conversant with the glorious history of the Rajputana Rifles spanning well over 200 years. The 1st Battalion of the Rajputana Rifles, now converted into the 3rd Battalion, the Brigade of Guards, had been raised on 10 January 1775 by Captain James Stewart as the 5th Battalion Bombay Sepoys. After the raising of the first battalion in 1775, other battalions followed in the subsequent years and since its inception, the regiment has had the unique distinction of participating in almost all the campaigns fought by the British, including operations on Indian frontiers and foreign lands. I learnt a great deal about the history, culture, traditions, ethos and food habits of the Rajputs and Jats, that is, the troops with whom I was going to spend a major part of my life.

After two weeks in Delhi, I found myself travelling in the first-class compartment of the Assam Mail, the train that would take me to Siliguri, thereafter in a civil hired Sikkim National Transport (SNT) to Gangtok, and further still in military transport ferrying me to my unit's location. Here, my new family awaited my arrival, similar to the tradition of family elders awaiting the arrival of a new bride in an Indian household. The first part of my journey in a first-class compartment of a train for the first time also literally transported me to an exalted world, imbuing a deep sense of achievement and pride.

4 RAJRIF, my unit, was stationed in the high-altitude area of Sikkim in those days and since it was snow-bound, and because of poor road connectivity, we could travel in a vehicle only up to a certain point called 'car post', a rather peculiar name for a location. I later found out that any point up to which a vehicular ambulance could reach for evacuation of casualties is called a 'car post' in military

parlance. Incidentally, the commonly known Willys Jeep was called 'Car 250 Kg 4x4 GS CJ3B' as per the Army inventory and I suppose the name 'car post' was derived from this. Though there were no cars in the field areas, this name was a classic example of military humour wherein you are continuously reminded of the things you have been deprived of because of the military service lest they just fade away from your memory altogether.

I was scheduled to spend the night at the car post before moving onward to join the unit at its designated location. As this was more of a transitory camp, I was given a cot into which I slunk shivering in the sub-zero temperature. My initiation into the unit was literally heralded with a 'hot and sweet' welcome, as I was offered a hot cup of tea and choorma, a delectable dish made of roti, sugar and desi ghee, popular in Haryana and Rajasthan, the areas from where a majority of the troops of Rajputana Rifles hailed, and which incidentally became my favourite dessert for the rest of my life. With the choorma melting in my mouth immediately, even in the sub-zero temperature at the picturesque Army post in the lap of the towering Himalayas, my initiation into the unit could not have been more flavoursome.

The sweet was, however, well balanced by a spicy treat, which was offered to me in the backdrop of the sun setting behind the snow-clad peaks. Thereafter, I was settled in a stone-walled hut with a steel door sans any windows and a lone glass-less lantern with a fluttering flame, a modification of the traditional lamp for allowing the sparsely available oxygen to reach and feed the fire. In fact, I could barely see the blanket-clad interior walls of the hut (with enhanced military knowledge now, I would prefer to call it an improvised bunker) in the fading light of the lantern. Notwithstanding the sumptuous choorma servings, I was really looking forward to the famous 'langar ka khana' (community kitchen food) that finally arrived in a steel plate (*thaal*). Apart from the usual serving of dal and vegetables, one of the *katori*s (bowls) contained a dish that I could not discern but still proceeded to take a bite from. The result was pure fire on my tongue, as the bowl contained whole red chillies and raw garlic fried in desi ghee, which aggravated the pungency of the chillies, leaving no respite for a man like me who was not used to consuming such a spicy dish. The soldier on duty was more eloquent when he said, '*Saab, RAJRIF mein aaye ho toh laal mirchi sehni aur kaale taare lagane hi padenge* (Now that you are commissioned in Rajputana Rifles, you will have to tolerate the hot chillies and wear black metal stars).' Like the officers and men in the Rajputana Rifles, I too got used to wearing the cool black metal accoutrements and eating the hot chillies on a regular basis, but the first time I encountered this fiery dish left an indelible memory of my welcome to the unit.

Befriending the Sleeping Bag

Anticipating the bitter cold at the high altitude in Sikkim, Bijee, my Naniji, had given me a thick quilt for the night, and extracting it from my canvas bed holder with leather straps (known as *bistarband*), I sneaked into it for the night in my cot. However, even my well-padded quilt was not sufficient armour against the biting cold. Watching my predicament, the senior JCO of the company, Subedar Lakshman Singh, came into the hut and asked me why I had opted for sleeping in the quilt instead of the sleeping bag issued to me at the camp. I replied by pointing out my reluctance to get into the sleeping bag as I had never used it before, and also that I was more comfortable using the quilt. His typical fauji reply was, 'If you sleep in a quilt, you are responsible for your own comfort as you have to slink inside it and keep adjusting it by continuously tucking in the sides to keep out the cold, but if you use the sleeping bag, this *jimmewari* (responsibility) is borne by the bag and you do not have to make any adjustments to combat the chill.' So, my first day as part of 4 RAJRIF began with a lesson on the value of the military-issued equipment/clothing in extreme climatic and terrain conditions as against grandma's love, and the balance between hot and sweet offerings for the palate.

Foundation of My Lifelong Professional Commitment to the Army

After spending the eventful eighteen hours at the car post, I reached the battalion headquarters location the next morning.

I was mesmerized by the natural beauty of the surroundings, the type I had seen only in the famous English movie *Where Eagles Dare*, starring Richard Burton and Clint Eastwood. I had my first encounter with the commanding officer of the battalion, Lieutenant Colonel (later Brigadier) Trigunesh Mukherjee, and I still remember the professional advice he offered me after the initial welcoming remarks. He told me very seriously, '**If you are in touch with your profession, [***pardon the language***] no son-of-a-b**** can touch you**', a statement that got deeply embedded in my mind and has stayed with me throughout my Army career. It also laid the foundations for my professional competence and diligence, with my motto being, 'Never let down my unit, my regiment, my army, my nation under any circumstances.'

I would like to think that my very first assignment as a newly commissioned Army officer literally took me on top of the world as I was posted at an altitude of 16,000 feet above sea level, and revelled in the experience where I was the only officer among jawans and JCOs, whose welfare I was wholly responsible for. This tenure of about twenty months also afforded me an opportunity to understand the hardy soldiers of a celebrated Indian regiment and the men I would eventually command. Thus, perched atop the gigantic Himalayas in Sikkim, the jawans and I exchanged snippets of our lives, value systems and family backgrounds with each other. These insights came in very handy during our various operations in the field and counter-terrorism encounters and during my time as a company commander and commanding officer in the Kashmir Valley years later.

I realized that but for my first posting in a tough station, I would not have learnt about the strengths of my jawans and how these brave men face rough weather and tough terrains almost throughout their lives as soldiers of the Indian Army and the fortitude with which they bear the adversities constantly occurring in an Army man's life. This tenure changed my perception of an Indian infantry soldier from a 'mean killing machine' to that of an extremely dedicated son/husband with unmatched commitment to the nation, a self-motivated and ruthless team person with unparalleled professional integrity, and above all, respect for human values and cultures.

With Brigadier Trigunesh Mukherjee—beginning of Army service, circa 1984

With Brigadier Trigunesh Mukherjee on the day of culmination of Army service, January 2022

Rajputana Rifles—Pride in the Unit through a Soldier's Eyes

One particular incident, which revealed to me insights about the soldiers' self-perceptions, had to do with the havildar to naib subedar promotion cadre, an examination where I was one of the assessors in charge of the viva voce examination. I asked Havildar Shayar Singh, one of the naib subedar aspirants the following question, 'Assume that you are in Alpha company and designated as the number one platoon commander, and the commanding officer has instructed that Alpha company will lead the attack, and the number one platoon will be the leading platoon within the Alpha company. When you issue orders to the men, a jawan comes up to you and says, "Our company always leads the attack, but this time, we will not lead." What then would be your reaction as the platoon commander to this statement by one of your jawans?' The response from the havildar had a deep impact on my sensibilities and made me realize the innate strengths of our soldiers. Forgetting that he was appearing for a test and that he should have thought of a prudent answer to impress the examiner (that is, me), the havildar instead seemed indignant at the suggestion that a jawan would urge his commander not to let his company lead the attack, and Havildar Shayar Singh solemnly told me, 'Sir, you are new to this battalion, so maybe I should educate you about its traditions. Every single jawan in this unit is ready to die fighting for the nation but not one of them will refuse to fight a war. So, in view of these non-negotiable principles of the soldiers of 4 RAJRIF, your question is irrelevant.' However, in order to ascertain the veracity of his claim, I repeated the question and insisted on a more candid answer. But he stood firm on his reply, admonishing me almost indignantly, 'Sir, let not these thoughts of yours reach the ears of the commanding officer because such a situation will never arise. It has not happened ever in the last 164 years of the history of this battalion nor will it ever happen in the future.'

Here, it may be pertinent to mention that the history of the 4th Battalion of the Rajputana Rifles dates back to Baji Rao Peshwa's Poonah Auxiliary Infantry raised in 1812 at Poonah (today's Pune), comprising men who were recruited from 'the other provinces of Hindoostan' and later converted into First Battalion, the Twelfth Regiment, a unit of the East India Company in May 1820. The unit has been in continuous existence since then and has never been disbanced or re-raised. In over 200 years of its history, the present-day 4 RAJRIF has been honoured with twenty-nine Battle and Theatre Honours. In addition, the unit has earned 113 individual awards after 1947 and 346 in the pre-Independence era. There have been seven occasions in its history when the unit, having taken over 200 casualties in its stride, hit back with renewed resolve. So, it was absolutely justifiable for Havildar Shayar Singh to be proud of his great regimental ancestry, and this conversation with him atop a snow peak taught me a valid lesson of using history as a motivation for achieving present-day goals. Also, the confidence bordering on insolence from the havildar re-affirmed in my eyes the resolve and resilience of the Indian soldier, and his strength of character, composed of both mental toughness and physical perseverance. The unimpeachable physical standards that the Indian Army soldiers are able to adhere to were apparent through the various tactical and operational exercises conducted at that altitude, but what astounded me the most was the level of tenacious resolve that they had imbibed and which they were able to sustain come what may. Thus, I learnt very early in my career that for a soldier, his attitude towards his occupation surpasses mere diligence to duty, almost touching obeisance to the nation. For him, the Army is not just a job but personifies a way of life, a sort of cloak of honour that wins him tremendous respect in his family, his community, his native place and the nation. Consequently, he will, under no circumstances, let down his platoon, company, paltan (battalion), regiment or the country.

As I delve more into the psyche and ethos of an Indian soldier, I am reminded of Mark Antony's final remarks in William Shakespeare's *Julius Caesar*,

'His life was gentle; and the elements
So mixed in him, that Nature might stand up
And say to all the world, THIS WAS A MAN!'

'Chiselling' in the Rajputana Rifles

As mentioned above, since my initiation into the Army occurred during chilly winters amidst heavy snowfall in the mountainous terrain of Sikkim, the conditions were appropriately tough for any structured training, and hence most of my lessons were learnt during 'on the job' training. On the very first day of my arrival in the unit, during the morning PT parade, it was snowing and visibility was reasonably poor. I recalled that the instructors at the NDA and the IMA, mainly captains, would come and stand behind the cadets during PT fall-ins. Expecting the same protocol as a second

61

lieutenant too, on reaching the PT ground, I stood behind the jawans who were already grouped into their platoon or company squads. Contrary to my expectations, the training-in-charge at the time, Subedar Major Nand Ram Saab walked up to me and the words he uttered then not only had a deep impact on me but have remained as a guiding metric for me ever since in all the operations I have been involved in throughout my nearly four-decade-long Army career. After wishing me 'Ram Ram Saab', he said, 'Saab, **Officer** *Hamesha Aage* (the officer always leads from the front)!' This incident thus conveyed in no uncertain terms that an officer is fully responsible for the safety and welfare of the men he commands not only during the operations but also during all aspects of unit life, as the men under his command will have unflinching faith in the officer's ability to lead them with utter disregard for his own personal safety, an honour code that always remained at the back of my mind during my entire service.

Every day in 4 RAJRIF was a new learning experience and our main teachers, who taught us the intricacies of Army operations, the manner in which various processes from cooking meat in the cookhouse to attacking a feature with stealth are planned and implemented, were the JCOs and non-commissioned officers (NCOs). These men of tremendous experience imbued me with an intense passion to diligently do my duty, while imparting a unique fighting spirit that would carry me long and far during the most perilous and arduous military operations in my life.

Why 'Tiny'?

Here, I would also like to narrate a very unique tradition that has come to be associated with 4 RAJRIF and has been sustained over the years. Any officer who is commissioned into this battalion is usually ascribed a moniker that is in complete contrast to his physical appearance and behaviour. For instance, one of my senior officers, Colonel Anil Kumar Suri, who is known for being a perfectionist and for the meticulousness with which he performs every task, was nicknamed 'Goofy'! Another senior officer, Major General Mohan

Deep Singh Ghura, who stands over 6 feet 3 inches tall, was named Shorty, and similarly, Lieutenant General Codanda Poovaiah Cariappa, who took over the charge from me as colonel of the regiment on my superannuation on 31 January 2022, also happens to be extremely tall and was named 'Mini'! In my case too, my height of 6 feet 3 inches determined my sobriquet of 'Tiny', a name that has stuck with me ever since and continues to be on my social media handles like Twitter (@Tiny_Dhillon), Instagram (@tinydhillon) and Facebook page (@TinyDhillon). In this way, 4 RAJRIF inveigles itself into the hearts and minds of its men, becoming an inveterate part of our lives and identities.

The following chapters, while delineating other memorable incidents of my Army life, also highlight the crucial role played by the families of soldiers in their lives and work, and the solid support system created by the collegiality of 'brothers in arms' and their near and dear ones that keeps the Army machinery so well-oiled and running smoothly at all times.

6

My Eventful Early Days in 4 RAJRIF

Standing up for Our Men

Another episode during my initial days as a recently commissioned officer once again brought home to me the immense responsibility that an officer has to shoulder for the men he commands. As I was returning to the unit location after a visit to the Brigade Headquarters in a one-ton, a patrol vehicle of World War II vintage, in snowy weather, I noticed a jawan walking ahead of the vehicle on the track that led only to our unit. On questioning, the driver told me that he was the dispatch rider who carried to and fro mail for the battalion. I instructed the driver, who was a frequent mover on this route, to offer him a lift, but the latter's insouciant reply was, 'This is Lance Naik Ram Singh, who never accepts a lift in a vehicle, so let him continue his march on foot.' On further inquiry, I learnt that Lance Naik Ram Singh's antipathy to sitting in any vehicle was the result of an accident in which a vehicle he had been travelling in skidded on the snow down a slope, and though he survived miraculously, Subedar Major Lakshmi Singh, who was accompanying him in the ill-fated vehicle, had unfortunately died. Traumatized by the accident, Lance Naik Ram Singh refused to sit in any vehicle thereafter and always opted to walk while performing his duty, regardless of the weather, distance or effort involved.

Notwithstanding the driver's narrative, I still advised him to stop the vehicle and ask the dispatch rider to get in. Much to our surprise, Lance Naik Ram Singh got in and sat down in the rear of the vehicle without any protest. The absolute astonishment on the face of the driver at this uncharacteristic move by the *'fauji dakiya'* (army postman) fuelled my inquisitiveness and I was determined to get to the bottom of this. When we stopped at the regimental police gate to report our arrival, and Ram Singh alighted from the vehicle and came up to wish me, I proceeded to ask him why he usually refused to travel in a vehicle and if so, why he had made an exception this time. He narrated the tale of the accident, which had terrified him so much that he could never bring himself to travel in a vehicle again, but the reason cited by him that had made him overcome his fear that day and agree to travel with me was, *'Saab, aaj to aap bhi gaadi mein baithe the* (Sir, today, you too were seated in the vehicle).' Obviously, the presence of his officer imbued him with enough confidence to override his trepidation and feel secure in travelling with his leader. The innocence with which he uttered these words in a rather matter-of-fact manner rattled me, making me realize how far my men were dependent on my judgement, and how much they were willing to risk even their lives on a simple command given by me. The unquestioning faith exhibited by soldiers of a military unit in their commander was an eye-opener for me, and I decided to justify this spoken or unspoken faith at all times, in war or peace. It also strengthened my earlier resolve to never let down my profession and my deep commitment to it.

The Religion of the Troops is the Religion of the Officer

Here, I would like to touch upon another very fine practice of the Indian defence forces, that is, the concept of 'Mandir, Masjid,

Gurdwara' (also referred to as MMG, synonymous with the acronym for medium machine gun, the long-range automatic firing weapon that is the mainstay of any offensive or defensive operation at the platoon/company level). This concept of MMG is more pronounced in the 'All India All Class' mixed troops composition units and headquarters, whereas the fixed class composition units have the place of worship associated with the religion of their troops. Headquarters and units with troops from other religions like Buddhism or Christianity also have the places of worship of these religions in addition to MMG. As the officers in the Indian defence forces can belong to any religion irrespective of the religion of the troops in the unit, the officers adhere to all the principles, traditions and practices of the religion of their troops. It is a popular adage in the defence forces that 'the religion of the troops is the religion of officers in the Indian defence forces'. All religious functions are thus celebrated together with full fervour and respect in the Army.

At a religious function with dharam gurus of all religions

At the mandir prior to superannuation from service, 30 January 2022

No One Is above the Law

Although the soldiers of the Indian Army are, by and large, known for their impeccable character and tenacity, a caveat here is that a stringent law is still needed to enforce discipline in a profession where the slightest intransigence could prove to be the difference between life and death for the individual, and victory and defeat for the nation. In this context, a military law prevails under which officers and soldiers can be tried for numerous offences and the Army has very strong internal mechanisms for delivering speedy justice wherein the punishments can range from a few days of extra duties, payment of a fine or rigorous imprisonment within the unit lines, to cashiering or dismissal from the Army or imprisonment in a civil jail for more grim and serious offences. These incidents of major violations and the resultant punishments have, however, been few and far between.

A unique way in which the Army ensures a high degree of discipline in its ranks is through the implementation of the concept of joint responsibility and joint action. Thus, a soldier almost never operates alone and the phenomenon of working as a 'buddy pair' or as a group implies that someone from within the unit is always keeping a watch on another colleague. While the main objective of this practice is to enable the safe rescue of a fellow Army man in case something goes wrong, it also helps prevent anyone from straying away from the straight and narrow path, even under the most compelling temptations. The guiding principle of law here is that offences are usually committed when the offenders believe that no one is watching them.

Stress and Anxiety—A Soldier's Constant Consorts

Few professions in the world are characterized by a greater degree of tension and trauma than the defence forces, and every soldier has to deal with the anxiety of separation from family even on occasions when the family needs them the most.

In recent times, the Army has also introduced unique tools and techniques to mitigate stress among all ranks by motivating and counselling them regularly to keep their heads above water. One such 'friend in need' is the Unit Panditji or Granthiji or Maulvi Saab, who visits various isolated pickets to impart spiritual support and lessons in the power of prayer. However, the most relevant adage that highlights the high spirits of a soldier doing duty in operational areas is still 'No news is good news'. The most common reply to a frequently asked question to a jawan '*Aur ghar mein sab theek thaak hai?*', is '*Sab theek hai, saab* (So, all well at home?, Yes sir, all well)'. This spirit of buoyancy not only permeates the entire atmosphere in a military unit but also keeps the soldiers consistently agile and optimistic, which is often manifested in their jovial and zestful attitudes.

Chicken Sandwich

In this same spirit, here, let me recount another hilarious incident that occurred while we were still in Sikkim, but planning to soon set off on our journey to Udaipur. The corps commander was visiting the unit in Sikkim, and Lieutenant Colonel Trigunesh Mukherjee was the commanding officer (CO) of the unit. In view of the vagaries of the weather, the optimal timing for the helicopter flying to our high-altitude venue was from sunrise till about 11 a.m., after which aerial journeys to the mountain locations were not advisable due to receding visibility and expansive cloud cover. Thus, senior officers visited us quite early in the morning to be able to conduct a brief but effective reconnaissance of the area of responsibility of a particular unit. Such visits by senior officers involved the aerial survey and briefing by the CO from a vantage point from where most of the area of interest was visible.

We got the intimation that the corps commander would land early in the morning at a particular helipad and would be there for an hour for briefing and discussion with the CO. The staff at higher headquarters also informed us that since it was early in the day, the corps commander would not have had his breakfast and he may be offered some light snacks while the briefing was in progress. As the CO was well-versed in his operational tasks, the briefing per se was not a matter of great concern. However, the issue of 'light snacks' led to an animated discussion on the prospective menu for the breakfast to be served to the eminent guest during his short visit. After many suggestions were considered and brushed aside, it was finally decided to serve him a simple but filling breakfast comprising a chicken sandwich, along with the usual accompaniments of additional slices of bread, butter, jam, eggs to order, juice and tea or coffee. The mess-in-charge, Havildar Ram Kishan, was given an extensive briefing on the chicken sandwich to ensure that the bread was fresh and the chicken was properly cooked. Complacent that nothing could go wrong with this simple fare, we left it to Havildar Ram Kishan to work his magic in the temporary cooking area located in a bunker conveniently tucked away from the main briefing viewpoint and turned our attention to more pressing matters.

On the day of the visit, I was assigned the critical task of pointing out the physical landmarks on the simulated enlargement hung up on a wall during the briefing. The CO and corps commander were facing the area in front, whereas, from my position, I had a bird's eye view of the entire area while also keeping an eye on the incoming mess staff from the makeshift cooking bunker, which would be hidden from the CO's horizon. Things were going absolutely as per plan until Lance Naik Ram Dhani, the mess waiter, emerged from the cooking bunker with a tray laden with the corps commander's breakfast. Lo and behold! I could not believe what I was seeing—as the waiter came inside and uncovered the much-debated dish, the 'chicken sandwich', there lay a steaming hot 'chicken' (roasted) on one plate and a plain buttered 'sandwich' on the other! The detailed instructions to serve a chicken sandwich had been innovatively interpreted by the mess staff, offering chicken 'outside' instead of 'inside' the sandwich. I was the only one who could see the potential disaster heading towards us from the kitchen towards the briefing bunker, but there was little I could do to remedy the situation. The CO looked at me in astonishment when the tray arrived but I just looked away discreetly. Mercifully, the corps commander di not seem to notice anything amiss and proceeded to thoroughly njoy the light snacks, asking for a second and even a third helping of the chicken part of the 'sandwich'. Interestingly, news of this unique meal spread far and wide and other units would often call us up to ask what we had served the corps commander when he visited our unit. The ingenious 'chicken sandwich' rustled up by the 4 RAJRIF chefs thus inadvertently became a huge hit and has dominated archival tales in the unit since then.

Taking a cue from the gracious behaviour of the corps commander, I never revealed my culinary preferences when I myself became the corps commander many years later, and happily ate whatever was served to me during my visits to various locations. I must admit that due to my non-disclosure of food preferences, I was actually served some of the most scrumptious delicacies. This positive and accepting attitude, which has helped us overcome many challenges and overlook hardships and adversities, is actually ingrained in all Army officers and jawans.

The Power of Positivity

This positivity was generally exuded by all our unit members but one of the most sanguine and cheerful persons in the unit was the quartermaster NCO, Havildar Bhawra Ram—a typical old-timer soldier with a perpetual smile on his face under all circumstances. In a unit, a quartermaster generally oversees all administrative tasks, including the management of rations, clothing and other daily needs of the troops. One day, as we were playing volleyball, we saw the rations vehicle parked in the campus and Havildar Bhawra Ram supervising the unloading of supplies. The weekly arrival of the supply vehicle was a significant event for us at the Sikkim station because it had to deal with various constraints such as difficulties in the movement of traffic posed by the high altitude, a rough geographical terrain and a lack of motorable roads to reach the forward posts. Hence, everyone was excited to see the food truck and the CO sauntered up to Havildar Bhawra Ram to inquire about the latest stock of 'fresh' rations or green vegetables delivered by the truck. This was, in fact, a constant query to the quartermaster because fresh vegetables are a rarity, and therefore something of a delicacy at high altitudes, which is why we had to largely rely on tinned vegetables that were abundantly available.

Motivated by the CO's interest in the inventory of 'fresh' supplies, Havildar Bhawra Ram started beaming and when the

CO asked what had arrived in the vehicle, he assured him that the supplies were so garden-fresh that they would reach the *aakhri jawan, aakhri post* (last jawan at the last post) in a crisp and fresh condition. Curious, the CO asked him again which uniquely fresh green vegetables had been sent for our unit this time, but his query was again met with the refrain that even if it took three days or more for the supplies to reach the last post, the vegetables would remain fresh and green. Havildar Bhawra Ram kept repeating his promise of the 'last jawan at the last post' receiving fresh greens and his positivity was hugely contagious as we started imagining all kinds of exotic fresh vegetables being served at the dinner table. Unable to restrain himself any longer, the CO absolutely insisted on knowing the name of the vegetable that was bringing such joy to the quartermaster. This time the quartermaster could not hedge and informed us that the green vegetable he had been flaunting so glibly was actually tinda (apple gourd), widely seen as a rather unappetizing component in the Indian thali. Havildar Bhawra Ram's attempt to hype the value of this rather staid vegetable was just a means of helping us keep up our spirits and enjoy whatever was available on the table.

This seemingly insignificant incident highlighted the power of a positive attitude, as personified by the quartermaster, aptly embodying the adage immortalized by Shakespeare's *Hamlet* that 'nothing is either good or bad but thinking makes it so'. It was this relentless optimism in the face of seemingly insurmountable odds that saw us through the toughest of situations, especially in Kashmir during the latter years of my tenures there, signifying the most challenging period in my professional life. It was again this positive attitude that saw me through the Pulwama episode, in which forty of our CRPF personnel had to make the supreme sacrifice, described in greater detail in a subsequent chapter.

From the Romantic Hills of Sikkim to Picture-Perfect Udaipur

It was soon time to move on from my first posting at Sikkim to our next peacetime destination, that is, Udaipur, which was our port of call from 1985 onwards. As a young officer who had never been to Udaipur, I was looking forward to this shift to the renowned City of Lakes with tremendous excitement and eagerness. Generally, the arrival of the Army unit at a particular location is preceded by an advance party, which takes charge of the accommodation and vehicles, and all other nitty-gritties entailed in the movement of an entire Army unit to its new designated posting.

As I mentioned earlier, the troops of the Rajputana Rifles are mainly from the states of Rajasthan and Haryana, known for their bravery and wrestling prowess. The man of the moment for us at this time was Havildar Sant Ram, also an accomplished wrestler, who had visited Udaipur ahead of us as part of the advance party, but for some reason had returned to Sikkim while the unit was still located here. And the moment we saw Sant Ram, we literally gheraoed him, bombarding him with questions about Udaipur, its sights and sounds, and the eccentricities of life that would permeate our stint in the lake city. However, we were in for some disappointment as Havildar Sant Ram, in accordance with his training and background as a wrestler, responded grimly, '*Wahan bahut bura haal hai* (things are in bad shape there).' Crestfallen, we looked at each other, not knowing how to weather this shock that had punctured all our expectations of moving to an exhilarating locale, and then gradually summoned enough courage to ask Sant Ram the reason for this anticlimax in our Udaipur sojourn. His response of '*wahan tamatar do rupay kilo hain*', restored our spirits, as for him, the picturesque city of Udaipur had lost its sheen merely for a mundane reason—the ubiquitous tomato, which was a daily staple in Sant Ram's diet, was available at an 'exorbitant' price of Rs 2 per kg in the city! Needless to say, our priorities were quite different from Sant Ram's, and we were again immersed in crafting our imaginary plans and agendas for our Udaipur posting.

In the next chapter, we move from Sikkim to Udaipur, which marked another momentous period in my life—it was here that I found my life partner and commenced yet another phase of responsibility and commitment, this time to my personal family in addition to my Army family.

7

Entering Matrimony

What Marrying an Army Officer Entails

As mentioned in the previous chapter, my sojourn in Udaipur almost entirely coincided with the beginning of my marital life, as I set off on a new journey with a companion who was going to be my support system for life. Here, first, I would like to narrate the sequence of events leading to my marriage, which will also—I hope—serve as a sort of tutorial or guide for young girls and boys for their career and life, enunciating what marriage to an Army officer signifies, as it entails forfeiture of a few personal comforts and a lot of sacrifice in terms of separation from the partner for significant durations of time, and uncertainties about life and future plans, especially for the wife. However, for an Army officer, the most rewarding aspect of marriage is the unflinching commitment of their spouse through difficult and uncertain times in life.

As I approached marriageable age and subtle pressure mounted on me to choose my life partner, my unambiguous brief to my parents was that they should do the scouting on my behalf, as due to paucity of both time and intention on my part to look for a partner, for me, an arranged marriage was really the way to go. I am perhaps saying it just to boost my ego, but the hard fact is that after spending four years in NDA/IMA (without mobile phones in those days) and nearly two years in isolated high-altitude peaks of the Himalayas, the choice before me was to either become a monk or settle for an early arranged marriage. I decided to choose the latter, as my profession was already decided, which, for all practical purposes, also meant spending half my life in the higher lands of the monks! While discussing the nitty-gritties of matrimony with my parents and Bijee, I specified that my would-be wife should be prepared to handle the numerous challenges that constantly confront Army families.

Initially, with my parents being in Nepal and me being posted in Udaipur, and none of us stationed in Punjab, coupled with the mandate that I had to get hitched to a Punjabi girl, looking for a suitable match was an onerous task, both for me and my immediate family. The responsibility for matchmaking and scouting for a suitable partner was thus passed on to my relatives who were based in Punjab. Their efforts paid off soon, and after they had zeroed in on a prospective partner for me, the formal proposal came from the family of my future wife, Nita, who was pursuing her masters in fine arts at the time. The meeting for 'breaking the ice' between the two families, fixed for 1 November 1986, the day of Deepavali, a festival of lights and good fortune, was planned by my Chachaji and Nita's Mamaji, who lived in neighbouring villages, and both the families knew each other well. The match was given a thumbs up by the elders in both families, with the common factor being *'munda te kudi dovein hi bohat sohne ne, badi pyari jodi banegi* (both the boy and girl are good-looking, and will make a wonderful match).'

The first meeting between me and my prospective bride was quite memorable. I was keen to impress the would-be bride, and decided to wear—with my limited income—'Dunlop' sports shoes and 'Hara' jeans ('Hara' was a very popular Japanese brand in those days, and a pair of Hara jeans would cost half of my monthly salary), which I had bought during one of my visits to Nepal. Despite the discreet pressure from both families, who felt that neither side had any reason to say 'No' to the proposal, both sides left it unsaid and the matter seemed to have hit a roadblock with no response from either side for a few weeks. At the personal level, Nita was still not sure and needed time to assess and reassess the proposal. Nita's family tried to persuade her to say 'Yes' to the proposal, pointing out that the prospective groom was not only a suitable match personally but was also promising professionally, as his 'gradings' in the Army courses were exceptionally high, and he had been an outstanding student in all the courses that he had attended so far. This discreet inquiry and description, acquired through some of Nita's fauji relatives, did wonders for my ego when I later learnt about it from my wife after marriage! However, she refused to be pressured into making a hasty decision, and perhaps needed time to think it over, as she was only about twenty years old and not too keen to jump at the first proposal that came along.

The photo that was exchanged, circa 1986

Nita Bajwa—the photo that made the difference, circa 1986; the rest, as they say, is history

First 'Encounter' with the 'Captain' of My Life

The initial first meeting between us, which had taken place at Nita's house on the day of Deepavali of 1986, was followed by an interesting corollary. After both of us were more or less agreeable to the proposal, our families too seemed keen for it to fructify into marriage, but strangely, neither side gave a clear confirmation, or positive or negative indication to take the discussion forward, leaving the matter in suspended animation, as it were. While they, that is, the girl's family, thought we would get back to them, we, on our part, thought that they would inform us of their decision. Soon thereafter, my parents returned to Nepal and I went back to Udaipur in this environment of uncertainty, with both sides adopting a 'wait and watch' attitude.

After a lull of about one and a half months, I returned to the village on leave in December, where my uncle was unwell and had to be taken for treatment to a nearby town. When I was on an errand purchasing medicines for him, I providentially ran into the car of Nita's Mamaji while crossing the road to enter a pharmacy. Her uncle, who was on his way to Chandigarh, stopped the car, and I wished him. After acknowledging my greetings, he politely inquired why we had not responded to the proposal. Taken aback, I said that we were fine with the match but were waiting for their response. Nonplussed, he said that they were also agreeable to our proposal but were anticipating that the boy's side would take the initiative in finalizing the match. Thus, just as a random newspaper notification in a bus had decided my career, this chance meeting on the road with Nita's uncle led to my marriage—I couldn't help but think that destiny is indeed an all-powerful force, or at least proved to be so in both my personal and professional life.

Immediately after our encounter on the road, her uncle changed track and instead of Chandigarh drove to Nita's parents' house to rekindle the discussion on the proposal. Things started moving at lightning speed after this encounter, and just a few hours later, Nita's family visited our farmhouse to 'seal the deal'. The slight recalcitrance on the part of Nita, who was mentally not fully prepared for marriage, had been neutralized by persuasion from her parents, who, by the way, were suitably impressed with my credentials, and also her two elder sisters, both of whom were married to officers in the defence forces, one to a Naval officer and the other to an Army officer. The crowning stroke was the fact that her grandfather and father's elder brother had participated in the First and Second World Wars, respectively, and the family thus respected and preferred their daughters to settle down with men in uniform. This thus proved the age-old adage that marriages are made in heaven, as through our long marital life, we have been blessed with love and commitment to each other. On a lighter note, in our case, the 'heaven' that decided our marriage was actually a beautiful countryside road in Punjab!

Wedding Vows

Here, I must point out that Nita's reluctance also stemmed from another issue, which initially ran like an undercurrent in our impending relationship; the fact that her future mother-in-law would be not her husband's biological mother but his stepmother. She discussed this issue with her friends, but they convinced her to shed her inhibitions and not use this as a flimsy reason for refusal. Moreover, the emotional succour that the two families derived from the fact they had roots and antecedents in the same region of Punjab was a strong influential factor in favour of the marriage. Thus, our next meeting on 17 December 1986 was for our engagement, with the date being a red-letter day in my life, as the date of my commissioning into the Army too had been 17 December, three years earlier. Thereafter, marriage followed in just two months, on 1 February 1987, which is again a special date, as it happens to be my birthday. The date was decided arbitrarily, as the bride's family sought time of about six weeks for the wedding preparations, and in keeping with the Sikh tradition of *Anand Karaj* or 'Act towards a happy life', wherein a marriage is solemnized generally on a Sunday morning in the *Gurdwara Saheb*, we chose the first Sunday falling after about six weeks of the betrothal ceremony for the wedding, which was incidentally 1 February 1987.

77

With regard to fixing the date for the marriage, I would like to narrate another very important coincidence. There is an Army ruling, probably from the British era, which authorizes an Army officer to apply for the married officers' accommodation only after he has attained the age of twenty-five. I really don't know the origin and logic of this ruling, but by design or destiny, I too decided to get married on the very day I was to turn twenty-five, which meant that my birthday and wedding anniversary would fall on the same day every year. This, in fact, resulted in a very interesting combination thirty-five years later on the day of my superannuation, when my sixtieth birthday, thirty-five years of marriage and retirement, all fell on the same day!

On the day of the engagement, my Naniji, who had come specially to attend the ceremony, was in for a unique treat as Nita prepared her trademark coffee for my grandmother. When Bijee expressed her appreciation for the coffee, Nita's demure but candid response was, 'Bijee, I can make good coffee but I know nothing about cooking regular meals!' This tête-à-tête between my Naniji and my fiancée set the tone for my wife's subsequent indoctrination into the kitchen, where she fulfilled her aspirations to become an enviable cook, learning the ropes the hard way!

Just-in-Time Wedding

Coming back to my Army responsibilities, since my marriage was fixed for 1 February, I had taken leave from 26 January (Republic Day) onwards, to ensure sufficient time for travel to be able to reach home well in advance of the wedding. However, though my leave had been sanctioned, two days before it was to kick in, the Indian Army got mobilized for 'Operation Brasstacks', when India and Pakistan were almost on the brink of a war in January 1987. The tension was eventually defused when the then Pakistani President Zia-ul-Haq visited Jaipur to watch a cricket match. But the days preceding this happy outcome were laced with tension on the border between the two nations. While on one hand, I was completing all my responsibilities before proceeding on leave, on the other hand, my unit was being mobilized to move towards the border.

In this backdrop, when prior to the departure of the unit, an 'All OK' and 'Ready to March' report was submitted to my commanding officer, Colonel (later Brigadier) Trigunesh Mukherjee, I was convinced in my mind that my wedding would have to be deferred and I would depart for the border along with my unit members. But Colonel Mukherjee did not seem to think so. I was quite shocked when he said almost matter-of-factly, 'OK, Tiny, see you after your marriage.' I averred that I would prefer to go with the unit but he asserted, 'There is no need for that, you go and get married, and in case you hear the news of war breaking out, just pack your bags and come straight to the border.' As I was all packed and ready to move to the border, I handed over my trunk and bistarband (bedding) to my Company Havildar Major (CHM) and left for my home with a small handbag, expecting to join my unit in action very soon. The excitement of being with the troops and the unit during combat causes an indefinable exhilaration and rush of adrenaline, a feeling I was destined to experience through most of my Army career later.

It was in this uncertain atmosphere that I eventually got married, and unfortunately, since most of the Army units had been deployed on the international border, none of my Army friends, and even the would-be co-brother (husband of my wife's elder sister), who is also an Army officer, could attend our wedding. Since I was mentally prepared to resume my duties immediately after the marriage, we cancelled all our plans for a honeymoon, and after spending just a few days together as a newly married couple, we headed back to my unit location. Hence, like all the landmark events in my life, the occurrence of my marriage too was closely associated with events in the Army, as it happened in the shadow of war.

Welcoming the New Bride into the Unit

Post-marriage, when I returned to join my unit with my wife in tow, most of the unit members had moved ahead towards the border, and only the ladies or Army wives were stationed in the Army housing facility at Udaipur. Notwithstanding the prevalent uncertainty and tense atmosphere of an impending war, all the ladies heartily welcomed the young bride and went out of their way to make her feel comfortable in the new environment, which was radically different from the comfort of her maiden home.

We travelled by the famous Chetak Express, the only train to Udaipur from Delhi in those days, and were expected to reach Udaipur Railway Station around 9 a.m. However, the train was running slightly late. Notwithstanding the fact that most of the unit personnel and officers were not in station, I was certain that the ladies would organize a traditional welcome for the new bride both at the railway station and in the unit. While we were in the train, I was briefing Nita throughout about the likely welcome she would receive at the railway station and was literally boasting about the affection that our unit officers and ladies displayed for each other. In the absence of smartphones and their ubiquitous picture galleries, I was trying to enthusiastically describe to her the personality of every lady likely to be at the railway station and also advising her on how to conduct herself. Although she listened to me patiently, she also gave me a rather haughty look, suggesting that as a master's student, she did not really need much tutoring from a husband who was a graduate. I was, however, convinced that we would get over this awkward tension as soon as she was surrounded by the love and affection of her new family at the railway station.

The much-awaited moment arrived, when the Chetak Express reached Platform Number 1 of Udaipur Railway Station. I was literally hanging out of the coach to see the welcome arrangements. But I almost fell off the moving train, and all my high hopes were dashed, when I could not spot a single soul from my unit on the railway station. Dejected, I picked up our bags and meekly told my wife that the anticipated welcome for her would probably be organized in the unit as the ladies may not have been able to come to the railway station. She acquiesced, exhibiting great dignity and grace, especially after my boasts which came to nought, and I realized that here was a life partner who would stand by me like a rock through the thick and thin of our marital and professional life.

With regard to the issue of why the welcome party was missing at the railway station, we learnt later that the ladies from the unit had actually organized a perfect reception for the new bride entering the 4 RAJRIF family at the Udaipur Railway Station much before the scheduled arrival of the train, complete with garlands, sweets, a welcome puja thali and tea at the railway platform itself. However, the delay in arrival of the train motivated the ladies to hurriedly change their plans and instead greet the newly married couple at the preceding station, the Maharana Pratap Station, where the train was due to arrive about 15 minutes before Udaipur Railway Station. So, they packed all the stuff and moved to Maharana Pratap Railway Station, but unfortunately by the time they reached there, the train had already left that station. They thus had to immediately rush back to the original welcome point, but before they could come back, our train had reached Udaipur and we had missed the welcome party. However, all's well that ends well, and as we were looking for a porter to help us with our luggage, we spotted all the ladies from our unit, frantically waving to us to return to the coach and de-board only when their arrangements were back in place. Hence, the dramatic merry-go-round from one station to the other ended happily and the reception that ensued was not only the most auspicious way to start our new journey but remains etched in our memories as one of the most memorable events of our married life.

Immediately on arrival in the unit, while I went to the border to join my unit, Nita, my bride, stayed alone in the Udaipur cantonment for a few months with all the other ladies of the unit. Initially, she did feel out of sorts as even our luggage had not reached Udaipur, but the intense warmth and caring attitude that characterizes Army wives across the country helped her tide through this difficult period. And I daresay that when I returned from the operational area after a few months, she had become so much a part of the unit that she hardly missed me. Such incidents reinforce the concept that the entire Army, including the wives of the officers, coalesce into such a close-knit entity that it is not just an extended family but almost like the intimate 'family'. One of my colleagues, Captain Bala Nair, had also got married around this time, and his wife too was staying with the unit in Udaipur. So every evening, these two young brides would visit a different officer's house to dine with the senior officers' wives, who would feed them affectionately.

Bond of Caring and Compassion

As part of the protocol, every fortnight, one officer was required to return from the border to the headquarters on duty to ferry some operational items and important letters back to the unit's location. In line with his compassionate nature, Colonel Trigunesh Mukherjee used to send a young married officer along with few married soldiers on this duty to enable them to meet their wives and children, even if for a short period, and to check on the welfare of the other families in the unit. This officer and soldiers' arrival was eagerly anticipated not only by their own wives but also by all the other ladies, as this symbolized a proxy meeting with the 'husband' and also usually brought good tidings about all the men stationed at the border. Since this was the pre-smartphone era, these rare personal meetings and letters sent by post were the only means of communication for the families of the soldiers.

Despite being so far away from their homes and loved ones, and the Damocles' sword of war looming over their heads, these women showed unusual daring and affection towards each other, not succumbing to fear but instead keeping their chins up courageously and acting as a tremendous support system for each other, also enhancing our mutual respect and bonding for each other.

The officers' wives not only provided support to each other but regularly visited the jawans' wives in the station to update them about the well-being of their husbands and resolve any issue they may be facing. This kinship among the families of officers and jawans was clearly visible even after the unit's return to the peace location, with the meetings of the jawans' wives continuing undisturbed until the unit moved on to the next field area. An Army wife rarely has to contend with the unpleasant thought of staying alone for months immediately after marriage in an alien land, because the *tarteeb* (drills) in the unit and the attitude of care and concern prevailing within the Army fraternity never let Army wives feel alone or neglected. So, all the young men and women wishing to marry an Army officer can rest assured that they would be marrying not an individual but an institution that will take good care of them at all times.

Another incident occurred with my wife during this period—she developed a medical problem and was admitted to the Military Hospital, and had to be administered an injection. She was paranoid about injections and all the ladies of the unit and even the officers trooped into the hospital to check on her and offer their support in this hour of crisis. As the compounder approached her with the menacing needle, Nita, despite being seriously ill, suddenly started jumping from one bed to another to evade the injection. She was ultimately pacified by a senior officer, Major (later Colonel) Hoshiar Singh Jatrana, who, just like her own father would have done, gently but sternly told her, '*Beta*, injection *toh lagwana hi padega, aaj ek lagwao varna kal teen lagenge*' (Child, you need this medicine. You can get injected once today or thrice tomorrow). The fear of this hat-trick of injections, coupled with the fatherly advice of Major Jatrana, did the trick and she finally agreed to take the shot. Thus, even though it pampers its members no end, the Army also never fails to mentor or chide them for their own benefit, as their parents or teachers would do.

First Sweet in Our Kitchen—*Munh Meetha*

Since Udaipur was our first port of call immediately after marriage, we initially ate from the Army mess and sent our tiffins to be refilled for every meal. This practice continued for about two months after which Nita decided that she must start cooking at home. Her first day in the kitchen signifies another interesting episode. The protagonist of this episode is the famous VJ of *Roadies* fame, Rannvijay Singha, an actor and a popular name with the youngsters, who is the son of Lieutenant General (then Captain) Iqbal Singh Singha and was about four or five years old at the time when his father was an officer in the unit. Since my wife always pampered the kid by showering him with chocolates and sweets, he visited her frequently, and he would admire her cosmetics and nail paints, which were part of her marital trousseau. Embarrassingly for her, one day, he went home and innocently questioned his mother, 'Nita Aunty has long nails and wears attractive nail polish, why don't you?', to which, even more embarrassingly for my wife, his mother replied, 'Nita gets her food from the mess whereas I do the cooking myself and thus have to keep my nails short.' This incident fuelled Nita's determination to learn cooking and stop relying on tiffins from the mess. Hence began her long and arduous training in the kitchen!

The first foray into the kitchen was for making a dessert, and Nita, along with another lady from the unit, decided to start her culinary journey by making halwa. Although neither of them knew the recipe, both the ladies entered the kitchen, armed with all the ingredients, literally ready for this new challenge. Since that day happened to be a Sunday, I was also at home. After about half an hour, when I could not hear any activity in the kitchen nor get the distinct whiff of the halwa, I came out of the bedroom to investigate. To my utter surprise, both the women were standing and staring at all the ingredients and brainstorming on how to go about the task of cooking the dish that they had very bravely embarked upon. Since I had much more experience of cooking halwa than the ladies, as I had learnt to rustle up many dishes in Army camps, I asked them to exit the kitchen and ended up making the halwa myself. Thus, the very first dish that emerged from our kitchen after our marriage was cooked entirely by me, and at the cost of sounding immodest, I can say that it was quite delicious.

Taking this halwa misadventure in her stride, my wife became even more determined to don the chef's hat at home, starting with the basic dishes of Indian cuisine. The first item on the menu was dal, but here too, Nita ran into a roadblock as for some reason, her dal would take inordinately long to cook. With the pressure cooker in our kitchen emitting endless whistles almost on a daily basis, the intrigued neighbours would often ask her, 'We finish our cooking in about half an hour but your pressure cooker keeps whistling nonstop; exactly what do you cook in it?' How could she reveal that she was basically resorting to trial and error with the dal, as at times, it would be overcooked and end up being totally mashed, while at other times, it would be undercooked and she had to restart the exercise of softening it in the pressure cooker? These experiments in the kitchen continued for some weeks but eventually, my wife emerged victorious and mastered various recipes through experimentation and her never-say-die spirit even in an era when there were no YouTube tutorials.

'Buddy' Admonitions

Another very important part of Army life is our 'buddy' or soldier who is almost like an officer's shadow or alter ego. He is a constant companion during peacetime, and also accompanies the officer during war. My buddy at that time was Naik Rann Singh from a place called Kankroli near the beautiful Rajsamand Lake in Rajasthan. He had completed about seventeen years of service and was in his late thirties at the time. He was extremely possessive about me and was also the keeper of my wallet when I was a bachelor. In fact, whenever I wanted to go out shopping or for a meal, I had to request him to give me some money from my wallet. On a few occasions, he even admonished me for overspending, and once when I asked for about Rs 20 for eating out, he chided me, asserting, 'What will you do with Rs 20? Try and keep your expense under Rs 15.'

This dual mother and father figure in my life became quite indignant after my marriage when he realized that control over the personal expenditure was slipping from his hands and my newly wedded wife was gradually taking control over my wallet. Whenever we asked him for money for shopping, he would part with it very reluctantly, and when we returned, he would take stock of the stuff we had bought, critically examining each item and doing mental calculations to determine if we had splurged during our shopping trip. We had to give him the complete account of our expenses, and my wife especially was on the receiving end of his censure, often being denounced by him, though discreetly, as a spendthrift. He frequently also advised her to imbibe the saving habit to be able to create a fund for buying a house later on. On one such occasion, when she asked him where she could get one of my shirts mended by a tailor, he lectured her on how she should learn sewing and carry out all such minor tasks at home rather than unnecessarily spending on these services. The care and concern with which my buddy Naik Rann Singh tried to handle my expenses and also guide my young wife to become a prudent homemaker is another example of the family values and compassion that characterize Army life and that make the entire unit a cohesive family living in a home away from home. Before we moved out from Udaipur a year later, Naik Rann Singh's daughter got married in his native village and my wife sent a nice Rajasthani saree as a gift from a 'didi' (elder sister) on her wedding, affectionately acknowledging the role of the disciplinarian father played by Naik Rann Singh for both of us.

In the next chapter, I will share some other key incidents of my life pertaining to both my personal and Army families.

8

'Trust' and Respect for Rules: A Non-Negotiable Value System

'Battle Honour/Raising Day'—Taking Pride in History

Army units always celebrate their Battle Honour days and Raising days with great pomp and show. These are the landmark days in a unit's history, where the currently serving officers, JCOs and other ranks re-dedicate themselves to safeguarding the *Naam, Namak* and *Nishan* (honour, loyalty and identity) of the paltan. 4 RAJRIF celebrates 'Keren Day' as their Battle Honour day, which falls on 12 February. In view of the scorching summer heat of Rajasthan, the outdoor training with troops is generally conducted during the winter months in deserts. In February 1986, while the unit was training in the deserts, a very solemn ceremony was organized to celebrate 'Keren Day' on the beautiful sand dunes of Rajasthan. In a literal embodiment of the popular phrase, '*Jangal mein mangal* (fun in the jungle)', the unit invited the legendary Rajasthani folk singer

Bungar Khan, who, like many among the Rajputana Rifles troops, was a native of the region, to entertain the troops and bring some joy and relief from the sweat and toil of the training.

The impromptu inclusion of Bungar Khan in the schedule of events and his mesmerizing performance, which had earlier enthralled audiences in over fifteen countries, became indelible memories for us as we enjoyed his folk music atop the makeshift stage created by collecting the desert sand in a heap and covering it with a fauji tarpaulin. Although I have had the opportunity of watching many performances by accomplished artists the world over, Bungar Khan's performance in the desert that evening wins hands down over all of them.

Legendary Indian artist Bungar Khan performing on the dunes of Barmer atop a locally made stage, February 1986

'Aye Meri Zohra Zabeen'—some lighter moments with Nita during a Battle Honour Day lunch, February 2010

Sand or snow—Battle Honour Day, February 2012; celebration spirits are always high

'Theirs Not to Reason Why'

An incident similar to the one wherein I got punished for keeping long hair in the NDA occurred again at Udaipur. Captain (later Lieutenant General) Iqbal Singh Singha was performing the duties of adjutant, and one evening when he was taking the report of the games fall-in, he perceived that I reported late by a few seconds. He thus pronounced the punishment of 'Round-the-clock guard check', which meant that I would have to check all the guards in the unit every hour throughout the night. Although I was sure that I had reported in time for the games, the adjutant thought otherwise and his perception could not be questioned. I commenced my punishment and started checking on the guards every hour. Since the entire exercise would take about forty-five minutes or so, it implied only a small break of fifteen minutes before I had to set off again to start the next hour's checking.

Since those days we had manually-wound wristwatches, which usually did not show the exact time, as a practice, the unit would run as per the timings of the quarter guard's clock, and the quarter guard NCO would visit the adjutant's office every morning to inform him of the time so that the adjutant could align his watch with the quarter guard's clock. The quarter guard NCO would give out the time by saying, *'Jab main kahoon* "TIME", *toh time hoga das baj ke teen minute . . . 5, 4, 3, 2, 1,* "TIME".' ('When I say "TIME", the time will be three minutes past ten o'clock . . . 5, 4, 3, 2, 1, "TIME".') In this way, the adjutant's watch would be aligned with the quarter guard's timings to the last second.

The next day, when the quarter guard NCO gave the 'TIME' to Captain Singha, he realized that his watch was ahead by a few minutes, and he had wrongly punished me the previous day. However, since the adjutant is always 'right', there was no way he would apologize to a junior unit member, and I had no option to protest against the punishment meted out by him or 'to reason why'. However, he decided to make amends in a subtle way, by inviting my wife and me to his place for dinner that evening. Thus, the unfair punishment I received was more than made up for by the opportunity to partake of the rather sumptuous dinner prepared by Mrs Baljeet Singha.

Nurturing the Concept of Unconditional Faith

The Army is not a profession but a bonding for life, and the everyday experiences that we have during the course of our careers provide a keen insight into the values espoused by the Army and the relationships nurtured by Army personnel and their families with each other. Life in the unit is a veritable depiction of the extent of mutual faith, or literally blind faith, that people in the Army have in each other. For my wife too, it was a new experience of absolute faith and respect. One incident highlighting this concept of trust occurred soon after our marriage. Like all young brides, my wife too had brought with her some of the gold and jewellery that she had received as part of the wedding rituals. She had a jewellery box full of various rings, bangles and other trinkets that accompanied her to her first post-marriage abode at Udaipur. After a few months of stay here, Nita had to go back home to appear for her post-graduation final exams. She put her gold ornaments in three zip pouches and asked me to keep the bags in a safe place before she embarked on the journey. I requested Captain (later Lieutenant General) Iqbal Singh Singha to keep the bags in safe custody in the locker in his office (although it is generally not done but seeing our helpless situation, he agreed). Neither he nor I checked the contents of the pouches and he just took them from me and placed them in his locker.

On Nita's return to the unit, Captain Singha asked me to collect the jewellery bags. I opened the locker and extracted the pouches but as became evident later, I took out only two pouches and inadvertently left the third one inside the locker only, for it must have been pushed to the back, thus evading my gaze. My wife too did not miss the third pouch, as she herself had not counted the trinkets and was not sure of the full inventory of either the jewellery items or the number of bags before asking me to deposit them in safe custody. This oversight on our part came to light three months later when Captain Singha was going on leave and had to hand over charge of his locker to another officer. During the process of handing over and taking charge, as they were checking the files in the locker, suddenly they came across my wife's jewellery pouch. Captain Singha called me, telling me that I had forgotten something in his locker. I checked with my wife, who said that she could not remember missing anything. Captain Singha then invited us to his home for dinner and promised to show us what we had forgotten to collect from his locker, leaving us in a quandary, as we still could not figure out what was missing from our jewellery collection. It was only when Nita saw the pouch that she realized that the gold in it was indeed hers, and she had not checked her inventory for the entire three months. This incident clearly shows the faith that Army personnel repose in each other, never doubting each other's loyalties or bona fide intentions, and always pitching in to offer support and assistance to colleagues and friends, even if it entails the safekeeping of expensive and prized personal possessions.

'Do Thy Duty and That Is Best'

Another distinct characteristic of life in uniform is the burden of responsibility as an officer and ensuring that the orders of the commanding officer are obeyed to the hilt, irrespective of whether one is individually a beneficiary of the same or not. In those days, hardly one or two officers in a unit owned a car, and most of the officers travelled on two-wheelers, including a few bicycles. Thus, in order to facilitate the travel of the wives and families of the officers and jawans to the hospital or railway station, for instance, certain military vehicles would be modified with cushioned seats covered with blankets and sheer curtains, and would be referred to as 'Officers' 1 Ton' or 'Jawan Bus'. When Nita was scheduled to go home for her exams, the CO, Colonel Mukherjee, told me that the Officers' 1 Ton should drop her to the railway station. He also told me to ensure that the vehicle was in good condition. When Nita was slated to leave for the railway station in the evening, the CO and other unit officers and ladies dropped in to say goodbye. The CO was ostensibly not very happy with the condition of the blankets in the vehicle and told me to see him in his office after dropping my wife at the railway station. When I reached the CO's office, he asked me in a fit of temper, 'Why the hell was a suitable vehicle not provided to the lady travelling to the railway station?' I told him, 'Sir, since Nita was travelling in it, I thought it was okay to use the old blankets.' This infuriated him further, and then I learnt the biggest lesson of my life when he roared, 'As an officer, it is not important, in fact, it should never be in your mind, as to who the beneficiary of your actions or orders is. An officer's actions are always based on absolute prudence and today, you failed in your duty as an officer to provide a respectable vehicle to a unit lady travelling to the railway station. You have compromised on the standards of the unit and the respect that we have for our ladies.' Suitably chastened, I learnt from this one statement of my CO that all my actions as an Army officer should always be above board and aimed at protecting the best interests of all whom I am responsible for, my jawans and my nation.

Being promoted to Captain with Colonel Trigunesh Mukherjee (CO)
and Suby Sir (Second in Command) doing the honours

When Providence and Prudence Went Hand in Hand

Another similar incident occurred when we were on our way to
Kashmir. I had already reached Kashmir and my wife was scheduled
to join me from Punjab and was booked on a flight from Amritsar,
which was getting repeatedly delayed or cancelled because of
a terrorist threat at Amritsar Airport. Since Amritsar was an
intermediate location for her, she was staying with a unit officer
posted there, Lieutenant Colonel (later Brigadier) Khazan Singh
Dalal. Lieutenant Colonel Dalal was not posted in the unit when
we got married and hence, neither my wife nor I had ever met him
or his wife before. Here again, I would like to clarify that I have
many relatives in Amritsar but the choice of staying with an unknown

unit officer was the only option considered and exercised. Lieutenant Colonel Dalal would escort my wife to the airport every day, where they would be told that the flight had been cancelled because of some impending threat. It was on the third day of their visit to the airport that they were told that the flight had finally arrived and was ready for departure. In her hurry to board the flight, my wife forgot her purse in the waiting lounge of Amritsar Airport. Interestingly, this purse contained the same pouch of gold that had been forgotten in Captain Singha's locker. On reaching Srinagar, she boarded an Army vehicle that transported her to our unit in Kupwara in North Kashmir. It was only on reaching Kupwara that she realized her purse was missing but could not recall where she had left it—in the aircraft, or at the airport, or perhaps even at Colonel Dalal's residence.

Providentially, since the purse had been forgotten at the airport (as we learnt later), in view of the prevalence of terrorism in Punjab, no one touched that purse, fearing it to have been a camouflaged bomb left by a terrorist. Hence, the airport authorities summoned a bomb squad to inspect the purse, and when it was opened, much to their amazement, the bomb disposal force found no incendiary device in it but a collection of gold jewellery. Since my wife's identity card was also in the purse, the security officer there, who happened to be a colleague of her father's, immediately realized whose purse it was, and thereafter, she was traced. We received a telegram within two days informing us that Nita's purse had been found at Amritsar Airport, asking us to identify the items in it and then claim it after suitable verification. According to her, the prospective list would include two bangles, three pairs of earrings and two rings.

My head clerk in the unit, Subedar Hardev Singh, typed the letter detailing this list, which was to be shared with the Amritsar airport authorities. However, before sending the list, the head clerk, also a soldier and an old hand who definitely had much more experience of married life than me, advised me to get the list re-checked by my wife, as wives tend to overlook or deliberately tend to underplay the loss, especially when the loss is due to their own oversight. And sure enough, when I asked Nita to reconfirm the items mentioned in the list based on her first account, she added a few more items to the list. The head clerk persisted, and asked me to get it checked yet again. Incredibly, I sent that letter to her four times, and each time, some amendment or addition was made in the list. Ultimately, the letter was dispatched from our end, and I requested one of my cousins stationed at Amritsar to collect the purse from the airport after producing the list of its contents. And believe it or not, when he claimed the purse and opened it, he found some additional items in it that had still been missed out from the list despite its amendment a number of times. What an unforgettable history that particular trinket bag acquired! Here again, another very important military lesson: 'Whatever is not checked is not done' was learnt early in life without having to go through a more stringent military way of learning.

Even more intriguing than the sequence of events leading to the recovery of the purse was the wisdom and confidence of the head clerk, who proved to be so right when he urged me to get the list re-checked and revised a number of times. I later found out that the JCOs and NCOs in the Army are a veritable treasure chest of information and experience, and keep imparting all their learning to officers during such key occasions, what is popularly known as hands-on experience or 'on the job learning'. These two incidents indicate that even though the officers in the Army and their families may at times be remiss or exhibit carelessness, the system in the Army can help overcome such challenges and ensure complete safety and security of both individuals and property.

Belying Trust, an Unimaginable Sacrilege for a Soldier

The security of Army life that I have referred to is also applicable for the home and hearth of a soldier—it may sound incredulous but it is a fact that Army personnel never lock their homes, even when they go on long leave. The whole house is left open and under the care of the watch and ward staff without any risk or possibility of an untoward incident. This faith and mutual trust among Army personnel, manifested in all aspects of their lives, is thus a remarkable trait and, in fact, the hallmark of the Indian Army. The core values that this sentiment emerges from are those of solidarity and protection for the country, come what may. It also symbolizes the trust that the entire nation reposes in the Army for the unconditional security it provides, which is why it is unthinkable for any member of the same Army to belie this trust in any way, least of all by failing to take care of the homes and household possessions of his fellow Army men.

The mandate of safeguarding the trust reposed in soldiers by their nation is actually a key lesson that is constantly imparted in the Army, not obtrusively but through actions and hands-on experience. And this emphasis on justifying the faith of one's countrymen is applicable across the rank and file of the Army, from top to bottom, from the jawans to generals. The motto behind this reality is: we trust you with our very life, so trust in terms of protecting our property and physical possessions is a very small part of the overall faith we have in the Army. These values also became an integral part of my entire career, and when I later became a CO, I was fully conversant with the reality that as a CO, almost 850 men owed their allegiance to me and would be ready to stake their lives at one command from me—how then could I betray this unshakeable trust in any way? Similarly, how could they be unfaithful to me for trivial things like material goods when they trusted me with their very lives?

Apart from the concept of trust, discipline too is an absolutely non-negotiable concept in the Army. The following incident underscores how actual or perceived indiscipline by any Army officer has inevitable repercussions.

The Redoubtable Mess Meeting

'Mess' as against the dictionary meaning, is a well-laid-out institution in all the military units where bachelor or forced bachelor (married officers staying single) officers dine. This is also the place where all the official and personal social functions are organized. For smooth running of the officers' mess in a unit, a mess committee is constituted from within the available officers who are assigned different duties such as food member, wine member, property member or garden member, etc., with the second in command (2IC) of the unit being ex-officio president of the mess committee, popularly called the PMC. There are regular mess meetings held to take stock of various aspects concerning the unit officers' mess including its smooth functioning. This somewhat interesting meeting took place in the summer of 1986, when our unit had just come to Udaipur a few months ago, the renowned Lake City, from its previous location in the high altitude of Sikkim. The CO was Colonel Trigunesh Mukherjee and Suby Sir was the 2IC. One of the biggest attractions of Udaipur, apart from its natural endowments, was that it epitomized the promise of good food, an inevitable enticement for young bachelors like me.

I must clarify here that 4 RAJRIF in those days was blessed with a posse of about a dozen bachelors, ably led by Ally Sir, the stylish young major, who, I daresay, still proudly flaunts his 'youthful' style. Our unit also had a fleet of 'Bultts' (the Bullet or Royal Enfield motorbike, for the less initiated), though Ally Sir preferred to zoom around on his trusted old scooter.

Since Zomato and Swiggy did not exist then, the bachelors would invariably disappear in the evenings, returning rather late for dinner, especially towards the second half of the month, purely for financial reasons! These truant evenings and erratic and staggered arrival timings of bachelors to the mess would result in the mess staff being kept awake late in the night. When the young officers made their late evening entry into the mess amidst shouts of '*Koi hai?* (Anyone there?)', their query would be followed by eerie silence, with the staff having left for good after waiting endlessly for the 'missing' bachelors. Eventually, the issue reached the 2IC, Suby Sir.

Sometime thereafter, we had a famous mess meeting, wherein as per tradition, the 2IC started mentioning various significant matters, initially in his typical *Lakhnavi* or *Allahabadi andaaz*, full of niceties and polished mannerisms. But his tone progressively became stern and finally, he came to the contentious issue, stating, 'Master (his way of addressing us when he was displeased, without undermining his otherwise extremely affectionate attitude), I have been informed of a matter concerning the bachelors who invariably come in very late for dinner and the mess staff has to keep waiting for them.' He would have gone on but suddenly something unprecedented occurred. Much to everyone's astonishment, 'Shorty' Ghura, a young Turk who had less than five years of service, interrupted the 2IC's speech, saying, 'Sorry sir, but that was my point; when we come in late to the mess, we do not find the mess staff waiting.' There was pin-drop silence for a moment, and then as if a dam had been let loose, the CO Colonel Mukherjee thundered, 'You bloody chaps . . .' (the rest of his endearments are not printable). Suffice it to say that the mess staff's complaint was given priority over Shorty's protestation, and all of us were told in no uncertain terms to remain within the limits of discipline and inform the mess staff well in advance whenever we would be late for our meals, and to strictly adhere to the anticipated time of our arrival. I daresay that these transgressions by happy-go-lucky bachelors were suitably curbed by marriage, which automatically instilled discipline in the lives and behaviour of the officers.

The following chapters weave the trajectory of my marital journey as it intersected with the inveterate challenges and responsibilities of my Army life.

Bachelor brigade of 4 RAJRIF ably led by then Major Ajit Singh (Ally Sir, third from left, front row) with Munna, Bala, Khevi, Goofy and Lochan; Shorty, Carie and Tiny in the second row

9

Tales of Endurance and Courage: Behind the Scenes Lives of the Family

The Arrival of Our Children—Father in Absentia

Parenthood is the most endearing blessing that one can be bestowed with. The opportunity to shower unconditional love on our bundle of joy evoked the same feelings, along with equal measures of anxiety and excitement, in both Nita and me as we awaited the birth of our first child. At that time, I was posted in Mhow as a captain and we had made numerous plans to celebrate the baby's arrival. Well into the fourth month of her pregnancy, Nita had gone home for the delivery whereas I was awaiting orders for my next posting, which had been somewhat delayed. However, I was constructively utilizing the God-given extended tenure at Mhow to prepare for my Defence Services Staff College (DSSC) entrance examination scheduled to be held in September that year. Meanwhile, I had already made plans to take leave coinciding with the due date of delivery, to be able to welcome the baby into our world.

In those days of STD PCO calling, I used to ring up Nita every Saturday evening and thereafter bury myself in my books for uninterrupted studies through the rest of the forthcoming week. About ten days prior to the expected date of delivery, when I had gone to wish one of my unit officers posted in Mhow and his wife on their wedding anniversary, on intuition I decided to call up Nita on my way back though it was a Friday instead of our usual calling day of Saturday. So, I went to my favourite PCO booth in Mhow town whose owner used to stay just above his shop itself. When I called up Nita at her parents' home where she was staying, I got no response. After repeated unsuccessful attempts and now plagued with worry, I called up the neighbours, who informed me that Nita had been taken to the hospital after developing labour pains in the evening. Since there were no mobile phones at that time, I had to wait for Nita's father to return home and respond to my call for updating me on Nita's health and well-being. I was frantically calling up every ten minutes, until around midnight when Nita's father, who had come home to pick up some essential personal items for her, informed me that she was fine and that the delivery was expected any moment.

With no immediate family to turn to in that moment of extreme concern, sitting twiddling my thumbs in an STD PCO booth in Mhow market, I had no other option but to keep ringing incessantly every fifteen to twenty minutes in the undying hope that someone would pick up my call and inform me about the well-being of my wife. By now, it was quite late at night and the shop owner wanted to pull down the shutters and retire for the day. However, due to the immense respect he had for the Armed forces, he told me to remain in his shop and keep calling whenever I wanted while he himself went upstairs. I was awake the whole night waiting in vain for the elusive good news. Finally, disheartened and exhausted after the interminable waiting, I left for home at around 7 a.m. to be able to attend a class for the young officers' course at 8 a.m. During the tea break, I rushed again to the PCO booth but the 'situation report', as we call it in the Army, had not changed a bit. This continued through the day and I got the news of the arrival of our son and of mother and baby doing fine only late in the afternoon. Wow, what a relief!

The anxious moments, however, did not end there. Immediately after birth, the baby contracted an infection. Thus, though it was a normal delivery, the mother and child had to stay in the hospital for ten days due to this unexpected health crisis for the little one. It was indeed a traumatic period for my wife; I managed to reach home only on the eleventh day after my son's birth, just as my wife and baby were getting discharged from the hospital.

In my case, duty almost made me miss my own wedding and accounted for my absence at the birth of our first child. Destiny, in fact, continued to test my resilience, as I could not attend the birth of our second child either. I was posted in the Manipur and Nagaland region at that time, which was a non-family posting. Again, like her first pregnancy, I had last met my wife when she was three months pregnant and I was supposed to come on leave in June to be with her during the time of delivery. Our daughter's birth also coincided with our unit's move from the North-east to Kashmir. Personal challenges in the life of a soldier and his family seldom get known to the outside world. The sacrifices made by Army officers and soldiers while dealing with the enemy on the border or terrorists in a counter-insurgency operation are obvious to everyone but the silent sacrifices made by their wives and families largely remain undocumented, unseen and therefore unrewarded. I have the utmost respect for these unsung heroes and heroines in the Army fraternity, who often fight their battles alone behind the scenes and hold the domestic fort while their male counterparts perform their duty outside the home.

I experienced this first-hand. The last month of my wife's second pregnancy coincided with the rising intensity of terrorist activities in the Kashmir Valley where terrorists' incursions against the security forces, including *fidayeen* or suicide attacks by the terrorists, were taking place at an increasing frequency. I was posted in a Rashtriya Rifles (RR) unit, which was involved in highly intense anti-terrorist operations in the Lolab valley near Kupwara in North-west Kashmir. The modus operandi of a fidayeen terrorist was to enter a post manned by security forces laden with explosives and target as many security personnel as possible to cause maximum damage and casualties before getting killed. My unit had moved into the Lolab valley only a day earlier and my company was deployed at an isolated post hugging the mountain ranges, where the nearest reinforcements or any assistance would take anything up to forty-five minutes to reach even by a vehicle. Mine was 'B' company, which was referred to as *'Bajrang Bali's* company' and accordingly, we had placed Lord Hanuman Ji's idol in our company mandir in a small structure located right in the middle of the post premises.

Lord Hanuman Ji's idol made of *ashtadhatu* (an extremely pure octo-alloy consisting of eight metals in equal proportion) was specially ordered from Jaipur.

The particular post where I was the RR company commander came under an attempted fidayeen attack on the night of my daughter's birth. The terrorists tried to storm into my company post in a fidayeen manner. I was a senior major at that time and was standing in the middle of the company post, next to the company mandir, while controlling the operation. An intense firefight was going on when suddenly my CO called on the radio set to inquire about the situation. While I was talking to him, I saw a rocket headed in my direction. I inadvertently shouted something that naturally upset my CO. The rocket landed very close to me and got embedded in the ground but did not explode. The next day when the CO visited my post along with the commander, he told me what I had shouted on the radio set the previous night. I had no clue of what I had uttered but the unexploded rocket still embedded in the ground next to the mandir was telling the story loud and clear. Notwithstanding, Punjabi is a very beautiful language, otherwise. We neutralized the attack without suffering any casualties on our side and blocked the entry of all terrorists into our post. I would credit this turn of events to the blessings of Lord Hanuman Ji and the 'lady luck' personified by our baby daughter, though I was not yet aware of her arrival into our world. After another four days, when I was engaged in a fierce counter-terrorist operation in the jungles, my CO received the good news of our daughter's birth but did not relay this to me; instead, he ordered me and all the officers involved in that operation to return to my company post after the operation.

We had already been engaged in operations for almost three days, and we perceived this message to be the harbinger of news of another impending large-scale operation. However, when we returned to the post, we were met by the CO, who had personally come down to the post along with the entire entourage of officers in the headquarters, to break the news of my daughter's birth to me. All the unit officers joined me and we had a small but roaring party to celebrate the arrival of my second-born. I myself could, however, visit Kupwara to make the STD call and talk to my wife and wish her only eighteen days later. The physical meeting was delayed for a good two months after our daughter was born, that was when I could proceed home on leave and actually see my daughter. The regret that I could not be by my wife's side during both her pregnancies and deliveries will always remain with me. This may sound like the sad incantation of a romantic husband or a devoted father, but I will have to live with the hard truth for my entire life that I was not present at the time of birth of both my children.

My first 'encounter' with our daughter was, however, rather uncongenial, as she was used to the soft and gentle voices of her mother and maternal grandparents. But the minute I entered the house and started talking to everyone in my loud Army baritone, she got ruffled and howled endlessly for a long time. She took some time to overcome her fear of my voice and she would start crying even if she heard the sound of my footsteps. I don't know whether I was naive or not, but it's a unique challenge that I faced and I am sure many fellow Army men too went through this. It's not easy to describe. No one can understand what it means. Being a father, I would always want to hold my baby daughter. It's not easy. When I see this in retrospect, I think it is but a small price to pay in the service of the nation. Notwithstanding my absence, my father-in-law, Sardar Atma Singh Bajwa, a retired police officer and an athlete par excellence during his younger days, held the fort at home in spite of his own eyes having been operated at the time of the delivery of our daughter. His sheer presence in the house boosted the morale of my wife whenever she felt low.

The late Sardar Atma Singh Bajwa, my father-in-law

Back from the 'Dead' Twice Over

The wives and families of soldiers are the epitomes of courage and sacrifice, standing behind their husbands, sons and brothers through every difficult situation, though their invaluable contribution to the careers of the men is seldom acknowledged, leave aside appreciated or celebrated. An army wife's life and what they have to endure never makes headlines but it's always the heartbeat of the main story. My life story, too, has been peppered with similar instances of sacrifice and valour exhibited by my wife, who underwent severe trauma on at least two occasions when she heard of my purported 'death', or rather news of my death, in the media. The first such incident occurred when I was posted as a major in RR in Kashmir and engaged in anti-terrorist operations in the Lolab Valley, and my wife was in her eighth month of pregnancy, expecting our second child. The Army had tragically lost a daredevil officer in one of the operations, who shared the same designation and a name very similar to mine, Major K.G. Singh as opposed to my name, K.J. Singh, and who also happened to be posted in Lolab in the neighbouring RR battalion. When his death was announced in a television news bulletin, his name was mispronounced as K.J. Singh, with the ticker in the news telecast carrying the scroll: 'Major K.J. Singh of Rashtriya Rifles killed in Lolab'. My wife not only heard this news on TV but also read it in the next morning's newspaper. Shocked and devastated, she had no reason to doubt that the news pertained to me as three of the key details were identical to my credentials—the name of the officer, the unit, Rashtriya Rifles, and the location, Lolab. Recovering from the initial shock, she decided to shield her ageing parents from grief as far as possible and attempted to conceal the newspaper from them. However, by this time, the subedar major in my unit, Sube Singh, had learnt of this misidentification and realizing the grim implications of the news for my pregnant wife, he urged me to call and inform her that I was fine. But that was easier said than done, considering that it was an era pre-dating mobile phones with a lack of any form of instant communication. In fact, we did not even have any access to a civil landline phone at our location, and I had to contact one of my counterparts in Kupwara, requesting him to convey to my wife that I was okay and that the news did not pertain to me. After experiencing several hours of mental torment in the belief that I was the casualty being referred to in the media, Nita eventually received the heartening news that I was alive and well. Yet the tremendous relief she felt when the false news was refuted was tempered by an immense sadness emanating from the realization that she may have escaped the blow of destiny but in her place, another wife and another family would be grieving the loss of their husband, son and father.

At the time, one of my maternal uncles, serving in the Border Security Force, was posted in South Kashmir. When he read this news, he immediately checked its veracity with the Corps Headquarters in Srinagar, where he too was told that Major K.J. Singh of the Rashtriya Rifles had been killed in Lolab, but on checking further, he subsequently found out that the officer who made the supreme sacrifice was actually from the Gorkha Rifles and not Rajputana Rifles. He also communicated to my wife that contrary to the announcement, I was alive and unharmed. In retrospect, however, it was obvious that such multiple communications from different channels can actually confound the confusion, causing more anxiety rather than relief.

The second incident related to my 'death' occurred when I was the CO of my battalion in South Kashmir in an intensely terrorist-infested area called Tral. Late on the evening of 18 August 2002, my brigade commander called, advising me to speak to my wife, who was at that time staying at the permanent base of the battalion in Uttarakhand. In this case, too, a ticker displayed during the television news bulletin averred that Colonel K.J. Singh had been killed in Jammu and Kashmir. However, this time, the reference was to a namesake of mine, Colonel Kanwar Jaideep Singh Salaria, Shaurya Chakra, Sena Medal, Commanding Officer 6 DOGRA, a great soldier who had made the supreme sacrifice in the Nowshera sector while fighting with the terrorists whereas I was in Tral in South Kashmir. Again, the STD lines at our post played truant and I could not get in touch with Nita to assure her of the TV news being untrue about me. Hence, I requested the CO of the neighbouring unit to urge his wife, who was also staying in the battalion base at Uttaranchal, to inform my wife about my well-being. Since it was quite late at night, at least by Army standards, he suggested that his wife would speak to Nita only the next morning rather than disturbing her at night. With the experience of the previous similar incident and knowing the distress that she would be going through on hearing this piece of news, I was determined to somehow inform her about my welfare immediately rather than let her suffer through the night. So, I called up on the Army line one of my dear friends, Lieutenant Colonel (later Major General) Anil Chaudhary, who was posted in the Army headquarters in Delhi, requesting him to talk to Nita, but he too suggested that she should not be disturbed at night. Restless and desperate to dispel the misperception about the mistaken identity, I did not give up trying to somehow get the news of my safety across to my wife. Hence, I called my maternal uncle on the Army line, who at that time was posted at the BSF headquarters in Jalandhar, to help out by ringing up Nita on my behalf, but he too advised me to be patient and not rattle her at night. By this time, it was well past midnight and facing a roadblock with all my three contacts, I thought it was best to let matters lie and convey the news to my wife only at daybreak or as and when our STD lines were restored. However, as luck would have it, though all three of my contacts had discouraged me from trying to get in touch with my wife late at night, each of them had had second thoughts and eventually, all three of them ended up calling her during the night itself.

Nita had, however, already seen the ticker on the TV news just as she was about to retire for the night, and once again went through an intensely torturous experience—the first thoughts flitting through her mind painted a desolate and insecure future where she would have to bring up her two little kids and manage the house without the support of her husband. However, once again she rose to the occasion, refusing to give in to emotion or break down and trying to rationalize her thoughts on how to handle the crisis. It was then that the phone rang—it was the wife of the CO of my neighbouring unit. Her short and sharp message was, 'Nita, don't worry, KJ is okay,' after which she disconnected the call. But my wife did not believe her and thought that she had called only to help her tide through the night. Then Lieutenant Colonel Anil Chaudhary and his wife called and they too said exactly the same thing and hung up. My wife was justifiably suspicious, not ready to accept that I was fine on the basis of those two brief and unusual calls, especially since one of them was from an officer posted in Delhi, who was not expected to be in the know about what was happening in my unit in Kashmir, especially after office hours.

To complicate matters further, my uncle too called around the same time, and his message was as cryptic as those of the other two callers, 'Don't worry, he is fine.' By this time, Nita was in complete mental turmoil, and instead of being relieved at the good news, she was convinced that the multiple calls had been made only to soften the blow as something was deeply amiss. She spent the entire night sitting up in bed next to the sleeping children, charting out a roadmap for navigating an uncertain future devoid of a secure livelihood and two kids in tow. But even in her hour of personal anguish and agony, she was determined to downplay her emotions and keep her chin up for the sake of the wives of JCOs and jawans in the unit's base location whose husbands were also involved in similar operations and situations. The ordeal for her ended only at about 5 a.m. when the STD lines of my unit were restored and I was able to call her myself. At first, she was absolutely incredulous on hearing my voice, and then all her controlled emotions were let loose, unleashing a volley of tears. My father and uncle, who were visiting her and were staying in another room in the same house, heard the uncontrollable sobbing, and since they had also heard the phone ringing a number of times at night, came to her room to investigate. When they learnt about the whole sequence of events, they too went through the same array of emotions as Nita, admonishing her for not sharing her feelings with them while trying to handle the situation alone.

With a sense of déjà vu stemming from past experience, my wife recalled another incident about confusion regarding the identity of a soldier killed in action during the Indian Peace-Keeping Force (IPKF) operations in Sri Lanka in 1987. At the time, the father of the soldier whose identity had been mistaken experienced the same intensity of emotions of grief and apprehension, then relief, and an indescribable joy on learning that his son was actually alive, finally followed by a sense of compassion and sadness for the father who had really lost his son and would not have the good fortune of learning that the news was false. Notwithstanding this, our hearts always beat for every soldier's life lost in the line of duty.

Imaandari, Wafadari, Zimmedari

Honesty, Loyalty and *Responsibility*—these three words form the crux of a soldier's value system. While the concepts of honesty and loyalty (to the unit, to the Army as a whole, and ultimately to the nation) are self-explanatory, the idea of 'responsibility' is very different in the Army as compared to civilian life. The incidents

I just narrated about the news of my 'death' on two occasions, and the evidence compelling my wife to believe them to be true but at the same time engendering in her courage and resolve to hide her own grief for the sake of the families of the jawans living in the same station is a classic example of the '*zimmedari*' that an Army officer and his entire family have to fulfil. It shows that as the CO's wife, who was more or less convinced that her husband had been killed in an operation in Kashmir, and was naturally worried about the consequences and implications of this turn of events for herself and her children, she still had thoughts for other women whose husbands were also posted in Kashmir and engaged in the same kind of perilous operations there as her own husband, and who needed to be protected from the trauma of news of the death of one of their husbands' colleagues while performing his duty. Thus, reining in her personal grief, she was determined to fulfil her responsibility as the CO's wife, maintaining a brave front and refusing to exhibit a weak image when they met her next morning so that their spirits too remained strong.

It is clear that the Army prepares not only the officers but also their families to behave responsibly and face any adversity or calamity, or indeed the worst possible outcome of any situation, and to still maintain their courage and composure in the face of all odds. The punishing Army training (what is often called '*ragda*') obtrusively prepares each one of its officers and jawans to bear any kind of physical challenge or hardship, but there are times when physical pressures are overshadowed by mental stress, and it is on such occasions that the unobtrusive training and emotional strength imparted by the Army system of camaraderie and 'brothers in arms' comes to the fore, enabling us to face any adverse situation with maturity and grace, as my wife was ready to do when she heard of my ostensible death. The most explicit aspect of this training is the NDA prayer that each one of us has to recite every morning throughout the three years of our training. Every word of this prayer is designed to imbue us with immense strength to confront even seemingly intractable situations, always motivating us to keep going regardless of any physical or mental obstacle. Here, I would like to recite the NDA prayer and derive the same succour from it that it has continued to offer me since I first heard it more than forty-two years ago:

'O God, help us to keep ourselves physically strong, mentally awake and morally straight, that in doing our duty to Thee and our country we may keep the honour of the services untarnished.

'Strengthen us to guard our country from external aggression and internal disorders.

'Awaken our admiration for honest dealing and clean thinking, and guide us to choose the harder right instead of the easier wrong.

'Kindle our hearts with fellowship for our comrades at arms and with loyalty to the men we command.

'Endow us with the courage which is born of the love of what is noble and which knows no compromise or retreat when truth and right are in peril.

'Grant us new opportunities of service to Thee, to our country and to the men we lead, and ever help us to place such service before self.'

10

Sharing and Caring: An Unwritten Rule
in the Army

Open-Door Policy for Seniors, Peers and Associates

The single-most important attribute of a soldier's life is to live and, if need be, die for the soldier next to him. The concept of benevolence and consideration for each other that prevails among Army personnel, especially those belonging to the same unit, is unmatched and many a time has proven to be the backbone of soldiering and *esprit de corps*. In this context, the first incident that I narrate here always evokes pleasant memories for me. It occurred around 1991–92, when I was posted as a captain in Mhow, a training establishment in Madhya Pradesh. Various officers from different units visit Mhow to imbibe training in short courses of a duration ranging from two to eleven months. At that time, I was there with my wife, prior to the birth of our children. Since I was a captain, I had been allotted a two-bedroom house. During my tenure there, two officers, who were quite close to me, one from my own unit and immediately senior to me, Colonel Anil Kumar Suri, also known as 'Goofy', and another good friend and younger brother of my unit officer Lieutenant General Iqbal Singh Singha, Captain (later Lieutenant General) Gurpal Singh Sangha aka Lally Sangha, came to Mhow to undergo a course of instruction of approximately three months' duration.

When I learnt of their travel plans, I went to the railway station to receive them. Neither of them had been allotted any accommodation by the institute where they had to undergo the course, and both had come with their wives and young children in the age group of one to three years. Since they were not able to arrange any accommodation to stay in, they came to my house and we offered them one bedroom each (with an attached washroom) in my apartment, as they needed both the privacy and the comfort of separate bathrooms because their families were accompanying them. My wife and I were thus consigned to sleep on the carpet in the drawing room.

The camaraderie and sense of belonging that we, as friends and colleagues, share with each other in the Army follows us everywhere and this Mhow episode was no different. For both the officers, partaking of the hospitality offered by their friend 'Tiny' was a natural corollary of the decision to undertake the course, and on my part, there was absolutely no doubt that their needs would take precedence over mine even if it meant making major adjustments for both my wife and me.

Like me, Lally Sangha is also a six-feet-three-inches-tall, well-built officer, and we are often mistaken to be brothers, or at least cousins. Lally Sangha had forgotten his name tab, an essential part of the uniform, in his unit and it would take three to four days for the new one to be made in the Mhow market. And guess what? He came up with the novel idea of wearing my name tab of 'KJS Dhillon' instead of 'GS Sangha' for the first four days of the course. The icing on the cake was when, after about a week or so, I informed both of them that I was trying very hard to arrange some accommodation for them in the Infantry School. Their very emotive and instant joint reply that left me speechless was, 'We are quite comfortable here, and you need not go out of your way to do anything for us.' A few months after this incident, Lally Sangha came down to Mhow again to prepare for the entrance exam of the Defence Services Staff College and stayed with me at our home. This time too, he got a room to himself, and as Nita was in the family way and had gone home for the delivery, I too managed to get a room for myself in my own home!

Availing of the CO's Home and Hospitality

It is not that only the seniors in the Army have the right to enjoy the unbridled hospitality of juniors. More often than not, it is the prerogative of the junior to experience the benevolence of the seniors. I experienced this first-hand when we were stationed in Udaipur, again during the early years of our marriage, and I got detailed for undergoing a course in the College of Materials Management at Jabalpur. It is a normal practice in the Army that when a married officer gets detailed for taking a short course during a field assignment or peace-time, he applies to the head of the institution where he would be taking the course for both accommodation and permission to bring his family along. Priority for providing the accommodation is given to the officers coming from field areas. I, too, put in an application for accommodation but my request was not entertained and the accommodation was refused, perhaps because I was moving not from a field area but from Udaipur, a peace station. However, permission was granted for my wife to accompany me and I was asked to make my own arrangements for our stay. When this reply was received, it was put up before the CO, Lieutenant Colonel (later Brigadier) Trigunesh Mukherjee, and he scribbled a note on the back of the letter, saying, 'Tiny to speak.'

This turn of affairs, wherein the CO was asking a young junior officer to speak to him was indeed a rarity, and I was really petrified, wondering what had motivated the CO to call me. So, I approached the 2IC Major Suby, and informed him of the summons from the CO. After analysing the case in detail and the probable reasons for the CO to summon me, he asked me if I had obtained the CO's go-ahead before seeking permission for taking my wife with me while attending the course at Jabalpur. This only magnified my concern as I had not sought this prior approval from the CO before joining the course. Although I entreated him to speak to the CO on my behalf, the 2IC said that since the CO had asked me to speak to him (the CO), it may not be correct for him (the 2IC) to do so, but he assured me that he would wait for me outside the CO's office while I went inside and tried to clarify the issue with the CO. He also promised me that in case the CO really lost his cool, he would walk in and try to defuse the situation. He advised me to be in total agreement with whatever the CO said, and not to show either my trepidation or confusion. So, with my heart in my mouth, I walked in to confront the CO. The conversation with him went something like this:

CO: 'Did you apply for this accommodation?'

Me (meekly): 'Yes, sir.'

CO: 'Why did you apply?'

Me: 'Sorry, sir.'

CO: 'You should have told me.'

Me: 'Sorry, sir.'

I was repeatedly apologizing as the 2IC had told me to humbly accept whatever the CO would say and not offer any explanation or argument. Little did I anticipate the rest of the conversation with him.

CO: 'Now, is your wife going with you?'

Me: 'No, sir.'

CO: 'Tell her to pack her bags, as she *is* going with you.'

Awestruck at this totally unexpected turn of events, I could not have even dreamt of what was to follow. Actually, the CO had summoned me not to admonish me but to tell me that his mother-in-law, Mrs Ganguly, had a house in Jabalpur, where she was staying alone after her husband had passed away. He was, in effect, suggesting that I could stay in that house with my wife for the duration of the course while his mother-in-law shifted to Delhi to stay with her daughter and grandchildren for our sake! Phew, what a turnaround from my original fears!

When we shifted into Mrs Ganguly's home, we found that she had ensured that the house was fully equipped with all provisions in the kitchen and refrigerator, and even made an arrangement with the milkman to deliver milk for us every day to ensure our comfort for the entire two months of our stay. This again is an example of the invaluable support system and brotherhood that pervades the Army, with everyone backing each other, irrespective of rank or seniority.

We were treated like privileged guests throughout our stay at Mrs Ganguly's home with even the neighbouring shopkeeper pitching in to make us comfortable. Since the milkman used to come as early as 5 a.m., we, being newly married, had no inclination to go out and collect milk at this unearthly hour, so I told him to stop delivering the milk and instead switched to purchasing powder milk from the local 'Mom and Pop' store. However, the proprietor of this store, at the cost of losing business from a customer, actually suggested that we should opt for fresh milk and offered to keep the milk delivered by the milkman at his shop and hand it over to us at a more convenient time. His wife would even go to the extent of not only collecting the milk on our behalf but also boiling it to prevent it from curdling. Thus, I learnt of the immense respect that Army personnel enjoy among the civilians and general public, with the latter willing to go to any length to bestow favours upon us.

With Brigadier Trigunesh Mukherjee (Retd), my first CO in Chinar Corps Commander's office, Diwali 2019

The Commander's Aura is a Motivating Factor

In the Army, a commander's relationship with his subordinates is not restricted to merely the passage of orders by the former and their unquestioned execution by the latter. This relationship is much deeper and almost akin to an unsigned bond of life between the two. An incident revealing the human and humanitarian aspect of Army life concerned our brigade commander in 1988—Brigadier (later Lieutenant General) Inder Verma, who had a very unique style of expressing his appreciation for some positive or courageous deed by any soldier under his command. He would summon the concerned soldier or junior officer to his office, where he had placed two bowls on his table—one was full of eclairs while the other would be laden with all sorts of dry fruits, including raisins, cashews, almonds and walnuts. When the soldier walked into his office, Brigadier Verma would enjoin him to fill up all the pockets of his uniform with the eclairs and dry fruits, and subsequently refill the bowls for the next round of appreciation for another soldier. As young officers, it was thus a big treat for us to be summoned by the brigade commander. Albeit, there were times when the summons were not for appreciation but for admonishment, and we would return from his office suitably chastened, though never with empty pockets, but the latter occasions were rare, and we invariably looked forward to every call to visit the commander's office in anticipation of the goodies we could gorge on! Needless to say, during any such interaction with the brigade commander, wearing an oversized snow coat with deep pockets, irrespective of the prevailing weather, was the order of the day for us!

These small but ingenious gestures extended by our seniors to us would go a long way towards motivating us to constantly do our best not just to win material rewards like the sweets and dry fruits but also to witness genuine appreciation and approval in the eyes of our senior officers. Such incidents also helped to dispel the rather unsavoury image of a forbidding Army general with a handlebar moustache and stern expression, carrying a twelve-bore gun that he would point threateningly at any intransigent person—an image perpetrated by numerous Hindi movies of the time, and one that most youngsters of my age in the Army initially often conjured up in their minds at the alarming thought of having to face an irate boss after some lapse in our duty. With time, however, we managed to overcome this apprehension and realized that Army brigadiers and generals too are human and do appreciate the good work accomplished by their juniors, and liberally offer accolades and rewards for it. I am narrating this incident especially for the benefit of aspiring young soldiers, who should enter the Army with an open mind, and be ready for both appreciation and reprimand, wherever due, which are handed down impartially by their superiors.

Humour in Uniform—Personal Gaffes and Challenges

Since Kashmir is such an intrinsic part of both my professional and personal life, my mind keeps weaving my personal experiences here into the tapestry of my life as an Army officer. A rather interesting though personally embarrassing episode occurred while I was posted in the Tral Bowl. The new brigade commander was visiting the battalion for the first time and after indulging in the normal pleasantries, he asked me as a matter of courtesy, 'How many children do you have?' I told him that I have a son and a daughter, following which his counter question was, 'Which class is your son studying in?' For the life of me, and much to my trepidation, I could not remember my son's class at that point in time and was deep in thought trying to recollect this piece of information, which should ideally have been top of mind. And as a balm to my confused mind, I heard my colleague, Major Shekhawat, answering on my behalf, informing the brigade commander that my son was in the fourth standard.

While a hugely embarrassing incident was averted at the moment, I still felt muddled in my mind, and in the evening when I made an STD call to my wife, a routine in those pre-mobile days, I asked her about my son's class. She said, 'He's in class three.' In immediate surprise, I responded, 'But Major Shekhawat was saying that he is in class four.' She asked, and I could sense the irritation in her voice, 'Who is Major Shekhawat?' She did not know any officer in the unit, since it was a new unit and I had taken over the command of the unit in Kashmir. I said that he was an officer in the unit, and in an effort to avoid any recriminations from her, I told her that I would re-confirm where he had sourced this inaccurate information. The next morning, I told Major Shekhawat in a seemingly casual manner, 'You were saying that my son is in class four, but actually he's in class three.' Laughing, he replied, 'Since you were getting stuck in front of the commander, I just bailed you out. I did my quick mathematics about your age and calculated that your son should now be in class four.' I felt instant relief and tremendous gratitude for this officer, who had not known me, and had never met either my wife or my son, yet who had come to my rescue in that difficult moment, offering what we in the Army call *'fauri ilaaz'* (immediate remedy).

Major Shekhawat with our son during one of the unit's functions

On a more serious note, this incident also highlights the extent of our commitment to our work, which keeps us so busy that we get to spend very little time with our families and often forget about their immediate challenges and routines in day-to-day life. Also, we have such unqualified faith in our families and our wives, and rely on them so heavily for keeping the family afloat, that we often fail to accord importance to the routine affairs that they keep managing on their own. It is such a boon for officers like me that we are blessed with wives who have the courage and gumption to single-handedly bring up the children, look after the home, resolve all the household issues and challenges, and also fulfil social obligations without burdening us mentally or physically with these duties. I must admit that we often take the family's contribution and support for granted, and it is only when we look at these instances in retrospect that we realize the magnitude of the family support available to us all the time, especially when we are posted in a field area. During this incident too, I was engaged in very difficult counter-terrorism operations in Tral in South Kashmir, and realizing this, my wife never shared any household problems with me but dealt with them on her own. Every time I called her, she would assure me, 'Everything is okay. You look after yourself, look after the unit, and do a good job of whatever you're doing.'

Happy family, Mhow, August 2005

With Nita and our son at Defence Services Staff College,
Wellington (Tamil Nadu), 1995

More Humour in Uniform

Our citizens also exhibit tremendous presence of mind. Once on my
way home on a short leave, I had requested my co-brother to pick
me up from Jammu Airport. The entrance gate to Jammu Airport in
the early 2000s was rather innocuous, and it could easily be missed
if you were not well acquainted with the area, while the road further
on leads straight towards the international boundary. My co-brother
got delayed and since there were no mobiles in those days, I could not
contact him. When he finally reached the gate and I got into the car
with him, I asked him the reason for the delay. He said that he had
missed the airport gate and kept driving ahead. And after travelling
for about ten to fifteen kilometres, he realized that something was
not right. So he stopped the car and asked a person who was working
in the fields, presumably a Sikh farmer, how far was Jammu Airport.
The farmer first looked at him incredulously and then replied wryly
in Punjabi, 'Jammu *wala ta pichhe reh gaya, agge ta hunn* Pakistan *de*

hi ne! (You have left Jammu Airport way behind, only the airports of Pakistan are ahead!)' His subtle sarcasm was not lost on my escort and is also a classic example of the rustic humour we often come across during our encounters with the diverse people of our country while operating in remote areas of India.

Coursemate—A Brother from a Different Mother

We also forge a lifelong association with our coursemates and friends in the Army, which keeps growing over time. I remember another incident that concerns then Captain Anil Chaudhary, who later retired as a major general. We were buddies since our youngster days, had attended our Young Officers' course together and shared many other pursuits and pastimes. When I was posted in Kashmir, also as a captain, soon after my marriage, my wife was accompanying me and we reached the Jammu transit camp quite late in the evening. I had written a letter to Captain Anil Chaudhary who was posted in Jammu at the time, informing him of the date and time when we would be reaching the transit camp. And sure enough, he was there to receive us. Since he was meeting my wife for the first time, he wanted it to be a special occasion and took us out for dinner. We spent an enjoyable evening with him and returned to the transit camp at about 10.30 p.m., and bid each other good night as my wife and I had to catch an early morning bus. However, just as I was preparing to retire for the night a few minutes later, there was a knock on the door. I came out and I saw Captain Anil Chaudhary standing there. Surprised, I asked him, 'Arré, have you left anything behind?' He said, '*Nahin yaar*, we could not talk freely in front of your wife, *mazaa nahin aaya*!' So I quietly slipped out, we sat on a culvert in the transit camp and talked non-stop for the next three hours, sharing and reminiscing over all the anecdotes of our childhood and bachelor days, and several other experiences of adulthood.

It is evident that in the Army, you may be physically separated from your friends and colleagues, but they are never far from your mind, and you can pick up the thread of memories and conversations just where you left it when you last met, regardless of all the momentous changes that may have taken place in your life in the interim. The bonding that we forged during our NDA training never leaves us. As they say, a cadet may leave the NDA but the NDA never leaves him. Recently, I attended the wedding of Anil Chaudhary's son in Chandigarh, who also happens to be my son's very good friend. I also met him again at a wedding in Jaipur where his newly married daughter-in-law warmly greeted me with the very welcome sentence, 'Uncle, Papa keeps talking about you from morning till night.' Incidentally, Major General Anil Chaudhary is one of the three people who called my wife to tell her that I was alive when there was a news flash of my namesake having been killed in action. Just a day before, we had attended the puja ceremony of Anil Chaudhary's granddaughter's birth.

The Army is thus not simply an organization where we perform our routine day-to-day jobs. It is also not just an institution that we enter in our teens and exit on retirement. In fact, we never exit the Army, at least mentally, as it is a way of life that pervades every aspect of our lives throughout life's journey. This is also what I told a student in Gujarat University, who asked me a question at an interactive session during my recent visit to Ahmedabad, 'Sir, how challenging is an Army job?' My spontaneous and honest reply was, 'Army *ek* job *nahin hai, mohabbat hai. Aur mohabbat mein* challenges *nahin hote, afsaane hote hain* (Being in the Army is not a job, it is like an unending love affair, and in love, there are only legends, not challenges).' So the afsaanas that I am narrating in this book personify my labour of love as a soldier, creating and re-creating memories for a life well and truly lived.

Duty or Family—An Easy Decision without a Dilemma

During a swarming operation (being explained in a later chapter) in the forest for flushing out terrorists, which occurred while I was commanding an RR sector as brigadier and was stationed at the forward-most post controlling the operation, my wife, mother-in-law and daughter decided to visit me in Kashmir for about five to six days. So, even as they landed at the sector headquarters, I could not come back to meet them for the next four days, as I was engaged in a highly intense operation with the terrorists in the forest. Thus, the ladies of my family, who were lodged at my headquarters, and who had come specifically to meet me were, unfortunately, unable to even see me. Meanwhile, my parent unit was stationed in Gulmarg in those days and the CO came to know of my family visiting me. He called up my wife, telling her, 'Sir (that is, me) is unlikely to come and meet you, as he is busy in a serious operation that cannot be aborted midway. So, why don't all of you come to Gulmarg and enjoy yourselves here during your vacation instead of waiting in vain to meet sir?'

The ladies readily agreed, and off they went to have a relaxing vacation instead in Gulmarg. In the meantime, my GOC, Major General Ravi Thodge (God bless his soul) came to know that my family was visiting me in Kashmir, but I had not returned to headquarters to meet them because I was busy with a swarming operation. He sent a message, urging me to visit the RR Force Headquarters to attend a conference. In the meantime, he also informed the CO of my parent unit to inform the ladies to have lunch with him and his wife before going to the airport to board their return flight. So, the GOC planned a meeting wherein he invited the ladies and me together to the headquarters, and treated us to an enjoyable lunch. Although we discussed the jungle operations prior to the meal, the real purpose of the lunch was to bring me and my family together. His hospitality, coupled with the commitment to continue the work and not let the operation suffer, offered me an opportunity to meet my family without compromising on my duties.

This generosity and planning on the part of the GOC again showcases the humane side of Army colleagues. Most of the time, we do not pay much attention to our mental well-being and needs, and often take many things for granted. But Major General Thodge realized that apart from being an operational commander, I was also a human with human needs and feelings. I remember this gesture till today, as it reminds me of the way in which we try to humour and please a child by catering to all his emotional needs, but perhaps even a grown-up fifty-year-old man has the same emotional needs as a child, and it is important to fulfil these needs, regardless of work commitments and duties.

When Lies Allay the Fears of Family

The tensions emanating from the intensity of anti-terrorist operations and their concomitant risks obviously cascade down to our families too. And an operation that I had led earlier as a brigadier in North Kashmir, when I was commanding a Rashtriya Rifles sector, is worth recounting here. This operation was undertaken in Lolab valley in a village in 2012, wherein we neutralized five Pakistani terrorists. I was there along with my GOC, Major General Ravi Thodge, leading that operation. Even as the encounter was going on full throttle, both my wife and father happened to call me on my cell during the operation. When my wife queried me about the noise in the background, I told her that a marriage procession was passing by and she was hearing the sound of crackers being burst. But when my father called up, the firing intensity had really gone up. When he asked me about the loud background noise, I told him that I was watching an English movie replete with violence and shooting! These examples of our interactions with our families during our field operations are intended to serve a dual purpose here—they not only show that we have to handle our families with tact and compassion in times of stress but also that during our field operations, we have to focus single-mindedly on the task at hand without getting swayed by emotions or family pressures. In effect, this is a by-product of the comprehensive training we undergo as cadets at the academy, which teaches us to preclude all distractions, and like Arjun concentrating on aiming his arrow at the eye of the fish in the epic *Mahabharat*, a soldier needs to be completely focused on his duties.

The Soft Heart and Sharp Mind of an Indian Soldier

The resilience and 'never say die' spirit of an Indian soldier is something that brings in victories even against heavy odds. I am reminded of an incident in August 1999 that happened immediately after the Kargil War when I was still posted in Rashtriya Rifles and was staying overnight at the Srinagar transit camp en route home for a short leave. I met a young medical officer, Captain Somnath Basu, in the officers' mess at the transit camp, apropos of which I have an 'early morning tea' incident later in the book. This young medico was a regimental medical officer (RMO) in 2 RAJRIF, who had been involved in the battle for the capture of a very strategically significant feature in the Kargil War. He was intrigued by the initials 'RR' boldly displayed on my uniform and questioned me whether I was also from RAJRIF. I told him that the RR on my shoulders was actually an acronym for Rashtriya Rifles, where I was presently serving in Lolab in North Kashmir, though my parent unit is, of course, 4 RAJRIF. The bonhomie we developed after this conversation led him to share a story with me about his experience as a proud unit member of 2 RAJRIF during the Kargil War.

The young doctor narrated to me that on the day of the most critical operation during the Kargil War, the commanding officer, Colonel M.B. Ravindranath (awarded Vir Chakra for his outstanding command during the Kargil War) apprised all the officers about the plan to capture the peak in just one night, and that he would himself be there to serve a hot breakfast to all the unit personnel at daybreak on the successful completion of the operation. However, the terrain was incredibly tough and the near-vertical climb immensely steep, with the rarefied mountain atmosphere causing a sharp drop in oxygen levels, and the absence of even a blade of grass to help in taking cover from direct observation or fire of the enemy weapons perched on the hilltop prevented easy access to the objective. Notwithstanding these constraints, the 2 RAJRIF team pressed home with the attack with a modified plan. The assault continued for two nights before the objective was finally captured.

Although the troops had been served a heavy meal the evening before setting off for the operation, most of the soldiers refrained from eating it as they anticipated that a full stomach would impede the tough climb to the peak. A few of them carried with them on their journey the puris that had been served along with the dinner. The doctor, who was accompanying the 2 RAJRIF team on this mission, revealed that one of the young jawans, who was his buddy, was left with only two puris even as the mission was nowhere near the end. Hence, strictly conserving the meagre food he was left with, he would break off a small piece of the puri and pass it on to the doctor every two to three hours, but refused to eat any of the leftover meal himself, as they negotiated the climb, slowly moving up the hill from boulder to boulder. While he gratefully accepted the food from the jawan during the mission, once they were back at their battalion base after the successful completion of the mission, the doctor summoned the jawan and asked him why he chose to go hungry himself while generously feeding his doctor buddy instead. The jawan's instant response was, 'Your life was precious, and we had to protect it at all costs, as you were the only doctor among us 100 jawans on that mission, whose services would be needed in case of any injury or casualty during the operation. If I had died, it would mean the loss of only one life, but if something untoward happened to you, it would endanger the lives of the entire company.' The doctor was visibly touched and supremely impressed by the ethos and commitment of the jawans and officers of the Indian Army. His eyes were visibly moist and his voice changed to that 'lump in the throat' tone when he was narrating this incident to me. This tale of selfless compassion and operational wisdom exhibited in the face of the enemy by a RAJRIF jawan reiterates not only the spirit of camaraderie and valour of that individual soldier but also the values and commitment that every Indian Army soldier possesses, which not only equips him both physically and mentally for the tasks that lie ahead but also teaches him to act and react rationally in every situation that he may confront during war or peace.

11

The Army Marches on Its Stomach: Exigencies of Sustenance and Survival in the Army

The quote, 'The Army marches on its stomach', which is attributed to both Napoleon Bonaparte and Frederick the Great, is a very apt recognition of the importance of integrating sound logistics in any pragmatic operational plans. It is also relevant here to invoke the play *Arms and the Man* by the renowned writer George Bernard Shaw, in which the battle-hardened soldier Captain Bluntschli preferred to carry chocolates in his pouch instead of additional ammunition. The cultivation of survival skills to deal with the non-availability of proper food and living off the land are the mainstays of a soldier's day-to-day life, especially during the prolonged operations in remote areas devoid of any habitat. The anecdotes in this chapter and some of the subsequent ones highlight this integral aspect of a soldier's life.

Story of Snow, Spirit and Frozen Oranges in Bhutan

The Indian Army has training teams operating in various countries outside India, and one such team functions out of Bhutan. I was posted in the Indian Military Training Team (IMTRAT), Bhutan in 1995–97 as a major. The incident I narrate here relates to a quiet Sunday afternoon in January 1996, when we were indulging in a passionate game of cricket, which was slated to be followed by brunch. Unfortunately, the vivacity of our game was marred by a human frailty as one of the Bhutanese soldiers posted at a forward location fell ill and needed to be evacuated on an emergency basis. Ironically, this human emergency coalesced into another practical exigency as the Indian Army helicopter that had been flown in from across the border to undertake the casualty evacuation could not carry the ailing soldier because the weather in the high-altitude area had packed up. The term 'weather packing up' in the mountains typically implies a rapid decline in visibility due to expanding cloud cover, which usually happens in high-altitude areas after mid-day.

In view of the deteriorating weather conditions, the helicopter pilots were forced to abort the rescue mission and decided to return to their base after refuelling at our location. On their way back, the radio detachment at a particular location in South Bhutan urged them to land there, warning that the weather ahead was getting progressively worse. With a view to hitting the plains of Hasimara, a small town situated on the bank of River Torsha in Alipurduar district of West Bengal near the border with Bhutan, the pilots persisted on their sortie, as they were keen on returning to their base before nightfall. However, they soon realized the futility of their overambitious goal, and with the visibility falling to near-zero precluding any chance of a safe landing even at Hasimara, the pilots had to return to the location where the radio detachment had told them to land. In the meantime, the weather in that area too had packed up. Suddenly, therefore, the helicopter went off the radar and lost all communication with the ground. When this bit of news and details of the sequence of events leading to the aborted landing of the sortie reached us in IMTRAT, we feared the worst.

However, after all the attempts to re-establish contact with the missing helicopter failed, I got a call from my senior that I, along with another officer, a medical officer and a few jawans, had to immediately launch a search and rescue mission.

I assembled my team and drove down during the wee hours of the night to the place where the last transmission with the pilots had taken place. On reaching the designated site, we contacted the radio operator and checked the tele-log, or telecommunication log, which clearly indicated the time when the transmissions had been made and the replies received from the pilots. With the weather continuing to play truant, the proposed rescue sortie could not be undertaken to search for the missing helicopter. Not wanting to waste any more time in waiting for the weather to clear up, we met the 'Dzongda', the local Bhutanese official, who in Bhutan performs the role equivalent to that of a divisional commissioner or the head of an area, and is the senior-most government official in a designated area. The Dzongda handed us a letter, which was tantamount to being the decree of the king, clearly stating that any help whatsoever we sought from anyone we came across during our rescue operation could not be refused.

Just after initiating the operation, the first hurdle our small team faced was the lack of any detailed maps of that area, and much as we tried, the only maps we could get hold of were some basic tourist maps that were of hardly any help in the hostile terrain and weather conditions. The situation was further compounded by the fact that the area had virtually no military presence per se but an extensive presence of members of the insurgent organization, the United Liberation Front of Asom (ULFA).

Exercising extreme caution, we commenced our search, simultaneously probing the villagers to assess if they had recently seen or heard a helicopter flying or landing in the area. We got a faint but clear lead on the third day of our search operation when the pilot of a foreign commercial airliner flying over that specific area intercepted a freak transmission, which he reported along with the rough coordinates of the likely transmission site to the Air Traffic Control (ATC) at Hasimara airfield of the Indian

Air Force. This provided us with a rough idea of the location of the stranded helicopter, and also the heartening indication that the communication system of the helicopter was at least intact enough to send out a transmission, which also suggested that the chopper was probably not damaged and that the pilots sending out the transmission were presumably safe. However, the weather gods continued to be unkind, precluding any scope of an aerial search. But now, with a firm lead to set us on our way, and also using the services of some Bhutanese guides, who were well-versed in both the local language and the local topography, the team located the stranded helicopter after about four days. By this time, additional choppers of the Indian Army had also come in to assist us in the search and rescue by aerial means.

The next challenge was to find the pilots, because when the rescue team reached the helicopter, it was found empty, lying deserted in the middle of a heavy snowstorm and extremely chilly conditions. In an effort to recreate the sequence of events, it was surmised that when the airborne pilots were unable to combat the weather, they decided to make the best of an impossible situation and started looking around for a flattish area large enough to facilitate the landing of the chopper. We later learnt that as they saw a hilltop above the clouds, and the undulating ground entirely covered by the snow, showing aviation skills of an extraordinary order, the pilots successfully landed the helicopter on that stretch of snow, above the clouds, and then just waited for the weather to clear enough for them to exit the helicopter. However, staying put in the chopper was not an option due to the unrelenting chilly breeze on the hilltop, and they were compelled to leave the helicopter to look for a warmer haven, which they found in a little grazier's hut a few metres down the slope. After shelter, the next priority was procuring food as all the emergency rations in the helicopter had been consumed and thereafter, the pilots only had snow for succour. So, they would melt a little bit of snow as they did not want to come out of the hut into the cold. Coming to the aspect of survival skills, incidentally, this would warm the cockles of many hearts, the pilots had picked up two or three bottles of the famous Bhutan liquor when they had touched down briefly for refuelling, which they kept consuming to boost both their body calories and body warmth.

On reaching the location of the hut, the rescue party could barely see a few metres ahead of them, as even the footsteps were covered with fresh snow. But plodding on with the effort, the team eventually managed to enter the hut and finally saw the two pilots huddled inside—shaking and shivering but alive and relatively unharmed. Although a helicopter with the mechanic had reached there as part of the rescue effort, which was used to evacuate the pilots, the stranded one flew off as a single-pilot helicopter with a mechanic on board, who had checked all the functional parts of the stranded helicopter before taking off. The pilots were straightaway ferried to a hospital at Hasimara, where they were subjected to a thorough medical check-up and pronounced hale and hearty though a little weak due to near starvation and the overall trauma caused by the situation.

But wait a minute; this was still not the end of the adventure, as before the search party could be evacuated, the weather packed up again! And the rescue team was left high and dry in the freezing cold. Fortunately, the team had a little bit of dry rations and, while climbing up the hill, had come across some orange orchards and bought some oranges from the caretaker there. Although even those oranges were now frozen and had to be thawed before they could be consumed, this challenge too met its match in the typical fauji ingenious minds! The boys would literally 'break' the frozen orange into segments, and hold it in their mouth till it became chewable.

Meanwhile, the team decided to wait for the rescue helicopter instead of descending from the slope on foot as the biggest challenge, however, was that if the rescue helicopter arrived after the weather opened up, it would not be able to locate the team in that difficult terrain. And even if it were able to spot the team, there may not have been a suitable place for it to land. So, in the face of this Hobson's choice in the snowy ordeal, before the team finally commenced walking, the helicopters were able to land and evacuate the team 'just in time' as they say. For this search and rescue operation in the snow and the perilous terrain, I, along with some other members of the rescue team, was awarded the Chief of the Army Staff's Commendation Card. I can proudly say that this was my first decoration as a soldier.

When we reunited with the pilots of the earlier failed sortie, they entertained us with their anecdotal experiences. They told us that when they had landed on the hilltop, the noise of the helicopter had attracted a local grazier boy, who came to investigate what had disturbed the peace in that deafeningly quiet and serene location. Assuming that he would bring them some assistance and perceiving that he was somewhat educated, they tried to communicate with him, though their inability to speak the Bhutanese language was a major hindrance. However, they still managed to get their message across to him, or so they thought, and in an effort to seal the deal, one of the pilots handed him Rs 500 and his Ray-Ban aviator sunglasses, asking him to return with some help. He thought that this would incentivize the boy to bring them aid, but it probably worked as a disincentive instead because the boy never came back, perhaps fearing that he would have to return the money and goggles. Later, when we reminisced over this incident, we realized in hindsight that perhaps the pilots should have just shown him the money, dangling it as an enticement to be won only if he returned with help. A great lesson in HR management, that is, incentives should be offered only on completion of the assigned task!

The Sweet and Salty Tale of Krackjack Biscuits

Learning in the Army is not restricted only to reading the précis or pamphlets taught in the courses of instruction. As they say, there is no age limit to learn and I learnt how, or how not to, behave as a divisional or corps commander when I was still a captain. This incident took place when I was posted as a captain at the Infantry School, Mhow, and Lieutenant General D.D. Saklani, a thorough gentleman and a great professional, was the commandant. He somehow had a personal liking for me as an instructor. He would invariably walk in to inspect the classroom activity whenever I was taking a class, just to keep an eye on the proceedings and I suspect, also to ensure that young instructors were doing their job properly.

Subsequently, after completion of my tenure at Mhow, I got posted to Samba in Jammu and Kashmir, a very small place but of immense strategic importance, while Lieutenant General D.D. Saklani was appointed as an adviser to the Governor of Jammu and Kashmir. One day, he was slated to visit Samba for a civil administration function but was to land at the Army helipad, and I was instructed to receive him at the helipad and offer him a cup of tea. The evening before his scheduled arrival, we received the information that General Saklani has a special affinity for Krackjack biscuits, so a packet of these biscuits should be arranged at any cost as an accompaniment to the general's tea. I told the mess havildar to procure the biscuits, but a while later, he came to inform me that the biscuits were not available in the mess and there was no stock even in the unit or the Brigade headquarters CSD canteen. The elusive biscuits could not even be found in the small local market of Samba, and we were at a loss as to how to fulfil the instructions of serving only that particular brand of biscuits. Finally, it was decided to send someone to get the biscuits from Jammu, which was about an hour and a half's drive from Samba. Major Ranjan 'Smiley' Mahajan was thus given a special vehicle and assigned the task of travelling to Jammu and bringing back the biscuits from there post-haste, to be served along with the tea to the visiting dignitary. And sure enough, the mission was successful, and the much sought-after Krackjack biscuits were procured after much effort by the unit.

As an anti-climax, General Saklani's first comment, when the biscuits were offered to him, was, 'Tiny, has the CSD stopped stocking all other biscuit brands except Krackjack these days?' Determined to get to the bottom of this 'hoax', I told him that we had specific instructions that he preferred only Krackjack biscuits, which is why we had made sure that they were served to him. Shaking his head in mirth, he said, 'I don't remember when and where but perhaps I had been served these biscuits in some unit a long time back, and as an aside commented that these biscuits were quite delicious.' His comment had been taken too seriously and since then, he was being offered nothing but this brand of biscuits wherever he went for an official visit. He also said that after this revelation to me, he was certain that his words would again be noted for eternity, and henceforth, he would be offered all other brands except Krackjack during his subsequent visits to any unit. After this rather unexpected conversation, I did not have the heart to apprise him of the 'sweet and salty' tale of the packet of Krackjack biscuits that had traversed to our unit all the way from Jammu! Unique indeed are the ways of the Indian Army!

This particular incident stayed with me and I gave clear instructions to my staff as divisional commander and subsequently as a corps commander that no food choice or habits would ever be told to the units under my command because a small instruction like this can mean unnecessary wastage of time, energy and resources at the unit end. I would much rather be like the corps commander who had visited us in Sikkim and enjoyed the 'chicken sandwich' offered by the unit as per their choice of menu and the availability of ingredients at their location.

Of Gastronomic Idiosyncrasies

While on the topic of food or the lack of it, I must also point out that whenever we undertook an operation in the Army, we always carried survival rations, such as gud (jaggery) and shakarparas, a sweet fried snack made of wheat flour. Also, since Rajputana Rifles troops are basically Jats and Rajputs, they prefer wholesome homemade stuff to pep up their energy, such as pinnis, choorma and puris, in addition to shakarparas, which are packed and carried on long-range patrols. I suppose in most of the regiments, they still prefer traditional food, because when I was undergoing jungle training with a battalion of the Bihar Regiment, litti chokha was very popular. I really relished this dish each time they served it to me. Its popularity among the soldiers from Bihar, in fact, compares with that of dal bati choorma, served in Rajputana Rifles.

In recent times, however, the popularity of some of the traditional foods has been waning, as many soldiers are now veering towards instant snacks like Maggi and chocolates, which may not be ideal nutrition options. In the Army, we also rely on 'Meals Ready to Eat' or MREs, which are like packaged, pre-cooked food. The contents of these MRE packets have to be just immersed in hot water, ending up becoming proper meals, including pulao, dal, sabzi, upma and halwa—with the halwa being an all-time favourite of the RAJRIF soldiers. They also cannot do without rotis, and no meal in RAJRIF is complete without rotis, as wheat is part of the staple diet in Rajasthan and all of North India. An anecdote regarding the sweet tooth of the RAJRIF soldiers and how the sugar is ingeniously saved from consumption as a snack in the jungles of Manipur is narrated in a subsequent chapter. We can thus say that the soldier is not only a superman but also a human who has normal likes and dislikes, small eccentricities and pleasures. Outside, he is very tough and always ready for a fight but inside, he longs for the small joys of family life, of good food and his favourite dishes, and of joyful interactions with peers and seniors.

KFC in the Rajwar Forest

The name 'Rajwar' represents a very small valley, close to the Line of Control, consisting of a few small hamlets encircled on all sides by dense jungles adjacent to the Bungus Valley, famous for its natural beauty and sprawling grazing pastures. The forested bowl with a small valley floor has only one narrow entry/exit towards the small town of Handwara in North Kashmir that connects it with the outside world. This area experiences heavy snowfall and was so isolated from the outside world in the earlier days that a local landlord used to look after all the day-to-day issues of the populace. He was respectfully addressed as 'Rajaji' and his descendants still reside in a very aesthetically built double-storey wooden house in Zachaldhar Village within the Rajwar bowl. As a brigadier, I was the RR sector commander and the Rajwar forest, notorious for nurturing hideouts of foreign terrorists due to its harsh topography and proximity to the Line of Control, fell within my area of responsibility. Readers must surely be wondering about the unlikely connection between the popular fast food joint Kentucky Fried Chicken (KFC) and the Rajwar forest.

As the RR sector commander, I avoided being dined in or dined out in a traditional manner, that is, from the officers' mess of any of the RR units under my command. In fact, I preferred to be 'lunched' out from the Rifle Company deployed in the most terrorist-infested areas and spend some lighter moments with the jawans over a song and a snack. During one such 'lunching' out after a very successful operation in the remotest company post in Rajwar, everyone was offered crispy, finger-licking fried chicken snacks that looked and tasted similar to the dish associated with KFC, the world-famous food chain. When asked about it, the cook just smiled and said that it was 'KFC Chicken' and refused to disclose the secret recipe in public.

After my tenure in RR, I was posted to a peace station and had the luxury of spending some leisure time with my family in a more relaxed environment. I have had a fascination for cooking since my NDA days and like to experiment with new recipes whenever I get the opportunity. On one such evening, as I remembered the delectable snacks, I was smitten with a desire to replicate them, but the first hurdle was my complete lack of knowledge of the recipe. So, I called up the company commander of that post, who told me that the particular cook who had rustled up the memorable dish in Rajwar was on leave in South India and no one else in the company knew the recipe. Undeterred by this next hurdle, I took the contact number of the cook and called him up with the hope that he would agree to share the recipe with me. And sure enough, the generous cook informed me of all the unique ingredients that went into the delicious dish. I will also take the liberty of sharing this recipe with my readers with the sole aim of emphasizing the ingenuity and creativity of our soldiers even under adverse weather, terrain and operational conditions. This secret recipe involved marinating chunks or drumsticks of chicken in a whipped paste of corn flour and crushed cornflakes, followed by frying of the marinade contents. The key ingredient is crushed cornflakes, which make it such a magical dish!

Tips and Tales for Survival in the Army

Apart from the importance of food for sustenance, I would also like to list here certain tips for survival in the Army. One of the key means of survival at high altitudes is recourse to fresh snow, which is absolutely pure and clear at that height and completely free of any pollution. The only pollution that may be witnessed in high-altitude army posts is around the barracks where we stay, maybe in the vicinity of the cookhouse, or the areas where we undertake our training. Also, since most of the Army pickets are on a hilltop, they can benefit from the water springs that spout out of cracks somewhere around the midriff region of the mountain. In the olden days, this water from the springs was usually lugged up to the post in a knapsack on the back. However, these days, pipelines have been laid at most of the places, which need to be maintained well, especially during winters as they burst due to the water freezing in them.

Most of the provisions are carried uphill to the Army posts by porters and ponies, which may be both army ponies as well as civilian ponies. While ponies are used for heavier luggage like ammunition and rations, water and other lighter accoutrements are invariably carried by locally employed civilian porters, who are an integral part of the body of troops deployed on a particular post, generally stay in nearby villages and earn their livelihood working with the Army units. During a snowfall, however, the services of the porters are normally discontinued to protect them from the risk of avalanches, and, as mentioned earlier, the fresh snow is melted and used instead to source water that is used for drinking as well as for cooking and even bathing.

In areas that receive plenty of rains but otherwise suffer from potable water scarcity, rainwater-harvesting is a viable option for sourcing water for daily needs. For instance, when I was posted in the Rashtriya Rifles in Manipur, which receives extensive rainfall during the year, the roofs of the houses were built with slanting tin sheets from which the rainwater cascaded and was collected in containers like drums or buckets. Moreover, since bamboo is commonly available in the North-east, we used to chisel bamboo sticks and tie them along the complete length of the tin roofs to create long pipes for transferring the rainwater from the roofs into the storage vessels below. This water would then be boiled to decontaminate it and make it fit for drinking and cooking. A water sterilizing kit is also provided to decontaminate the water where boiling it may not be feasible, especially when on a long-range patrol. This kit basically has two tablets, one blue and the other white, which have to be added to the water bottle one after the other in a specified sequence with a specific interval of time in-between the two immersions. I used to always get confused as to which tablet, blue or white, has to be added first till I made a code for myself. My code was 'Water Bottle' meaning white tablet to be followed by the blue one, corresponding with the initials 'W' and 'B', of 'water bottle'.

These survival tips and drills are an integral part of Army life across the country, with the peculiarities of each region being mapped into the specific requirements of Army life in that particular region. Acknowledging the importance of survival on a daily basis, with little external support, I too, like all other faujis, have honed my survival acumen and learnt various skills, especially in cooking. I am, in fact, very proud of the absolutely round rotis that I can make. I can also cook both non-vegetarian and vegetarian food, as well as desserts. Cooking is a key skill, as trained cooks are available only in the posts, and when we move out for operations in small teams, each team cannot be assigned an independent cook, and someone from within the team has to be able to cook. Also, when these teams are out in the field, all members are considered equal, and there are no hierarchical divisions among them. Each member, be they jawans or officers, is expected to perform all routine chores and share responsibilities across the board, starting from cooking to performing guard duty. This is how we build bonds for life in the Army and also justify the famous phrase 'band of brothers'.

Truth about the First Cooked Meal

Another anecdote that has to do with food concerns the wife of one of my colleagues, Captain Bala Nair, who also got married around the same time as me. His wife is an Army officer's daughter. When they set up their home a few days after their marriage, they invited the CO, Colonel (later Brigadier) Trigunesh Mukherjee, and, since we were also newly married, Captain Nair invited us too for a really lavish meal at their place. Post dinner, the lady, who was naturally very excited and enthusiastic about the party, straightaway asked the CO, 'Colonel Mukherjee, how was the food?' And since we were in Udaipur, Rajasthan, our hosts had served the special local cuisine. Colonel Mukherjee's response to the lady's question was as candid as her question. He said, 'Lal maas and gatte ki sabzi were very nice. But for the other dishes, you need a little more practice.' This virtually reduced the lady to tears. She said, '*Yehi to Bala bahar se lekar aaya hai, baaki to maine khud banaya tha* (these two were the only dishes Bala brought from outside, all the rest were cooked by me!)' Notwithstanding, Mrs Bala Nair is an excellent cook today and the Nairs are wonderful hosts.

The CO in any Army unit is a father figure and he has all the right to politely, or even sternly, convey his appreciation or otherwise to anyone, as every statement uttered by him is literally like a law in that unit. Albeit, the CO in a unit is not an appointment but an institution who would always call a spade a spade and never mince his words. Hence, if a CO praises it, the implication is that the food is really deserving of admiration. This is actually a double-edged sword, for appreciation of any lady's culinary skills by the CO will also preclude any subsequent criticism of her cooking from the husband.

The next section of the book takes us to Kashmir, a land of exquisite natural beauty and hugely talented people, but also a land ravaged by violence and terrorism. In view of my multiple tenures in various capacities here, Kashmir has virtually been a second home for me, and I describe my various experiences and escapades as an Army man doing duty in Kashmir in the following chapters.

12

Kashmir: The Land of Natural Beauty, Culture, Art, Hospitality and *Kashmiriyat*

Kashmir—An Overview

It was the September of 1988 when, having finished the peace tenure in Udaipur, our unit moved to the Kashmir Valley.

I will delve into my Kashmir experiences from the next chapter onwards but before that, I would like to talk about this mesmeric place, its wonderful people, rich history, amazingly beautiful landscape, culture, art, craftsmanship, hospitality and above all, the *Kashmiriyat*. Kashmir, as we all know, comprises a beautiful valley, approximately 135 km long and 30 km wide, with the Pir Panjal mountain range towards the south and south-west; the Shamshabari mountain range towards the north-west and north; and the Great Himalayas towards the north-east. The heavenly beauty and serenity of the land was very aptly described by the Mughal Emperor Jehangir when he quoted Amir Khusro, '*Gar Firdaus bar rue zamin ast, hami asto, hami asto, hami ast*', which translates into English as 'If there's heaven on Earth, it's here, it's here, it's here'.

Kashmir, in addition to being famous for its mountains, lakes, springs and the mystic shrines that are nestled among them, has been a spiritual land since time immemorial and has been known as *ReshéVer*—a land of saints and sages. Buddhism and Hinduism flourished in the Valley until the fourteenth century CE. Hindu dynasties like the Karkota, Utpala and Lohara ruled Kashmir before the preachers and invaders from central Asia came and Islam took root here. Kashmiris are very intelligent people, known for their artistic attributes with interests in poetry, *sufiana kalaam*, music and performing arts. Kashmir has always been a home to a very intellectual and educated society. Sharda Peeth has been an ancient centre of learning and lies in Sharda Village, along the banks of River Kishenganga (now across the Line of Control in Pakistan-occupied Kashmir [PoK]). Sharda Peeth has been mentioned in various historical and literary texts and has a significant spiritual and cultural importance as scholars travelled long distances to access its vast library and texts. All the religions, i.e., Hinduism, Islam, Christianity, Buddhism and Sikhism have contributed immensely to the essence of Kashmiriyat. I am sharing a few words here with my readers about some famous Hindu temples, Muslim shrines and Sikh Gurdwaras in Kashmir that add to its rich heritage and culture.

Hindu Temples and Shrines of Kashmir

Sharda temple, dedicated to Goddess Sharda (Goddess Saraswati), is one of the most revered Hindu temples, which has a close architectural resemblance to the Sun Temple of Martand. The temple symbolizes the elegance and zenith of the medieval era temple architecture of Kashmir, which was deeply influenced by Indo-Greek and Bactrian styles. As mentioned above, the Sharda temple now lies in ruins in PoK.

The temple of Martand near Anantnag, as per its Sanskrit name '*Martand*', is dedicated to the Sun God or *Surya Dev*. The Martand temple built on top of a plateau, mostly in ruins now, has a collonaded courtyard with the main shrine in the centre and is surrounded by eighty-four smaller shrines. The entrances of the shrine are huge, which adds to the grandeur of the temple, with all the walls in the complex having intricate figurines of different gods and goddesses, such as Vishnu, Ganga and Yamuna.

The Avantiswami temple near the town of Awantipora, presently also the headquarters of the Army's Counter Insurgency Force (Victor), was built by King Avantivarman of the Utpala dynasty in the years 853–855 CE on the banks of River Vitasta (Jhelum). Originally known as Viswasara, the town of Awantipora was also a capital at the time. The Avantiswami temple is smaller in size but has a striking resemblance to the older Martand Sun temple.

Amarnath cave is a very revered Hindu shrine in Kashmir, located in the Great Himalayan mountain range, at an altitude of nearly 13,000 feet above mean sea level. During the months of July and August every year, hundreds of thousands of pilgrims from all over the world trek to the holy cave to worship the naturally formed ice stalagmite, the Shivling. The pilgrimage or yatra concludes with the holy silver mace (*Chhari Mubarak*) reaching the holy cave that coincides with the Hindu festival of Raksha Bandhan. I consider myself singularly honoured to have visited the holy cave on fifty-nine occasions and received the blessings of *Baba Barfani*. In the year 1989, my company was deployed along the northern route to secure and maintain the arduous foot track and also provide immediate medical assistance to stranded pilgrims, including servicemen and ex-servicemen. To achieve this task, we constructed a wooden log bridge on a mountain stream at Sangam, the confluence of two routes, a few days prior to the commencement of the yatra. Once the yatra started, I walked along the complete route up to the holy cave for fifty-seven days continuously, offered my prayers and returned to our company base at Baltal by the evening. Later in 2019, as Corps Commander of Chinar Corps, I participated in the performance of the *Pratham Puja* (the first prayer) of 2019, along with the then Honourable

Governor of Jammu and Kashmir, and visited the holy cave again along with National Security Adviser Mr Ajit Doval, and the then Chief of the Army Staff General Bipin Rawat, taking my total *darshans* and blessings at Amarnath to an incredible fifty-nine!

I have always been blessed to be part of Sri Amarnath Ji Yatra on many occasions

At Sri Amarnath Ji Holy
Cave, July 1989

Sri Amarnath Ji Holy Cave,
Pratham Puja, 1 July 2019

The Jyeshteshwara temple, or Shankaracharya temple as it is popularly known, is perched on top of Shankaracharya Hill (which was known as Gopadari Hill in olden times), next to the famous Dal Lake in the centre of Srinagar. The stone temple, built by Jaluka, the son of Emperor Ashoka, is dedicated to Lord Shiva and is believed to date back to 220 BCE. The existing structure is largely believed to have been made by Gopaditya around 4 CE. The seer Adi Shankara is supposed to have visited the temple in 8 CE, which is how the temple got associated with the name Shankaracharya.

The Kheer Bhawani temple is a highly revered Hindu shrine, situated in the Tulmul Village, about 22 km from Srinagar. The temple, made of white marble, sits in the middle of a hexagonal sacred 'Nag' (meaning 'spring' in Kashmiri) and is surrounded by a large number of Chinar trees, which render a very peaceful aura to the place. The water of the Nag is said to change its colour, signalling the portent of the future. While the hues of pale blue and green are supposed to be a good omen, red and black colours reflected in the water of the spring are considered to be inauspicious. Goddess Ragnya, an incarnation of Goddess Durga, is the presiding deity of this shrine. The temple is named after the popular Indian dessert made of rice, milk and sugar, kheer, which is offered to the goddess.

Pandrethan or Paani Mandir, an ancient Hindu temple inside the Badami Bagh Military Cantonment in Srinagar, is situated about 100 yards away from River Jhelum. This temple is very close to my life, as I have always paid obeisance here before the commencement of and on the termination of all my tenures in Kashmir. The great mystic saint Lal Ded was born in Pandrethan. The Pandrethan Shiva temple is also known as the Meruvardhanaswami temple, as it was built by Meru, a minister of King Partha, who ruled Kashmir in 10 CE. The square stone shrine is like a little jewel sitting in the middle of water that can be accessed via a footbridge. There are huge Chinar trees all around, lending gentle shade to the surroundings. The roof of this temple is still in place and is unique as it has been chiselled out of a single block of stone, which is artistically carved.

Paani Mandir, Badami Bagh Cantt, Srinagar; puja in the temple, 2019

Paani Mandir, Badami Bagh Cantonment, Srinagar

Rani Mandir, the shrine of Shiva, is perched atop a tiny hillock in the famous tourist destination town of Gulmarg, known for being the world's third highest skiing resort with powdery snow runs. The Apharwat Summit near Gondola II, standing at a height of nearly 4400 metres above mean sea level, has the longest ski slope in Asia. The Rani temple was built by the Dogra ruler, Maharaja Hari Singh, in the early twentieth century. His better half, Maharani Mohini Bai Sisodia, was an ardent believer in Lord Shiva and used to offer prayers here, which is how the temple derives its name of 'Rani Mandir'. Many Bollywood movies have been shot in the surroundings, and it is also the location of the popular song, *'Jai Jai Shiv Shankar, kaanta lage na kankar'* from the 1970s movie *Aap ki Kasam*.

As commanding officer—paying our respects at Rani Mandir, Gulmarg, May 2002 (Young Captain Manish Sanga, Adjutant, on the extreme left)

Many Kashmiri towns, villages and locales have the word 'Nag' suffixed to their names, for example, in the case of Anantnag, a town in South Kashmir, Anant means 'infinite' and Nag means 'spring' in Kashmiri. Thus, Anantnag means 'infinite springs'. There are many springs around Anantnag, including Nagbal, Salak Nag, Kokernag, Verinag, Mattan Nag and Malik Nag. Verinag, a spring at the base of the Pir Panjal mountain range, located approximately 25 km from Anantnag, is a major source of the enchanting Jhelum River, which originates from Verinag in South Kashmir and meanders through the Valley till it finally enters PoK at the Kaman post near Uri in North Kashmir.

Anantnag also houses a beautiful shrine at Mattan, surrounded by huge Chinar trees, which must be hundreds of years old, and has a huge Shivling at the centre of a rectangular natural spring. The blue-green water of the Nag is full of fish of different hues, which are considered very sacred. In fact, most holy springs and lakes have fish in them that are never killed or eaten. According to folklore, there exists a fish in this spring that wears a gold nose ring. Only the lucky ones get to spot it. And those who do are truly blessed by the gods!

I would like to particularly thank my Twitter friend Namrata Wakhloo (@SrinagarGirl) for some well-researched and valuable inputs on the Hindu temples and shrines in Kashmir.

Muslim Shrines of Kashmir

Dargah Hazratbal, a seventeenth-century mosque, is situated in the locality of Hazratbal on the northern banks of the famous Dal Lake. It is the most revered shrine in the Valley of Kashmir not only among Muslims but also among people of other faiths. According to local belief, the shrine houses a relic, *Moi-e-Muqqadass*, or the sacred hair of Prophet Muhammad. The shrine is the most preferred mosque for Friday prayers.

Dastgeer Sahib, also known locally as Daechh Gandein, is a 200-year-old shrine situated in the Khaniyar locality, which was built in memory of Sheikh Syed Abdul Qadir Jelani. The *ziyarat* (pilgrim site) of Dastgeer Sahib is visited by many people, irrespective of their religious faiths. Devotees tie threads at the shrine, which are untied once their wishes are fulfilled, a practice commonly followed even by the Kashmiri Pandits visiting the shrine.

Charar-i-Sharief is located at a distance of 32 km from Srinagar, on the way to Yusmarg, another beautiful tourist resort in Kashmir. The shrine was built more than 600 years ago in honour of the Muslim Sufi saint, Hazrat Sheikh Noor-ud-din Wali, who was a benefactor saint of Muslims and made many contributions in the field of poetry. His followers also called him by various other names, including Alamdar-e-Kashmir, Sheikh-ul-Alam, Sharkhel-e-Rishia and Sheikh Noor-ud-Din.

The shrine of Khanqah-e-Moula, also known as Shah-e-Hamadan, is one of the oldest Muslim shrines on the banks of River Jhelum in Srinagar. This shrine is believed to contain the *Khanqah-e-Moula* (the secret of Allah). The architecture of the wooden shrine draws inspiration from Buddhist, Hindu and Islamic styles.

The Ziyarat of Baba Reshi is a popular shrine situated in the village of Baba Reshi near Al Pather Lake, close to Gulmarg in Baramulla district. The shrine is named after the well-known Sufi saint Baba Payam-ud-din Reshi, who was also a courtier of the king of Kashmir Zain-ul-Abidin. This popular shrine is frequented by locals and tourists alike. Childless couples also come here to pray for the fulfilment of their wish to have a child.

The shrine of Makhdoom Saheb is located below a magnificent fort at the base of Hari Parbat in Srinagar. This shrine is named after the revered Sufi saint, Sheikh Hamza Makhdoom, a scholar and a mystic saint of a high order. Thousands of people, irrespective of their religious beliefs, visit the shrine to pay their respects and receive the blessings of its deity.

Sikh Gurdwaras of Kashmir

Sikhs are a very intrinsic part of Kashmiri society ever since the rule of Maharaja Ranjit Singh and even earlier. There are many gurdwaras across Kashmir. Gurdwara Chatti Patshahi aka Gurdwara Chhevin Patshahi, named after the sixth Sikh guru, is located on the banks of River Jhelum and Dal Lake, outside the Kathi Gate of Hari Parbat Fort. The site of the gurdwara is believed to be the house of Mai Bhagbhari, who had for long been yearning for a glimpse of Guru Hargobind Saheb, who fulfilled her wish and not only visited her but also appeared donning her gown. This gurdwara, one of the most important Sikh shrines in Kashmir, comprises a rectangular hall with the sanctum sanctorum in the middle and a spacious terrace in front. The campus of the shrine also houses an old well that is said to have been dug on the orders of Guru Hargobind Saheb.

Kashmiri Art, Craft and Artisans

While the natural beauty of Kashmir is unmatched, its most precious resource is its people and their craftsmanship. Kashmiri artisans are also renowned worldwide for their craftsmanship and skills, including embroidery, carpet-weaving, woodcraft, papier mâché, metalware, tapestry, *numdah*, *gabba* and wicker craft, to name just a few.

For the non-initiated, Kashmiri carpets symbolize the finest, most intricate and exquisite form of weaving artistry. The exclusive range and depth of their designs, their opulent look and feel and the vivacity of colours make them coveted possessions for many with a keen eye for aesthetics.

Woodcraft in Kashmir has a great range of artistic expressions but the most famous among them is walnut wood-carved furniture and an ancient art that entails the use of pine wood-cut pieces put together in geometrical designs on the ceilings of rooms called *Khatumbandh*, which is also remarkable for the fact that it is invariably done without the use of nails. Kashmiri walnut wood furniture, which is highly sought after, is made from walnut trees that mature to the age of more than 250 years and are thus considered ideal for furniture carving. Once sawn into planks, these wooden pieces are subjected to a process of seasoning that ensures the removal of all moisture from the wood. While the carving uses different designs based on the choices of customers, the most common ones among them include engraved, raised, through-cut and plain designs. The carving process comprises the initial etching of the basic design or pattern on the plain wood after which the craftsmen use very fine chisels to incorporate an embossed look.

Papier mâché, like other arts, has been passed down for generations and was originally known as *Kar-i-kalamdani*, meaning 'the case of a pen'. The two stages involved in creating papier mâché include first making the raw paper pulp and forming a soft mash, and then moulding the latter into visually pleasing objects of the desired shapes. This step is called *sakhtasazi*. The next step is called *naqqashi*, which involves painting very intricate floral or figurine patterns on the surface of the object created. Traditionally, the colours used in this painting work were obtained by grinding and soaking various vegetables and mineral dyes, but these days, most artisans use synthetic colours to maintain cost-competitiveness.

Kashmir's 'Chinar' leaf gold jewellery is one of the main attractions for tourists who are charmed by this lightweight and aesthetically crafted jewellery. The silverware industry of Kashmir produces some of the finest and most minutely embellished pieces of craftsmanship denoting traditional Kashmiri motifs like the Chinar and lotus. Some of the more popular silver items include samovar, a typical Kashmiri kettle used to brew and serve Kashmiri kahva or salted tea called 'noon chai', flower vases, photoframes, cigar boxes, glasses and cutlery items. However, in view of the rising prices of gold and silver in recent decades, some of the silver artisans have switched to using copperware. While the designs, motifs and techniques used in copperware largely remain the same as those for silverware, the commonly produced copper items include samovars, pitchers, kitchenware, hookahs and serving trays/bowls.

Kashmiri tapestry constitutes a delicate rug made of framed canvas boasting varied designs ranging from birds or flowers to landscapes, which are made with needlework embroidery, mostly using cross stitch or chain stitch, also known as *aari* work. These rugs are generally used as wall hangings. *Numdah*, an inexpensive floor covering that helps to beat the winter chill in Kashmir, is a felted rug made of unspun wool or a cotton-wool mix embroidered with fast colour threads in floral motifs, either in chain stitch or appliqué work. The embroidery not only adds vibrant colours to the rug but also binds it together. *Gabba*, on the other hand, is a poor man's carpet, made of old used blankets intricately embroidered in chain stitch with colourful threads.

Kashmir experiences a very harsh winter but the local people know how to beat it while going about doing their daily chores as usual. The Kashmiri male dons a loose-fitting robe-like garment called *pheran* and hides a fire pot made of baked clay called *kangri* to keep himself warm. The pheran, which is now widely popular even in other parts of India during winters, is, in fact, also worn by Kashmiri women and children, apart from men. Kashmir also spins world-class pashmina from the wool of the mountain goat (found in Ladakh), which is used for weaving and embroidering exquisite shawls. Each pashmina shawl is intricately embroidered by hand, and it can, therefore, take months to get one made. The embroidery work is usually done in winter when the farming work gets stalled due to the intense winter.

Cuisines of Kashmir—*Mehmaan Nawazi* (Hospitality par Excellence)

No discussion or deliberation on Kashmir would be complete without the mention of its mouth-watering rich cuisine and the famous Kashmiri hospitality. Wazwan, the most famous multicourse meal in Kashmiri cuisine, is a very unique and embedded ingredient of Kashmiri culture. Wazwan can comprise up to thirty-six dishes of mutton, chicken, fish, fruits and vegetables. Its preparation is not merely a recipe but an art that is considered a matter of pride in Kashmiri culture and identity. Almost all the dishes of Wazwan are meat-based, using lamb, chicken or fish, including the most prominent traditional dishes like Rista, Goshtaba, Kebab, Roganjosh, Tabak Maaz, Aab Gosh and Nate-Yakhni (Yakhni is a gravy made of yogurt and spices). Although Wazwan is predominantly a non-vegetarian spread, the Kashmiris have also ingeniously adapted many of these recipes to make vegetarian dishes like Dum Olav (dum aloo), Kashmiri Baingan (brinjals), Kashmiri Paneer (cottage cheese), Haak Saag (a leafy vegetable cooked in mustard oil), Nadru Yakhni and Nadru Monji. Nadru or lotus stem, believed to be a fat-free vegetable, is available in all the lakes of Kashmir, but the ones found in the Dal Lake are considered to be really delectable. There is a very subtle difference between the traditional ingredients used by Kashmiri Muslims and Kashmiri Pandits to prepare their respective variations of Roganjosh. Kashmiri Pandits use heeng (asafoetida) and fennel powder instead of ingredients such as onions, tomatoes, garlic, shallot or mawal that are used in the Muslim version.

The Kashmiris also have a unique fondness for their lamb, chicken and fish-based dishes though that in no way undermines their love for chutneys and home- or locally-baked breads like lavasa, girda and telvor. Kashmir produces one of the best saffron varieties in the fields of Pampore, which is the most aromatic ingredient in the famous sweet Kashmiri tea called kahva, which is usually brewed and served in a traditional kettle called samovar, as described above. The salted tea or noon chai, also called sheer chai, is an 'any time of the day' beverage, and is best consumed with the traditional breads.

Some of my personal favourite eating places in Srinagar are Jan Bakers near Dal Gate for their ever-so-delicious plum cakes. When I was a young captain posted in North Kashmir in 1988–90, we used to have a game of croquet and the loser used to pay for the plum cakes especially brought from Jan Bakers in Srinagar through the bus driver plying daily from Dal Gate to Chowkibal. Jan Bakers continue to be at the top for their plum cake, though they also offer a range of other bakery items. However, recently, Moonlight Bakery has caught up, especially for their famous walnut fudge. As regards Wazwan, a lot of people would prefer the old and famous restaurants in the city, but I would put my money on the lesser-known Shamiana restaurant, closer to Dal Gate.

The Tulip Garden—A Splash of Amsterdam in Kashmir

All of us have seen or heard of the world-famous Keukenhof tulip fields of Amsterdam in the Netherlands, made famous in India by the Amitabh Bachchan and Rekha-starrer Hindi movie of 1981, *Silsila*. However, a splash of those colourful, rolling tulip fields is now available in our very own Srinagar. Taking nothing away from the famous Nishat Bagh, Chashma-e-Shahi, Shalimar Bagh and many other beautiful gardens of Srinagar, the Tulip Garden is the newest entrant and situated on the lower foothills of the Zabarwan Range just below the Chashma-e-Shahi Garden, with an overview of Dal Lake. This tulip garden, built in a terraced fashion on a gradually sloping ground of nearly 30 hectares, is the largest of its kind in Asia. It also flaunts many other flowers like daffodils, ranunculus and hyacinths, in addition to tulips. An annual tulip festival is organized at the onset of the spring season in March and April every year, which is a big hit with tourists, and hotel and flight bookings are absolutely full during this period.

Thus Kashmir, with its incomparable natural beauty, is also a land of many rich treats and unique talents that have been passed down for generations, enthralling both locals and visitors alike.

13

Entry into Kashmir: A Heaven Burning

Eventful Journey to Kashmir

In September 1988, our unit commenced its move from Udaipur to the Kashmir Valley. Kashmir, at that time, seemed quite peaceful, ostensibly living up to its popular sobriquet of 'heaven on earth'. We moved to Ahmedabad in the military convoy, as we had to board the Military Special train from Sabarmati Railway Station. I was awestruck by the very name Sabarmati, which as we all know, is a highly renowned place in the history of India, being home to the Gandhi Ashram. This journey by the Military Special train clearly entailed touching upon more than one famous location.

Here, I must mention the unique characteristics of the Military Special, which is also referred to as 'rolling stock', a term that I actually came to know of much later, when I was posted in the Weapons and Equipment Directorate of the Army Headquarters. At the outset, I must confess that it takes forever for the rolling stock to get positioned at the starting railway station because of the complex management involved, as at any given time, numerous military units are moving to and from field/peace stations spread across the length and breadth of the country. However, once the rolling stock is placed, the railway authorities constantly push the unit members to load up soonest lest demurrage charges are levied on the unit. Loading of the Military Special train is an extremely well-orchestrated exercise as the personal baggage of the entire unit's personnel as well as the essential equipment and (in certain cases even vehicles) have to be laden on to the train. In this case, we spent ten to twelve hours to fully load the Military Special at the Sabarmati Railway Station. Those were highly memorable days for all the officers, with most of us being accompanied by our families. My wife and I were newly married and thoroughly enjoyed ourselves, revelling in the idiosyncrasies of an Indian railway station by day (as I had to check the status of the evasive rolling stock from the station master every day) and visiting local restaurants in Ahmedabad to sample Gujarati cuisine by night. The Army provides you such exciting opportunities to see the remotest areas and beautiful locales in India, meet wonderful people, understand the different cultures and taste exquisite cuisines from across the country. It was also the first time I saw a revolving restaurant when we visited Patang, the restaurant located on the top floor in a multi-storeyed building in the heart of Ahmedabad city. Needless to say, I hardly remember what I ate there as for me the entire focus of the evening was on the sights observed from the vantage point, literally perched in the middle of the sky!

Finally, after much action and activity, D-Day arrived and the Military Special was ready for take-off. In Army lingo, the Military Special is characterized by the phrase '*Chali to chali, nahin chali to nahin chali*'. If it moves, it can cover hundreds of kilometres at a stretch, but if it does not move, it can stay put in the same place without budging an inch for three days at a stretch. Another important aspect of a unit's move by the Military Special is that during the journey, fresh rations for all the officers and jawans on board the train are collected from various military cantonments that fall on the route of the train. This entails constant contact with not only the military stations' supply depots but also the concerned railway station masters so that the latter allow the train to be parked at a decent platform for a reasonable duration, enabling the ration collection party to go to the supply depot, collect rations, complete the necessary documentation, return to the railway station and distribute the rations to all the company cookhouses in the different coaches. This complex management of the Military Special train in an era of 'no mobile phones' was a Herculean task in itself. However, the most difficult job always was to get a decent parking place at the railway station because the station master had his own priority of ensuring the unhindered and scheduled movement of passenger trains. Hence, the most suave officer exhibiting highly polished and persuasive manners was nominated to deal with the railway authorities. His job would start at least seven railway stations earlier where he would rush to the cabin of the station masters of every railway station en route and speak to the station master where the train had planned a halt for the replenishment of supplies, on the railway telephone network.

The journey, however, began with a characteristic speed breaker, as it were. We were scheduled to start at around 6 p.m. on the stipulated day. In preparation for the long journey, my wife took a relaxing bath and dozed off, anticipating waking up at a new destination. However, when she got up from her slumber at around 11 p.m., asking me where we had reached, I had to reluctantly inform her that we were still at the Sabarmati station, as the process of changing the rail engine, or 'Power', as it is called in Railways lingo, was taking unduly long due to a delay in the arrival of the engine. A Punjabi stand-up comedian, while explaining the journey by Military Special trains, had very aptly described the situation as, '*Challaunge taa pahunchaange* (We will reach only if the train starts).'

Notwithstanding the delay, it did start finally and the journey was enlivened by a food competition among the various Rifle companies of the unit travelling on the train, as a result of which we were lucky to be served an assortment of mouth-watering dishes every day. Some JCOs, officers and ladies were assigned the responsibility of judging the food items served during the competition, with exotic prizes being awarded to the winners of the culinary contests. Another highlight of this train voyage was its passage along the Ranthambore National Park, the famous sanctuary in Rajasthan, wherein all the binoculars came out and everyone was peeping out of the windows, with the train driver having been requested to move slowly. Although we did not spot the beast, the experience of traversing through 'tiger land' was no small achievement.

Tea-time Tales

Ultimately, on reaching Jammu, we boarded our civil trucks and set off for Srinagar, the last leg of the journey, from where we were scheduled to travel to our final destination, the unit location in the Kupwara district of North Kashmir. An incident that occurred at the Srinagar transit camp is worth recounting here. During our staging halt at Srinagar, the officers were staying at the Srinagar Transit Camp while the other ranks were housed at the Old Airfield (OAF) a little distance away. The Srinagar transit camp is also the starting and terminating point for the road convoy to and from Jammu for the normal military transients going on or returning from leave. Since the road convoys usually left for Jammu from the Srinagar transit camp at 5 a.m. in order to reach the destination before last light, the Kashmiri civilian orderlies in the transit camp would serve morning tea to the transient officers in their rooms at the unearthly hour of 3.45 a.m. Thereafter, the same orderlies would serve breakfast in the dining room by 4.30 a.m. or so, after which they would help the officers in loading their luggage on to the trucks, and the Jammu convoy would finally march off by 5 a.m. However, on this particular occasion, due to our long haul the previous day from Udhampur to Srinagar, the commanding officer had decided that our convoy would leave for Kupwara at the much more reasonable time of 9 a.m. Hence, we were deep in slumber when there was a knock on the door of our room in the wee hours at 3.45 a.m. Since I (then a captain) was sharing the room with a senior, Major 'Horsey' Jatrana, the onus of answering the knock fell upon me. I grumpily opened the door only to find a civilian orderly standing there with two cups of tea. Peeping out from his quilt, my room-mate 'Horsey' Sir asked me who was visiting us at that preternatural hour, and I replied that it was the waiter with our morning 'cuppa'. Since we were scheduled to leave much later, Major Jatrana advised me to send him off with instructions to serve the tea at the more decent time of 7.45 a.m. Unperturbed, the orderly just walked in and left the two cups on the table with the ingenious suggestion, '*Sahab, idhar hi rakh ke ja raha hun, paune aath baje pee lena* ('I am leaving your cups of tea here. You can drink them at 7.45 a.m.).' We were both dumbstruck by his gumption!

This incident stayed with me, and when, thirty-one years later, I visited the same transit camp as the 15 Corps commander, I was gripped with nostalgia, and especially went to the same room on the first floor that I had occupied as a young captain. I also asked to meet the same tea boy, whose face I still remembered vividly. The gentleman in question, Abdul Hamid Khan, who had been a mess waiter more than three decades ago, had retired as a head steward after putting in forty years of service at the Srinagar transit camp. Delighted to meet him, I hugged him warmly and also gave him a small award for his adroit behaviour and the tea that he had served on the cold winter night during my first official visit to Kashmir.

Kashmir—'Heaven on Earth' or 'The Lost Paradise'?

Coming back to the situation in Kashmir in 1988, as our unit settled down in our new location and we got busy with our routine training activities, we noticed an undercurrent of hostility and tension. Although in 1988, the scourge of terrorism had not started, the issue of alleged animosity against India and Indians among a few members of the local population was quite visible in normal day-to-day life. It would thus be a fallacy to say that trouble in

Kashmir started only after 19 January 1990, the date synonymous with the exodus of Kashmiri Pandits from the Valley. Various indicators of trouble brewing, such as selective and targeted eliminations, incidents of intimidation, availability of weapons, infiltration of trained terrorists into the Indian territory and exfiltration of young Kashmiri boys to Pakistan-occupied Kashmir (PoK) for secessionist training, were already apparent in 1988 and 1989.

There were very few uncommitted reserve military formations or units in the hinterland as most of the combat/supporting arms units were deployed on the Line of Control (LoC) with only the headquarters and a few softer support elements stationed in the hinterland. Further, since the deployment on the LoC was basically intended to withstand any conventional enemy attacks, a majority of the troops were focused on dominating the enemy approaches or guarding the main axes so as to prevent any loss of territory to the enemy rather than occupying all the gaps and countering infiltration as is being done nowadays. The Rashtriya Rifles were not present in Kashmir during the initial phase of terrorism and came in much later; initially as a relocation from the state of Punjab, which itself was going through a very intense phase of terrorism in those days, and later as a newly raised counter-insurgency force. This fact was exploited by Pakistan, which started indulging in the exfiltration of young Kashmiri boys, imparting them training in terrorism and sending them back post the training, armed with heavy weapons. Providing security in the hinterland and maintaining law and order on the Valley floor was the responsibility of the state police and civil administration.

Beginning of Terrorism—When Did It Happen?

Another issue which is often flagged is that of the 1987 Assembly elections in Jammu and Kashmir, which is considered a trigger for the advent of insurgency and terrorism because it is alleged to have been a rigged election, post which the National Conference came to power and Farooq Abdullah became the chief minister.

However, yet another indicator that has often been ignored is the conduct and outcome of the 1989 Parliamentary elections, for which the separatists or the subsequent terrorists had issued a boycott call. The following data pertaining to the 1989 elections provides some key insights on the prevalent security situation—of three Parliamentary constituencies in Kashmir, only 5.48 and 5.07 per cent of the total votes were polled in Baramulla and Anantnag, respectively, whereas the Srinagar seat was won uncontested by the National Conference. The outcome of a conspicuously low voter turnout in the face of a boycott call is an indication of an environment of fear, threat and intimidation, and the presence of undesirable elements in the Kashmir Valley in 1989, a fact that is often glossed over and the entire narrative is shifted to the issue of who *was* or *was not* **the chief minister on 19 January 1990**.

As regards the other seats in the state, the polling percentages in Udhampur and Jammu were approximately 40 per cent and 57 per cent, respectively, while in Ladakh, about 86 per cent of the total votes were polled. In these constituencies, multiple parties were in the fray, and the elections were keenly contested—this also highlights the stark contrast between the Jammu and Ladakh regions vis-à-vis the Kashmir Valley, with the former characterized by remarkably close contests among various political parties and people exercising their franchise fearlessly as compared to the fear prevailing among voters in Kashmir.

Thus, the 1989 elections in Jammu and Kashmir, which are hardly discussed, represent a strong portent of things to come and the impending terrorism. There were clear signs that things had started deteriorating even before and at the time of the 1989 Parliament elections, there was a perceptible fear psychosis. The call for an election boycott was also more or less adhered to in totality. Further, selective killings had also started in 1989, and intriguingly, the then chief minister resigned on 18 January 1990, followed by the declaration of Governor's Rule in the state. It is not a coincidence that the infamous date of the exodus of the Kashmiri Pandits fell just a day later, that is, on 19 January 1990. The atmosphere in the region was highly toxic, as open announcements were being made asking Kashmiri Pandits to leave, and a few prominent Kashmiri Pandit personalities like Justice Neelkanth Ganjoo and Lassa Kaul were also assassinated. Justice Ganjoo was targeted and killed by terrorists on 4 November 1989 because, as a sessions court judge, he had awarded the death sentence to the accused, Maqbool Bhat of the Jammu Kashmir Liberation Front (JKLF), in the Amar Chand murder trial in August 1968. Justice Ganjoo was among the early Kashmiri Pandit victims of terrorism in Kashmir. Lassa Kaul, director, Doordarshan Kashmir, was shot dead by terrorists on 13 February 1990 because he did not bow down to the terrorists' threats of not broadcasting Indian programmes on Doordarshan Kashmir and leaving Srinagar.

The Fateful Day of 19 January 1990

These incidents led to the build-up of violence in the Valley in 1989 and 1990, and need to be analysed in detail. It is not that the terrorism and anti-Pandit sentiment just came to the fore one fine day. Since our unit was posted in North Kashmir, we were very friendly with the local population in our area. I recall an incident concerning the caretaker of a local Shiv temple in the village next to our unit's location. The caretaker, a middle-aged Kashmiri Pandit, was also a teacher in the local government school, which was very close to where our battalion was stationed. This panditji used to frequently visit our battalion mandir with his family, and his wife and daughters used to socialize with the families of our officers as the ladies from the Army community also often visited the Shiv temple to pay obeisance. It was obvious that an extremely congenial environment prevailed around the temple. However, on the night of 19 January 1990, the panditji came over to the battalion headquarters and informed us that some of his students, who had presumably joined the terrorists' ranks, had come to secretly inform him that his family was now a target and the terrorists were planning to neutralize them. Being forewarned of things, the panditji rushed to our unit for help, and the unit eventually helped evacuate his family. However, many others not located near the Army garrison may not have been that fortunate.

In addition, the patrols were sent to evacuate a few more Hindu families in the nearby regions that may have also been targeted by the terrorists. These efforts were, however, constrained by the fact that the Army's interaction with the civilians in the villages far away from their location was very limited and the troops did not have much knowledge about the habitations of the Kashmiri Pandits. Notwithstanding these challenges, the Army tried its best to save as many families as they could. I, along with my troops, personally evacuated a few Kashmiri Pandit families to safety.

The forced exodus of Kashmiri Pandits from Kashmir adversely impacted not only the historical social fibre of Kashmiri society but also the future of Kashmiri generations. As most of us may be aware, Kashmiri Pandits were the backbone of the education system in Kashmir and they occupied the most prestigious and influential places in academia at the functional level, such as that of teachers in the primary and higher secondary schools, professors in colleges as also the decision-making or senior executive level appointments like deans, chancellors and vice chancellors at universities. The exodus of Kashmiri Pandits thus left a void in Kashmir's education system at all levels, from the primary schools to universities. This is not only being felt currently but will also impact the future of Kashmiri youth in the years and decades to come in the competitive educational environment in the country and globally too, especially at the entry level of professional colleges and universities. This human tragedy of our lifetime reminds me of a famous couplet by the renowned Urdu poet Muzaffar Razmi, which poignantly summarizes the reality of Kashmir after the forced exodus of Kashmiri Pandits from the Valley: *'Ye jabr bhi dekha hai, taarikh ki nazron ne, lamhon ne khata ki thi, sadiyon ne saza payi'*, which roughly translates as 'Enough injustice or oppression has been witnessed by the eyes of history, wherein for a mistake made by a moment, centuries to come have been punished.'

Why Was the Army Not Called in?

Questions are often raised as to why the Army was not called in to prevent or at least counter the assault on Kashmiri Pandits.

There is a definite need to clarify certain important aspects and present them in the correct perspective, so that doubts or apprehensions are put to rest. I must reiterate here that Jammu and Kashmir had not yet been brought under the Armed Forces Special Powers Act (AFSPA) nor had it been declared a Disturbed Area at that time. As I stated earlier, during the late 1980s and early 1990s, most of the Army units stationed in Kashmir were primarily deployed on the LoC with only the headquarters and certain softer support elements in the hinterland; most of those also closer to the LoC. As a matter of constitutional responsibility, in the states where AFSPA and/or the Disturbed Areas Act have not been imposed, the maintenance of law and order remains the sole responsibility of the local police under the state civil administration. Notwithstanding this, the Army regulations allow the state or Central civil authorities to requisition the specified number of Army columns for a specified period of time in a specified area for 'aid to civil authorities' by a written order of the civil administration to bring an adverse law and order situation under control, to help maintain essential services in case of a natural breakdown or a man-made situation such as strikes by certain employees, during natural calamities such as earthquakes, and any other type of aid that may be needed by the civil administration. It is pertinent to mention here that any such 'aid to civil authorities may include the provision of Army manpower, heavy earth-moving equipment like dozers/excavators, and medical assistance that includes doctors, nursing assistants, medicines, ambulances, casualty evacuation, etc.' Regulations of the Army, paragraphs 301 onwards, lay down the guidelines for the routine aid to civil authorities.

All Army columns are employed with the guiding principles being 'use of minimum force' and 'acting in good faith'. All such requisitioned Army columns are to be compulsorily accompanied by a nominated magistrate, who is supposed to assess the gravity of the situation and thereafter give written or verbal instructions (only in an emergency and it is followed by written instructions) to bring the deteriorating situation under control. The nominated magistrate accompanying the requisitioned Army columns is also responsible for derequisitioning the Army columns, giving the time of derequisition immediately after the situation has been brought back under control. Therefore, in Jammu and Kashmir, during the period prior to the imposition of AFSPA in September 1990, it was the sole responsibility and prerogative of the civil administration to assess the situation and take action to requisition the Army for 'aid to civil authorities'.

Exfiltration of Youth and Infiltration of Militants

Another aspect that is usually overlooked is that numerous weapons had already been smuggled into Kashmir long before the carnage against the Kashmiri Pandits and targeted killings, including that of Muslims, had begun. A few villages, especially in districts like Kupwara and Bandipora close to the LoC, had been penetrated by the terrorists and almost half the youth in some of these villages had been indoctrinated by the separatists and sent for training to PoK. Large numbers of people had thus gone missing from these villages long before the exodus of Kashmiri Pandits took centre stage. The date 19 January 1990 became famous—for the wrong reasons though—only because of the magnitude of the event. But it comes as a surprise that anyone can feign ignorance about the events preceding this violence, especially someone in power who would have access to more information than ordinary citizens. The steady deterioration in the situation was amply clear and it is highly unlikely that the state administration and its intelligence agencies were unaware of this situation, as it did not come about overnight but was the outcome of a sustained and planned effort by external elements to foment terrorism in Kashmir.

There were clear indications of the festering terrorism, as many local buses would halt at the bus stops with the conductors attracting passengers by shouting, 'Muzaffarabad'—the destination for aspiring terrorists, who were being lured to visit the training camps in PoK. Although these buses may not have physically plied to Muzaffarabad, these incidents were open markers of how Kashmir was rapidly descending into a morass of terrorism, and yet things were allowed to reach a point of no return. The question of whether this was a combination of incompetence and collusion on the part of those holding high offices at that time needs to be deliberated and discussed, and the responsibility fixed.

Interestingly, both Syed Ali Shah Geelani and Syed Salahuddin belong to the higher caste 'Syed' of the Kashmiri Muslims and had earlier contested elections under the purview of the Indian Constitution, and it is only when they lost the elections due to the alleged rigging during the Assembly polls in Kashmir in 1987 or otherwise that they veered towards separatism and terrorism. Indian democracy allows any citizen of the country to contest and win elections. The very fact that these people were in the electoral fray implies that they were keen to be part of the democratic process in India and had they won, they would have been members of a legally elected framework under the Indian Constitution instead of members of separatist groups questioning the validity of the Indian Constitution and posing a threat to it—the irony of the situation is quite palpable! It is also a moot point as to whether the dominance of a single party in Kashmir and its alleged efforts to prevent others from gaining political credence and mileage has adversely affected the polity of the state and pushed others nurturing political ambitions into the wilderness of terrorism. Would the situation have been strikingly different had these separatists been embraced by the political system and allowed to thrive inside it rather than being left to sabotage it from the outside?

After the incidents of 19 January 1990 and post the imposition of Governor's Rule, Army columns were requisitioned virtually every day to launch cordon and search at various locations all over the Kashmir Valley. An anecdote from one such operation is reprod iced later in this chapter. The number of militancy-related incic ents occurring in the Kashmir Valley was so huge that the security fc rces present in the Valley per se were considered inadequate for hanuling the situation and additional forces were desperately needed.

It was on 10 September 1990 that the Armed Forces (Jammu and Kashmir) Special Powers Act (AFSPA) 1990 was enforced, which was deemed to have come into effect on 5 July 1990. The arrival of certain additional security forces, relocation of the few Rashtriya Rifles (RR) battalions from Punjab to Jammu and Kashmir, as also the raising of additional RR units and their deployment across the entire Kashmir Valley helped bring the situation somewhat under control. In this way, the Central Government of the day made efforts to control the situation by moving security forces into the troubled state. But for these urgent measures, many had assumed that Kashmir would soon gain 'Azadi' (independence) from the Indian state. Thus, suggestions that all the turmoil in the state took place after 19 January 1990 are misleading and most accounts of the situation connote that the disturbance had started much earlier and the state was allowed to degenerate into a hub of terrorism and violence. The Jammu and Kashmir Disturbed Area Act 1992 also came into effect in 1992. In addition, the LoC, which had initially been extremely porous, thereby permitting infiltration of weapons and terrorists and exfiltration of potential terrorists, was also further reinforced with additional troops immediately and later fencing in the early 2000s. Additional Army formations and Central Armed Police Forces (CAPF) were moved in and deployed to restore normality in the Valley floor, which led to a significant decline in the terrorism graph. The implementation of all these anti-terrorism measures helped restore a modicum of order and peace over the next three decades in the Valley.

When Not Being Promoted Proved to be a Blessing in Disguise

Here, in the midst of all the tumult and uncertainty that hit the Kashmir Valley with such brutal force, it would be apt to end this chapter by narrating an ostensibly minor but heart-warming incident—it is interludes like this that help motivate soldiers and keep them going in their challenging day-to-day lives and feisty missions. This incident occurred during the initial stages of terrorism in the chilly month of January 1990, and as discussed earlier, my unit, being part of a reserve formation, was available as the Immediate Response Force for any counter-terrorism operations across the entire Kashmir Valley.

In those days, the rank of second lieutenant was the first commissioned military rank. Second lieutenants, who were referred to as 'Mr' in the unit, would get promoted to the rank of lieutenant in peace stations and directly to captain in the field areas, after completion of two years of service. One of the young second lieutenants in our unit was Ranjan Mahajan, popularly known as 'Smiley' for his extremely infectious smile, who had been commissioned in December 1987. Since Kashmir was a field area, Smiley was due for elevation to the rank of captain, the first promotion of his Army career in December 1989. However, the promotion did not come through, as the CO, the sanctioning authority, was away on a short leave. The officiating CO was a stickler for military decorum and firmly believed that an officer's promotion was the sole prerogative of the CO, and not of anyone officiating in his absence, and thus Smiley was not promoted to the rank of captain. Smiley could do nothing about this but smile, and wait for his turn and the CO's return from leave.

Soon after the imposition of Governor's Rule, the requisition and employment of the Army to aid civil authorities increased manifold. On one such occasion, within a week of the imposition of Governor's Rule, on 27 January 1990, our unit was tasked to move to Tral as part of a major counter-terrorism operation. Tral was a tiny village in South Kashmir, but in huge disproportion to its size, it is notorious till date for having nurtured or housed the maximum number of local or foreign terrorists in South Kashmir. The officiating CO had created a small 'hit team' (akin to the erstwhile Commando platoons) under Second Lieutenant Smiley. The unit debussed about 2 km short of Tral Village at approximately 3.30 a.m. and all the Rifle companies moved towards their respective locations for executing their plan before first light.

Smiley's hit team was instructed to stay at the debussing point next to the road till he received further instructions to 'hit' as per the emerging situation. It was a freezing cold January morning in Kashmir and it was snowing heavily. In consonance with the typical hospitality that is part of the Army culture, a jawan from his hit team asked Smiley if he would like a hot cup of tea.

He, of course, warmed up to the idea, following which the brass kerosene stove sitting in a one-ton vehicle (a one-ton was a World War vintage petrol vehicle) was lit up to prepare the tea. Since it was an important operation, the corps commander, a very strict disciplinarian, wanted to be personally present at the operational site and was driving into the village with his cavalcade at the very moment when the flames from the stove leapt into the air and were clearly visible to him in the distance. Seeing a burning stove inside a petrol vehicle, the corps commander, already being a strict disciplinarian, completely lost his cool, halted his cavalcade near the debussing point and asked for the senior-most officer at the spot to come forward and give an explanation for this transgression.

Suddenly, everyone started looking for the 'senior-most officer' and Second Lieutenant (fortunately not yet promoted to captain) Smiley emerged from the shadows with the black cotton epaulettes on his shoulders as part of the RAJRIF uniform not showing his rank in the dark. The corps commander thundered, 'Who are you?' 'Second Lieutenant Ranjan Mahajan, sir,' came the quick and subdued response from the 'senior-most officer'. There was a discernible silence after which the corps commander muttered, 'Second lieutenant, hummm, grrrrr, hunnnn' and just drove off. Obviously, he did not wish to target a junior officer and had been looking for someone at least of the rank of captain to take him to task. Till today, Smiley remains ever so thankful to the then officiating CO for not having promoted him as captain; otherwise, he may have been literally skinned alive by the corps commander for the sin of brewing tea inside a petrol vehicle on that night of the counter-terrorism operation in Tral. This incident notwithstanding, the ever-so-efficient and professionally sound Smiley rose to become a major general in the Army.

This operation was to be followed by many others in the coming days as Kashmir progressively became a hotbed of terrorism, keeping our unit perpetually on our toes and in the thick of anti-terrorism operations. The subsequent chapters delve in greater detail into the volatile situation in Kashmir and the chain of events that followed.

14

Rashtriya Rifles: RR, *Sirf Naam Hi Kaafi Hai*

The First Encounter

As described earlier, my unit moved into the Kashmir Valley in September 1988, which was also my first visit to Kashmir. Thus began my unique voyage, as my life was slowly woven into the socio-military fibre of the exquisitely beautiful locales of Kashmir, which is now an indelible part of my life and soul. This lifetime cruise has been dotted with a fair share of ups and downs but has never even for a second been lacklustre or uneventful, for either the right or the wrong reasons.

Although this particular incident happened when I was in my unit, it laid the foundation for my subsequent tenures in the RR, hence I will narrate it as a foreword to my experiences with RR, a force like none else. In 1990, when incidents of violence were taking place on a regular basis, we were getting deployed all over the Kashmir Valley in small teams. We had started operating in certain key areas including Kupwara, Handwara, Bandipora, Baramulla, Sopore, Tral and the outskirts of Srinagar. Therefore, the involvement of the Army kept increasing progressively in Kashmir in order to keep the situation under control. As its role expanded, the Army got involved in more and more counter-terrorism operations, resulting in the recovery of huge caches of arms and ammunition and the apprehension of a large number of terrorists. The RR had been raised for operating in Punjab during the 1980s. Later in the 1990s, some battalions were lifted from Punjab to Kashmir to help restore normality, especially in South Kashmir, where initially there was no Army presence. Slowly, however, the RR became a main counter-insurgency force in Kashmir, and some of its units were also relocated from Manipur and Nagaland to Kashmir after the signing of the Naga Peace Accord.

The first encounter is always significant, which always leaves a permanent impression in mind. You always remember it throughout your life. My first encounter with terrorists was while we were patrolling the Bungus Valley in Kupwara district, close to the LoC, one of the prominent infiltration routes for terrorists. Like the rest of Kashmir, which is replete with unexplored natural beauty, the Bungus Valley, essentially a grazing ground, is even more beautiful than the better known and more popular hill destination of Gulmarg, meaning the 'meadow of flowers'. While we were on a reconnaissance patrol to this area for the first time, the patrol leader was Lieutenant Colonel K.J. Singh Kang, a soldier par excellence, with a tremendous aptitude for reading and, more relevant to this anecdote, a prolific golfer, whereas I was the patrol 2IC. When we were climbing up to the Bungus Valley, Lieutenant Colonel K.J. Singh was leading the patrol and I was immediately behind him. We had already been treading up this treacherous mountain trail for six to seven hours and on reaching the top, K.J. Singh paused for a second, stretched out his hands and exclaimed, 'Oh my god, that's a seventy-two-hole golf course!' I, a non-golfer at that time, was a little behind him and hence could not see what lay ahead, but the sight I witnessed a few seconds later cannot be described in words. Bungus was truly amazing!

The Bungus Valley is a vast grassland biome with flora at lower altitudes of around 3500 metres and has two major grazing pastures called Bod Bungus (Big Bungus) and Lokut Bungus (Little Bungus), with their length running into several kilometres. These grasslands are covered on all sides by spurs jetting out from the Shamsabari mountain range covered with a beautiful coniferous forest. Nomadic graziers, or *Bakharwals* as they are locally called, come to this area from the plains or the lower hill areas of Jammu along with their livestock during summers and return during winters due to heavy snow in this area. The log huts (known as *dhok*s) of these Bakharwals remain unoccupied in their absence and act as transitory housing facilities for the infiltrating terrorists.

Coming back to my life's first encounter with the terrorists, on my second or third such patrol to the Bungus, I was the patrol leader and we bumped into the terrorists resting in a dhok in Bungus while they were infiltrating Kashmir. In fact, while we were moving as a patrol, they were hiding in a small dhok. They had probably seen us coming and just as we approached their hut, someone in the patrol urged me to halt close to their hiding place. The suggestion for a halt came because the area was a little open and not located in the thick of the jungle. The operations in the current scenario are virtually in complete contrast to those days because today, the Army patrol does not halt in an open area but chooses an area that is under forest cover to avoid being observed and becoming easy targets for terrorists.

After we halted, my patrol 2IC, the subedar saab, ordered a member of the patrol to make tea for everyone. Hence, a few of the jawans started scouting the area around to collect dry wood for a fire to make the tea. The terrorists probably thought that we were encircling their hideout, and in panic, they started firing at us from a distance way beyond the effective range of their weapons. We immediately returned fire and a brief firefight ensued. Although there were no casualties on our side, the operation was an eye-opener for me. I learnt the grim lesson that counter-terrorist forces cannot afford to be lax or complacent even for a moment and have to perpetually remain on alert because, unlike an open war, the adversary in this case is operating clandestinely rather than confronting us directly in battle. With each such operation, we became wiser and sharper, with the result that today, counter-terrorist operations are executed with surgical precision, and each member of the team is fully trained and prepared to perform the task assigned to him.

Honing the Rashtriya Rifles into an Indefatigable Force

It is apt here to discuss my multiple tenures in the Rashtriya Rifles in the north-east parts of India and Kashmir. The Rashtriya Rifles is a counter-insurgency force where everyone is sent on deputation for about two or two and a half years, before returning to the parent unit, which, in my case, was the Rajputana Rifles. I was posted in the Rashtriya Rifles unit deployed in Manipur in the late 1990s. On my first day in the unit, as I was taking over charge of the company, a particular instrument was reported missing from the Company Kote (which, according to some, is an acronym for Keeper of Technical Equipments)—a secure place where sophisticated equipment such as weapons, compasses, night vision devices, radio sets of various kinds and so on are stored. The particular instrument I am referring to could not be located in the kote at the time though it had been entered in the ledger inventory and was supposed to have been there. The young officer who was handing over charge of the company to me was about to move to another unit on posting, and he happened to be my junior and also one of my students in the Young Officers' Course when I had been an instructor at the Infantry School, Mhow. The officer apprised the CO, Colonel (later Brigadier) S.D. Nair, and me of the missing instrument, which was worth about Rs 2000, as per the ledger entry. The officer kept saying that he had never seen the instrument and did not even know what it looked like, to which the unyielding CO replied, 'It looks like Rs 2000', implying that the officer would have to pay up to compensate for the instrument before being allowed to leave the location. I still remember the look on the officer's face as he realized that the amount would have to be deposited, though subsequently, the instrument was actually found in the kote itself and the officer got his money back. However, this episode suitably emphasized the immense sense of responsibility and care that every Army man must display throughout his tenure, with every single error of omission or commission carrying a strict punishment. As mentioned in a previous chapter, the concept of *Imaandari, Wafadari, Zimmedari* is always an integral part of a soldier's life.

Another similar incident pertains to the beautiful Loktak Lake in Manipur, famous for its floating islands. However, when I was posted there, the beauty of these islands was somewhat marred by the fact that they were often used by insurgents for 'rest and recoup'. The insurgents would arrive at the lake, place their weaponry securely in polythene bags and lower them into the lake waters while spending a short sabbatical on the floating islands. One evening, we received information about some insurgents staying in a particular house on an island. We decided to launch an operation in the night to apprehend the insurgents, but when we entered the targeted house on the island, we found nothing there and had to abort the operation. This probably happened because the island had only one entrance from the mainland and the insurgents there had got wind of our plans when they saw our Army vehicles approaching the island from this entrance, which gave them an advance warning and thereby sufficient time to escape.

Our effort came to nought as we could not find either the insurgents or any real-time evidence of their presence on the island and had to return to the unit. However, on our return, when we did a count of our arms, ammunition and other essential equipment, we found one bulletproof *patka* or helmet of the jawan missing from our inventory. The CO of the unit was Colonel S.D. Nair still, the same CO who made the officer pay for the missing item, a stringent disciplinarian, who refused to let the matter lie and insisted that we return to the venue of the operation to recover the missing patka. This was a huge challenge, as going back to a location where one has just carried out an anti-insurgency operation is fraught with risk because perceiving that the operation is over, the insurgents are likely to have returned to the spot and would ostensibly be more armed and better prepared for any further operation. But there was no way we could ignore the CO's order, and therefore headed back to the island, though with reasonable precautions, such as keeping the headlights of our vehicle off.

As luck would have it, the insurgents who had relocated to a safer place earlier during the night had now returned and they were present in the target house on the island. We found them nonchalantly having dinner at the dining table, and swiftly moved in to apprehend them. Taken completely by surprise, they became an easy catch for us, and though we could not find the missing patka, we ended up with a successful operation. Thus, this operation, which had initially threatened to end up as a botched exercise due to both loss of equipment and the failure to apprehend the insurgents, instead became a successful one due to the insistence of the unit commander to adhere to the rules of engagement and not leave anything behind at the site of the operation. Obviously, nothing succeeds like success! However, the more important lesson from this episode was reaffirmation of the ethos of the Indian Army, that is, 'the Indian Army never leaves anyone behind, not even our dead'. This is the single-most important principle that sets us apart from many other armies. A case in point is that of the Pakistan Army, which, during the Kargil War, not only left the dead bodies of their soldiers on the heights recaptured by the Indian Army but also refused to own them and take their mortal remains back even when such an offer was made by the ethical Indian Army. Later, the Indian Army gave Pakistani soldiers a decent burial as per their religious beliefs and practices.

My company was located in Churachandpur district in South Manipur about 40-odd km away from the battalion headquarters. Since that area is prone to ambushes by insurgent groups, carrying out any operation there using vehicles is an absolute no-no. However, vehicles are still needed for other routine tasks such as transporting rations and ferrying letters and salaries. In this context, we had to undergo a peculiar exercise every fortnight called 'half link'. This mandated that those who had to go on leave would move from the company base to the battalion headquarters on foot, whereas those returning from leave would also move on foot from the battalion headquarters to the company base, and the movement of only one vehicle would be allowed for carrying essentials to and fro. This exchange of supplies and personnel proceeding on or returning from leave at a mid-point in the area is known as half-link. It is one of the most awaited events in the company, as it not only signified going on leave but also heralded the arrival of much-awaited rations, and even more so, mail and bags carrying the salaries of the men posted in the company. Such small actions also indicate how a delicate balance is always maintained between the safety and welfare of men that is the hallmark of all Army activities.

Last-minute morale boosting talk before an operation by RR troops

Come Hell or High Water—Thoughts of Family Are Never Far Away

Coming back to family, a major operation was launched just four days before my wife's birthday, when we received information about thirty-odd heavily-armed insurgents camping in a village in South Manipur in Churachandpur district. I received a call from my CO, Colonel S.D. Nair, at about 11 p.m., conveying this critical piece of information about the presence of the insurgents in the particular village, which was notorious for being their regular haunt, and which had, at one time, also been a training camp for insurgent groups. When the CO asked me my plan, I suggested that since the village was located on a hilltop, and also since sunrise in the eastern part of India occurs rather early, we would be deprived of the surprise element while approaching it. I recommended that I would approach the village with a small team while a number of other teams would lay ambushes all around the target village, covering the tracks leading down from the village to counter the insurgents running downhill. Hence, I approached the village with just ten men, including myself, and carrying very light weapons. We had an exchange of fire during our approach as the insurgents could see us approaching and trained their guns on us. We returned the fire, but there were no casualties on either side. However, our post dog, which always accompanied and led the patrol, proved to be our saviour that day. He was ahead, along with the scout leading the team, while I was right behind him, and the remaining eight men, in turn, were following us. As we neared the village, this dog sensed something amiss and sat down at a location just a few metres from the village. Immediately on cue from the dog, I gave the order to 'deploy'. The insurgents, who were observing us from their perch on top of the hill, were waiting for us to come as close as possible and thereafter to open fire on us at an opportune moment. But when they saw us halt and deploy, they probably realized that we were going to encircle the village and they opened indiscriminate fire upon us with machine guns and grenade launchers to preclude our move. With relentless firing from their side, a bullet hit the dog's leg while the rest of us escaped unscathed. While I could see the insurgent firing the machine gun from the hilltop, the bullets were not hitting me but going over my head.

'Plunging Fire'—The Fire That Doesn't Hit the Target

'Plunging fire' is basically an exposition of a key element of physics. When a bullet leaves the barrel of the gun, it travels on a straight path up to a particular distance, after which it starts dipping down because the velocity declines due to various environmental factors, as also the effect of gravity. As a result of this, the bullet would fail to reach the target if fired with the barrel pointing in the straight line of the target. Hence, the sighting systems of all long-range weapons are designed such that the barrel keeps pointing slightly upwards as the range increases, thereby launching the bullet or the projectile not in the line of sight with the target but at a slight elevation in a parabolic flight path. The weapons' sighting systems are thus designed to ensure that both the target and the person firing the weapon are at the same height. However, when the bullet is fired from a height, the force of gravity takes it downhill faster, thereby affecting its parabolic movement and often missing the target. I had been an instructor at the Infantry School and had been teaching the concept of 'plunging fire' in theory during the training to all my students, but that day, for the first time, I witnessed the practical application of plunging fire and that too from the target end in a face-to-face encounter with insurgents. Interestingly, the latter ostensibly enjoyed an advantage over us because of their elevated location, but they became inadvertent victims of the rules of physics. I could see the man firing at me; he too could see me and was in a position of advantage vis-à-vis me. And yet, his bullets did not hit me because the plunging fire made him miss his target and the bullets whizzed past above my head. It was clear that there is a world of difference between theory and practice, and the proof was right there in front of my eyes!

The lesson about the principle of plunging fire has since been deeply ingrained in me and has also become an intrinsic part of both our training and last-minute briefings while preparing for any operation in the mountains. As they say in the Army, 'The more you sweat in peace, the less you bleed in war'; that is, if you train hard and train well, you will suffer fewer casualties in war. This adage was proved without a doubt on that fateful day atop the Manipuri hillock.

During this encounter with the insurgents on the hilltop, which lasted for about ten minutes, we had to fire indirectly as they were above us and difficult to target from downhill—we fired what is called 'a two-inch mortar', which is technically a short smooth-bore weapon used for firing high explosive bombs at a high angle that burst on impact. Unable to face our mortar assault, the insurgents fled from their position. We then mounted a chase but since we had hurriedly assembled for the operation the previous night, we were carrying only dry rations with us and had no cooked meals. The insurgents ran along the ridge line towards the south whereas we had anticipated that they would run downhill and had accordingly positioned our ambushes. My small team doggedly continued the chase along the ridge but soon ran out of water, and all possibility of getting cooked food receded in the absence of water. Even the water springs that could be used for refilling our empty water containers were located downhill while we were running along the ridge. The chase continued through the night and the next morning, we were pleasantly surprised to see a helicopter overhead with our CO, Colonel S.D. Nair, hanging out, firing from the air with a machine gun, successfully neutralizing four insurgents whom he could spot from his aerial position in the helicopter.

Soldiering On an Empty Stomach

The chase continued and by this time, we had not eaten for more than thirty-six hours, with access only to the dry rations that we were carrying in our backpacks. Since dry rations mainly comprise sugar, tea leaves, potatoes and dals, they cannot be consumed unless cooked. As an aside, I must reveal here that since the troops of the Rashtriya Rifles are overly fond of meetha (sweets), when taking off on an operation, in order to prevent the jawans from consuming all the sugar on the way, we pre-mix the sugar with the tea leaves—an ingenious way of combating their incorrigible sweet tooth!

Meanwhile, the operation in Churachandpur district was still not over. The next morning, I was offered an onion and the sugar pre-mixed with tea leaves as breakfast, and after this unusual and paltry meal, we set off on our hot pursuit again. Fully aware that the insurgents were only a short distance ahead of us, we did not want to give up and sustained the chase despite our severely diminished rations and energy. The next evening, just as we were about to call it a day, we had another short contact with the insurgents, which revived both our hopes and energies yet again. Since we were inside the thick jungle, our radio sets were getting affected by what is called the 'screening effect' (being a line-of-sight communication device, a radio set gets affected by any intervening features like buildings, mountains or even thick jungle) and we were not able to communicate as we were also running low on batteries.

The next morning, I was compelled to call the battalion headquarters, asking for replenishment of our food supplies. I could get through to the headquarters only by climbing a hill to revive the radio connection, and the call at the battalion was received by Major (later Colonel) Anil Kumar Suri aka Goofy, an officer from 4 RAJRIF, also on deputation to RR along with me. Having lost all communication with us for the last thirty-six hours, he was intensely worried about our team and asked me to clearly specify our location so that he could send food supplies. My immediate response was, 'Sir, rations can come later, what is critical at this point is that the wife of a jawan who is accompanying me on this operation was critical and admitted to a hospital at his native place. So, can you please check about her condition and convey "all ok" and also please convey to her that her husband is all right?' On a personal note, I said, 'My wife's birthday is approaching and can you please call on the STD line and wish her from my side?' Thus, even in such dire situations, facing death in hostile locales and deprived of food and water, we still always have thoughts for our families. In fact, we often used to go on an area familiarization patrol with Churachandpur as one of the intermediate points to call up home on the STD lines so that the jawans could talk to their family members. In those days, this was the only way of keeping in touch with our families.

Coming back to the seemingly endless operation in the jungles of South Manipur, except for a few morsels, we had not eaten for the last three days. On the fourth day, we met a group of woodcutters who were carrying some food. However, here we faced a new challenge —a language problem—as in Manipur, the spoken dialect changes every few kilometres. So we requested for food using sign language, and mercifully they fed us some rice and dal, which, hungry souls that we were, we devoured rather gratefully. But after partaking of their food, when we offered money in return, they refused to accept it.

This put us in a quandary, as we had never faced a situation earlier where locals did not accept money from us in return for any item we bought or asked for. After little more gesturing and sign language, we realized, much to our amazement, that in our hot pursuit of the Manipuri insurgents, we had reached closer to the Myanmar border, and in all probability, they were Burmese woodcutters (probably illegal), who were ready to feed us but they did not recognize Indian currency and were thus reluctant to accept it. However, we were determined to compensate them for their kindness, and I asked one of the jawans to gift them his watch, which they readily accepted. Of course, when we returned, I had to buy the jawan a new HMT watch from the CSD canteen, but it was a small price to pay for the wholesome food that we had obtained after four days of intense toil and sweat on empty stomachs in the jungles!

Rashtriya Rifles—Never a Dull Moment

In the Rashtriya Rifles, every day offers a new challenge cum learning and I would like to cite another instance, which also underscores the imperative for alertness and constant vigil in anti-insurgent operations. This incident occurred in Manipur, when I was commanding a Rashtriya Rifles company as a major and we were on an extended search and destroy mission of fourteen days' self-contained duration. When we returned to our post after the operation was completed at the end of two weeks, the subedar saab, who was at the post during my absence, handed me a letter, which immediately created a feeling of foreboding, as insurgent organizations in Manipur and Nagaland, especially the Naga insurgent groups, still follow the archaic convention of sending warning letters to military posts. This missive had been sent by one of their commanders, who had probably met me earlier posing as a common civilian—he pompously communicated in the letter that his group had almost ambushed us, but since he had met the 'Sahab' earlier, that is me, and had found me to be a decent person and moreover, our company jawans were very respectful to the locals, they had refrained from opening fire at us during our stopover near their hideout in the jungle. 'So, the next time you go on a patrol in the forest, remember to be more careful,' concluded the letter ominously. While this epistle, on the surface, reinforced the imperative for us to always be on our guard during counter-insurgency operations, at a deeper level, it made me realize, somewhat tragically, that insurgents too are human and vulnerable to human emotions, notwithstanding the grossly inhuman and macabre acts they perpetrate against innocent people. It was this slim glimmer of hope emanating from subdued human feelings, and the rare victory of the insurgent's heart over his head, that I internalized in my future strategies, and also used as a basis for some of my subsequent tactics to deal with terrorists in Kashmir, such as Operation Maa, Taleem se Taraqqi, Khairiyat Patrol and Humsaya Hain Hum, which I will describe in a later chapter.

Thus, a counter-terrorism operation is like a mind game in itself, and one learns the lessons gradually, honing the capability to tackle terrorists through a combination of personal experiences and on-the-ground training.

Rashtriya Rifles—Kimberlite that Turned into Diamond under Pressure

Rashtriya Rifles as an organization has grown from its modest beginnings as simply being called a '*Rif Raf* Force' by the naysayers to probably the world's most professional counter-terrorism force. I was singularly lucky to have served in RR as a company commander for three years in the North-east and subsequently in Kashmir during the most challenging times in the most difficult and terrorist-infested areas. Having commanded and seen the RR force from very close quarters as the RR sector commander and finally as the corps commander, I can say with utmost professional integrity that the nonpareil dynamism and professional ethos engendered in RR have catapulted it to a position even higher than that of some of the finest and oldest regular units in the Indian Army. His emulatory 'fire in the belly' commitment to fulfilling the task at hand and the motivation with which he goes about achieving this objective literally makes an RR soldier one of the most professional, meanest 'man machines' designed to serve the motherland. I daresay that even the most dreaded terrorists baulk at the name of RR and the epithet, '*RR—Sirf naam hi kaafi hai*' has not been earned without reason. The RR crest, consisting of the Ashoka Chakra with two crossed bayonet-fixed rifles nestling against each other, overlaying the RR motto '*Dridhta aur Veerta*' (Courage and Valour) just beneath them, is an authentic depiction of the concept of brothers in arms in the service of the nation. I am sure that likening the Rashtriya Rifles to a kimberlite stone, which has metamorphosed into a diamond in an environment that demands the highest order of military precision and alertness from its soldiers 24/7/365, would be no exaggeration.

Debriefing the RR troops after a successful operation, Kashmir 2011

15

My Homecomings in Kashmir

Nations Go to War; Defence Forces Merely Fight on the Front

The Kashmir situation has been so much in the news that it is often a subject of animated discussion among people. During one such discussion with a fellow traveller on a journey I was undertaking just after the commencement of the Kargil War, he asked me, 'Sir, what will be the impact of this Kargil War and situation in Kashmir on the prices and availability of mustard oil in the country?' Taken aback, I asked him, 'Why are you concerned about mustard oil, of all things?' He replied that he had a small business wherein he was dealing in mustard oil and was naturally worried about the effect of the war on the product that was the mainstay of his livelihood. His microcosmic interest in just the aspect of the economy that had direct implications for the future of his business indicated the huge disconnect between the actions of the government and the defence forces on one hand and perceptions among the common people on the other hand.

This gentleman's simple statement also got me thinking about the huge repercussions of any conflict situation or war. Basically, it is nations that go to war, and this war is not only fought by the defence forces of the countries concerned but the general public also contributes directly or indirectly (and usually with little awareness about it) to the war effort, which means a comprehensive national power is applied to win wars. Wars are thus the outcomes of a combination of military might, economic matters, diplomatic efforts and domestic issues, and therefore entail the contribution of each and every citizen. Also, the best way to prevent a war is to be fully prepared for it because such extensive preparation by a nation will deter any enemy from initiating a war against it. The seemingly trivial conversation was thus actually a vital eye-opener for me, as it made me realize the imperative to create awareness about the circumstances that lead to war between countries and the ways in which war can be averted. The prevalence of numerous media and instant communication channels in today's globalized world easily facilitates the spread of such awareness, but most of these means of communication were conspicuous by their absence prior to the 2000s.

I must humbly admit that in 1999, the nation went all out to support the war effort during the Kargil War. I was, for instance, a personal witness to the huge number of colour televisions, blankets, clothing items and numerous other products lying at the Srinagar transit camp, donated by concerned citizens for the forces. There were also innumerable bundles of non-perishable food items like biscuits, noodles, dry fruits and cans of edible oil (including mustard oil) and ghee, among other things. Teams had to be specially constituted to distribute these supplies equitably to various units across Kashmir and Ladakh during the war. This *nazaara* (sight) of supplies donated by our citizens for the forces nurtured in me feelings of both pride and gratitude for the invaluable support extended by the people of the country to the war effort.

Army Drills Save Lives

The incidents I narrate constitute a modest effort on my part to create awareness among young readers aspiring to join the forces, about the high-level and in-depth preparations that go into making our Army war-ready and fully prepared to face any eventuality to protect the territorial integrity and sovereignty of the nation.

One of the incidents I recount here concerns a fidayeen attack on my post in Kashmir and the various tactics we utilized to thwart such incidents. In this context, it is important to explain the concept of 'Stand To', a practice that was conventionally followed during the two World Wars and also the initial Indo–Pak wars, in which the attacks were usually planned during first light, that is dawn, or last light, that is, dusk, depending on the particular objective of the attacking forces. Thus, during these two periods, armies used to carry out a drill called 'Stand To', wherein every soldier would get into a trench from which he would be expected to defend his post against an enemy assault. A commander would come to check his preparedness for the ensuing battle and question him regarding the arcs of fire, that is the area in front he was responsible for guarding.

'Stand To' was regularly practised during my tenure in RR at Manipur, wherein each soldier had to rush to his designated bunker in the least possible time. When we went to Lolab in North Kashmir, I reached my company post quite late in the evening. And the first thing I did, even before having a cup of tea or taking a break, was to order the 'Stand To' drill. We began the drill by about 9 p.m. and could finish it by only about a quarter to eleven or so, because it was a new area and dark, as a result of which it took us time to make all the adjustments and figure out the exact locations that each soldier was supposed to move to.

Incidentally, the moment the troops got back to the respective barracks, after everyone was duly informed of his area and his bunker, just at 11 p.m., the post was fired upon. Since we had just practised the 'Stand To' drill, every jawan at the post knew where he had to go, and every soldier was in position within the next 30–45 seconds.

Consequently, the fidayeens who were targeting to breach the post could not succeed. This incident, therefore, emphasizes the importance of carrying out Army drills diligently and seriously.

One thus cannot afford to be negligent or lax at any time, especially as an officer commanding a team or small team in such areas. Based on my experience and training, my word of advice for the young officers or youngsters wishing to join the Forces is, 'Never take the easier wrong, always take the harder right.' And these lines are direct excerpts from the NDA prayer, which every cadet has to recite every morning during the three years of training at the NDA. Even today, after all these years, reciting this prayer has become second nature for me. It was actually this very adage that saved lives on that fateful day.

Invisible Fidayeen—The Ghost Who Walks

Here, I want to cite another incident, also related to the 'Stand To' drill, which occurred again in Lolab. In this case, I was the officiating CO of the Rashtriya Rifles battalion, and a new young officer had just been posted at a particular post called Devar in South Lolab, which was notorious for its concentration of terrorists. As the officiating CO, I wanted to visit the officer who had just come in from a peace station and discuss critical aspects of his area of responsibility with him, while also checking if things were fine and he was ready for the potential tasks that lay ahead. When I went there, the CO's protection party, called the 'Quick Reaction Team' (QRT), of twenty-odd boys was with me.

Akin to the incident narrated above, even before having a cup of tea or taking any kind of break, I told the post commander, 'Let's do a "Stand To"', asking him to specify the exact locations of the bunkers for members of my QRT, if something untoward were to happen in the middle of the night. The JCOs in the post told me that the involvement of the CO's QRT in the 'Stand To' drill was not required as the troops at the post were adequate to deal with any situation. They entreated me to relax and allow them to exhibit their hospitality to a guest. But I was not very enthused by their respectful gesture and told them, 'There are no guests in the combat zone, and everyone has to be a part of the team.' So, on my insistence, they agreed and we carried out the 'Stand To' drill, which helped identify the specific positions for each member of my QRT, allowing them to settle in at the post comfortably and yet be fully prepared for any eventuality. And sure enough, at about 11.30 p.m., the post came under terrorist fire.

When the firing started, each member of my team went to his respective designated location. Incidentally, I was wearing a *pathani* suit (salwar-kameez) as my night dress. Without stopping to think about the implications of my dress, I picked up a weapon and started running towards the bunker that had been earmarked for me during the 'Stand To' practice. Suddenly, when I was going past the cookhouse, that is a kitchen or the '*langar*', as we call it at the post, I heard the sound of someone cocking a rifle.

As I heard the noise of the rifle cocking, it immediately occurred to me that since I was wearing a pathani suit, could I be mistaken for the fidayeen? So, I returned to my cabin post-haste, and to avoid wasting time, pulled on the combat dress, that is trousers and jacket, on top of the pathani suit itself. Anyway, the fire was suppressed after about 30–40 minutes and everything seemed to be all right. The troops did well to counter the terrorists' fire and as per the initial report, no fidayeen was allowed to enter the post.

Notwithstanding the initial inputs by everyone, our biggest concern was to find out if anyone had entered the post or not. So when the 'All Correct' or 'All Ok' report was being taken, I heard some commotion outside the kitchen. On checking, I was told by the JCO that the cook was adamant that a fidayeen had entered the post. The cook said, 'I saw him personally and was loading my weapon to fire at him but the fidayeen ran back towards the company commander's hut.' The cook also described in no unclear terms the 'fidayeen' he had seen—'*Woh pathani* suit *mein saadhe chhe* foot *ka dadhi wala banda tha, woh toh meri* rifle *sahi* time *pe* fire *nahi ki warna maine usse ek* minute *mein maar diya hota* (He was a six-and-a-half-feet-tall, bearded person dressed in a pathani suit—unfortunately my rifle did not work otherwise I would have eliminated him in minutes).' Obviously, he had mistaken me to be a terrorist when I went past the kitchen in my pathani dress. So, without a word, I took off my jacket, exposing the pathani suit underneath, and asked the cook expressionlessly, 'Is this the purported fidayeen?' At first, he was nonplussed; then realizing the truth, he exclaimed, laughing, 'So, you are our "fidayeen."' I nodded in agreement, saying, 'Thank god your rifle did not fire.'

This incident reiterates how seriously we need to take all our drills and practices, and implement everything we have learnt during our training. Also, alertness and presence of mind are critical in any situation. In my effort to save time, I probably did not anticipate the consequences of rushing out in my unconventional dress.

On a lighter note, I would like to recount what my RR sector commander, who later on rose to become the vice chief of the army staff, said to me one day, 'Tiny, you attract fire wherever you go!' Fortunately or unfortunately, this happened to be true as it continued to happen with me throughout my life. There were many incidents when I was directly in the line of fire from terrorists or insurgents, and I could have easily lost my life each time, though like a cat with nine lives (and definitely more than that in my case), I am still around! Touch wood!

An Unending Tryst with Kashmir

Seeing destiny repeatedly take me to Kashmir, I cannot help but feel that I must have shared a close bond with this place in my last life too, which has carried on throughout this life! Kashmir has become an inseparable part of my DNA. In fact, I was approved for the rank of brigadier and was in the US on official duty when I received the news of my posting as the commander of a brigade in North Kashmir. I called up my father and told him that I had been posted to Kashmir and would be going there on promotion as a brigadier. His instant reaction was, '*Wahan par tere naanke hain? Baar baar jaata hai* (Do you have your ancestral maternal home in Kashmir that keeps drawing you there? Why do you keep going back there every so often)?' His statement is not without valid justification, as a large part of my professional life has been spent in Kashmir, and I can vouch for the fact that I know more about Kashmir than my own village back home in Punjab. I may not know my neighbours or their families in my village, but I practically know each and every village in Kashmir. In fact, the local Kashmiris who know me intimately actually tell me, 'You are an honorary Kashmiri.'

Unlike officers of the Indian Police Force, who belong to the cadre of a particular state, Army officers do not have any such cadres, but all the police officers in Kashmir jokingly tell me, '*Aap toh* Army *mein Kashmir* cadre *ke ho* (You are a Kashmir cadre officer in the Army).' I have served with these officers for several years. For instance, I have known most of the senior police officers since they were newly commissioned SPs and I was a captain or a major. We have literally grown up together. I have also had the occasion to meet and befriend the very who's who among the politicians, journalists and other opinion makers because we have been meeting each other numerous times during the course of both work and personal interactions. And all of them invariably know me as an 'officer for and of Kashmir'!

Swarming Technique—Mobile Warfare in Jungles

As RR sector commander, I was responsible for carrying out counter-terrorism operations in Rajwar and Haphruda forest, the most dense forests in North Kashmir. I suspect that most people believe that mobile or mechanized warfare through the use of tanks and other mechanized platforms, whose usage entails speed and accuracy, is absolutely different from the sluggish slow-moving counter-terrorism operations in the dense jungles in high mountains with near-zero visibility. But I am a firm believer and proponent of the idea that the mobility of mind, speed of operations, operational acumen, visualization of the evolving situation and competence of the commanders are needed in both. In the jungle, the speed one needs is not through the tracks or engines, but in terms of the mobility of mind. And though in the jungle, we may not be covering long distances of hundreds of kilometres that modern weaponry can do, but even if we are covering just 2 km, mobility of mind is crucial in the stealth of the jungle. Thus, we had to change both our strategies and our mindsets while carrying out counter-terrorism operations in the forests. Here, we very successfully applied what is called a 'swarming technique', which is used to flush out the terrorists from the jungle.

Lieutenant General Syed Ata Hasnain, PVSM, UYSM, AVSM, SM, VSM and Bar (Retd) was the Chinar Corps Commander when I was the RR sector commander in the Rajwar forest of North Kashmir in 2010–12. Lt Gen. Hasnain has written on 'Applying Swarming and Small Team Operations in J & K' in DefPost in January 2014. With his permission, I reproduce certain excerpts from his article for an easy understanding of the technique.

For years on end we have heard about 'small team operations' but the Indian Army has experimented with it just a few times. Not too much is documented about successes and wherever they have been executed it is primarily the Special Forces or a few Parachute Regiment units which have had the will to implement this most essential aspect of counter insurgency operations. This is not to take away anything from the courageous experiments of some outstanding officers and men of the Rashtriya Rifles who adapted this concept with much spirit and élan in South Kashmir, cleaning out some areas in the bargain. Small team operations in the Indian Army's context have invariably been covert in nature, just as they need to be but coordinated multiple teams in swarming mode has seldom been tried out.

The military situation in J & K today calls for the adoption of the concept of small teams in big measure and this can promise a transformation in the conflict as we witness a much reduced presence of terrorists in the hinterland. The fact that most contacts in the last few years have seen the elimination of only two to three terrorists (except in the vicinity of the LC) confirms that the days of large bands of terrorists roaming the countryside are well behind us. The Army has assessed this correctly and put an end to large-scale Cordon and Search Operations

(CASO) in the villages and towns . . . There are remote mountainous hideouts where covert approach is difficult. Jungle strongholds exist as in Rajwar and Hafruda forests where hard to discover dugouts act as hideouts. Then there are hideouts in peripheral villages around major towns such as Sopore, Anantnag or Pulwama. The Army's favourite mode of domination in built up areas is the ambush although rarely does it get a success. In the prevailing situation foreign (Pakistani) terrorists like to remain in hideouts closer to the LC as it facilitates easier infiltration and later exfiltration at the end of their contractual period. The situation begs for 'swarming' operations. These need to be understood and rehearsed if a measure of success is to be achieved.

. . .

Two units of RR provided two sets of 75 teams of six men each; that makes almost 450 men at one time being deployed. Orders for the RR Sector deploy one set for 72 hours in the jungle and then progressively turnover all 75 teams with the next set of teams; no break between operations. The men were briefed to ensure that 96 hours of self-sufficiency would result in only 72 hour operations and then 72 hour refit. There was to be no search; only static deployment in small cordons taken up in the form of ambushes with adequate command and control to ensure that 'swarming' remained coordinated on ground to avoid fratricide. Nothing happened in the first 72 hours except the muted cursing by the RR teams as they prepared themselves for a long haul.

The terrorists having withstood the might of many regular and RR units over a couple of years expected the conventional search and destroy mission to be called off after the first 72 hours. They appreciated that resources from the nearby villages would once again build up into their hideouts before the next operation was launched by the RR; and that could be any time from the seventh day to three months.

By the fifth day an odd intercept indicated that the terrorists were indeed getting surprised; no soldier seemed to be in a hurry to get out of the area. The 72 hour turnover by the two groups was done meticulously and seamlessly; spread out over a large jungle area; the turnover itself was contributing to the deception. On the seventh day, an element of desperation could be sensed; more SMS and voice messages reporting the

paucity of food and water with no indications of the RR stepping down.
It is around this time that the first of the many contacts commenced. By
the 13th day the logistics situation of the terrorist cadres was getting
fairly stretched; the communication intercepts revealed plans of breaking
out and conducting fidayeen like acts; all troops were then put on a
higher status of alert for potential suicide type attacks. None occurred; the
terrorists were simply not up to it. The two units ably assisted by some
Paratroopers and a ghatak platoon of another RR battalion comprising
tribal troops (best jungle fighters) formed the operational element and had
a field day as multiple contacts commenced with the terrorists deciding
to break cover in sheer desperation. Many were eliminated while a few
did escape the dragnet. It was a great achievement for Kilo Force under
*General Thodge and **Brigadier 'Tiny' Dhillon of the RR Sector** proving*
how mindsets about tactical operations can easily be broken for effect.

These swarming operations used to last for as long as forty to
fifty days at a stretch. Swarming basically signifies a tactic deployed
on a given area with the objective of tiring out the adversary by
saturating his combat stamina in an extended operation that could
go on for long periods at a stretch. The entire team, including
myself as the commander, would be involved in the operation in the
jungles during this period. One saving grace in this tough challenge,
however, was that we always received freshly cooked food from the
multiple kitchens running out of many RR posts around the area
of swarming, wherein anything up to 1200 officers and men were
deployed in the jungle at any given time. Colonel Prashant Nikam,
my deputy commander, in charge of procuring and providing cooked
food to the troops involved in the operations, was an enthusiastic
officer with unique ideas to keep the morale of the troops high.
He would add unique popular items in the meal packets every day,
such as Frooti, eclairs, chocolates, choorma and even laddoos from
famous outlets like Haldiram's. This effort was intended to keep
both the nutritional value and morale of the troops high. On the
other hand, the terrorists stuck in our dragnet were crying for food
after a few days. We intercepted a message from their handlers trying

to motivate them by promising that biryani was awaiting them the moment they were able to link up with the other terrorists in Rajwar forest. My message to my small teams operating in the jungles was very clear that '*Biryani khane nahin denge*'. We ensured this by neutralizing any terrorists coming in to meet them with packets of biryani and not allowing them to get out of our '*Chakravyuh*'.

Well done, boys—during a swarming operation with the young tigers on ground zero

Shaking a leg with the jawans as RR sector commander at a company-operating base

Shaking a leg with the jawans in traditional style

Party *toh Banti Hai!*

After the conclusion of one of these almost fifty-day-long swarming operations, I called my deputy commander, Colonel Nikam, informing him of the success of this extended operation and the need to boost the spirits of all the men and young officers who had participated in the operation over such a long period even during the rains. To express appreciation for their efforts in the operation, it was decided that the jawans' *bara khana* (community feast) would be organized at the battalion or company level. But for the officers, I decided to have a debriefing conference at the Sector Headquarters followed by a brunch. Since the profile of RR is largely that of very young officers, the guest list comprised mostly enthusiastic captains and majors, exhibiting a lot of infectious 'josh'.

The entire responsibility of organizing such events fell on the shoulders of the deputy commander, who is also responsible for funds and keeps an eye on the inflow and outflow of money. I eased his problem a bit by suggesting a simple menu of chana bhaturas and biryani, and the time for serving the brunch was set at 12 noon so that the party could be wrapped up by afternoon, enabling all the officers to return to their respective locations early. I ordered additional crates of beer on payment and much in contravention of the original plan, though the party started at around eleven, lunch had not been served even at 4 p.m. Everyone had a roaring time, singing and dancing—a great way of busting stress—and the celebrations were followed by a serious game of basketball at 4.30 p.m. among the officers, which proved to be the icing on the cake after the boisterous celebrations we had during the entire day. This party, after an intense fifty-day-long operation in the forest with some officers still nursing blisters on their feet, proved to be an ideal outlet for relieving stress and fatigue. It also became a hugely-talked-about event, and at all the posts I subsequently visited, a common request I received from the rank and file was the call to have another brunch party at the sector headquarters, where officers from all the units would be invited. It also gave grain to the idiom, which is an integral part of Army life, that 'all work and no play makes Jack a dull boy'.

A day to remember with the young tigers

These large-scale operations were a success due to the very professional conduct by each and every soldier involved in them. Here, I remember one such soldier, Lance Naik Patey Tassuk of the Brigade of Guards, serving with an RR battalion deployed in Rajwar during my tenure as sector commander.

Lance Naik Patey Tassuk—The Instinctive Hunter

Having been in active operations since my captain days of 1988 and subsequently as a major in RR in the North-east and Lolab and then a commanding officer in Tral in South Kashmir, I was really fortunate that until I was RR sector commander, I had never lost any of the officers or jawans under my command despite being involved in numerous encounters with insurgents and terrorists in many successful operations. However, this record was sadly broken when we lost Lance Naik Patey Tassuk in an operation in the Rajwar forest. Tassuk, who hailed from Arunachal Pradesh, was a daredevil soldier and a fearless hunter by nature. He had already been awarded a Sena Medal (Gallantry) during his tenure in the Ghatak platoon of the RR battalion, which was operating in the Rajwar forest. Lance Naik Patey Tassuk got the second Gallantry award, another Sena medal posthumously for an operation in Rajwar. Having lost a soldier for the first time in my command, I will always remember Tassuk as the most daring soldier with a hunter's mindset.

The next call of duty for the CO, however, was to ensure proper documentation for the fallen soldier so that his wife and children could get access to all the benefits they were entitled to. As soldiers come to RR for a tenure of two years or so, the documentation of their earlier service period is generally done by their parent unit and all the records are held in the respective Regiment's Records offices. In this case though, the CO was on leave and the adjutant told me that all of Lance Naik Patey Tassuk's service documents must be in order and we could start the process of compensation for the family. I have a very strong sense of ominous intuition or 'black intuition' as I call it, when something is not right. Ultimately, taking care of these things is the responsibility of the CO, but as the brigade commander, I too had a responsibility and, acting on my hunch, I asked the CO, who had immediately rejoined duty after cutting short his leave the moment he came to know of this incident, to recheck all Tassuk's documents prior to processing the case with the Records office.

A thorough back-check was carried out by his unit and we found that he had had another child but was yet to get the latter's details published in his record book. We suspended the process of documentation until details of the child were published. Thereafter, we called up the Records office and urged them to complete the publication of details of the child's birth before initiating the process of handing out the benefits to his family. Meanwhile, we also needed a birth certificate for the child. So, I called up a brigadier colleague of mine, whose relative had been in the government of Arunachal Pradesh, and requested him to facilitate the issuance of the birth certificate for Lance Naik Patey Tassuk's son on priority. The urgency for the issuance of the birth certificate was conveyed to the divisional commissioner who issued the birth certificate within a day after checking all the records. He faxed that birth certificate to us, and we sent it to the Records office, where it was duly processed, ensuring that the compensation and future benefits in education would cover his wife and both children. As an institution, we never lose contact with our bravehearts' families. Tassuk's wife was given a job in the state health department and his kids, now aged thirteen and eleven years, respectively, are turning out to be well-rounded students. Tassuk may not be around today, but the Army is dedicated to making his dreams for his kids come true.

Welfare for a Soldier—The Concept Redefined

As officers, we have multiple commitments towards our men. I especially brought this issue of 'welfare of troops' to centre stage when I was the CO and had taken over the command of my battalion in Kashmir during 'Operation Parakaram'.

My first message during the first *Sainik Sammelan* to the unit that I was commanding was to redefine the concept of 'welfare' during my command. For me, welfare for a soldier does not mean that he just gets good food, or timely leave to visit home, or a comfortable pre-booked air or train journey home. It also does not mean providing him a comfortable stay in the barracks, or adequate clothing and other provisions. All this was not 'welfare' in my book. These were simply part of my duty towards my men, as they were a soldier's entitlements. As their commander, I was obliged to ensure that they got nutritious, balanced food, a comfortable and well-equipped barracks to sleep in, and all the requisite equipment and clothing on time. I was also supposed to ensure efficient communication between the soldiers and their families so that rumours did not create panic. These were not, in the technical sense, the benefits or welfare; they were simply a jawan's authorizations and as officers, it's our duty to ensure they are provided to him. My definition of welfare instead was to make such operational plans that the unit completes its assigned task without suffering any casualty and every soldier goes back to his family hale and hearty. I, as a commanding officer, would have a long-term plan for the social security of the family in case the soldier had to sacrifice his life in the line of duty. In the unit that I commanded, a jawan, Lance Naik Umashankar, had lost his life on the Line of Control before I joined the unit. The deceased soldier's father was an alcoholic and his wife had died earlier, leaving behind a minor daughter and a son. The CO at that time, the late Colonel I.N. Mitra, sensing that the children may not be brought up well by the grandfather, had the family adopted by the unit and ensured that the soldier's mother (we all called her 'Mataji') along with her minor grandchildren stayed with the unit and were provided quality education in Army school. The CO of the unit was nominated as *ex officio* caretaker of the children and also the account holder for all their bank accounts. I, during my tenure as CO, did my part of the duty and now the boy has joined as a soldier in the same unit and the daughter was married to a bank official and is happily settled in her new life. That's the long-term social security I am talking of.

Similarly, in the case of Lance Naik Patey Tassuk, my definition of welfare was that his family should get all their entitlements. As an aside, I must admit that because I stayed away from my family and children during most of my career, I may not have done these things for my own children as everything was being handled by my wife whenever there was a requirement for any documentation or other things in school or college. The blind faith reposed by the men in their officers is, in fact, an unwritten honour code between an officer and the jawans, in line with the famous phrase in the Army, '***Mere peechhe* move**', signifying that the jawan would unquestioningly, and with absolute trust, follow the officer. It is thus a tradition in the Army that all the men follow the leader and the onus is on the leader to ensure the welfare and well-being of the team that is walking behind him in such earnestness and trust. An officer thus has to justify this faith at all times and behave like a fully responsible leader to actually earn that faith.

'Experienced' Young Major Who Took on the '*Zorawar*'

Here is an input in first person from Colonel Neelgagan Singh, who worked with me as a company commander in the jungles of North Kashmir as a major when I was the RR sector commander as a brigadier. I quote the words of Colonel Singh as narrated:

> '*I vividly remember that pleasant evening of July 2011, as I was sitting in my office at Handwara; the CO called me and told me that there was confirmed input/intelligence about the presence of two foreign terrorists in a particular village in our battalion's area of responsibility. Normally, we would take all such "confirmed inputs" with a pinch of salt, but this "TINY" (pun intended) intelligence input was from the "Zorawar" (Zorawar was the code name for the sector commander, Brigadier Tiny Dhillon). And that definitely set a bell ringing because Zorawar was a man of few words himself but his piercing eyes spoke louder than words.*
>
> '*I gathered my men and equipment, and proceeded to cordon off the house and its adjoining cowshed. The cordon stayed in place through the night, and with each passing moment, I became more and more convinced that this was also one of those "confirmed inputs" which never come true. Since my company 2IC, a young officer with just about five or six years of service behind him, started looking a little tense by around midnight, I had to assuage his nerves by telling him, "Main tere ko dhai saal ke experience se bata raha hoon . . . is mein koi nahin hai (I am telling you, based on my experience of two and a half years, that there is no one inside this house)." Little did I realize that the input about the presence of foreign terrorists had come from someone with "dhai dashaks" (two and a half decades) of experience.*

'The next morning, the search party conducted the search as per the standard operating procedures (SOPs) that had been laid down for such operations, and just as I suspected, nothing was found. At around 11 a.m., I lifted the cordon and sent back the reinforcements. When I called up the adjutant asking for clearance for disengagement, he told me that a Search and Rescue dog was on its way from a unit located over 70 kilometres away and that the cordon would continue. Full of ire at what increasingly seemed a wasted effort, I blasted the adjutant on the phone, expressing my displeasure at now having to wait there for a dog. That's when the adjutant said, "Sir, yeh Zorawar ka hukum hai (Sir, this is an order from Zorawar)." Obviously, no further questions were asked.

'The terrorists were actually hiding in a hideout carved inside the false ceiling of the ground floor and the wooden floor of the first floor of the structure used as a cow shed. They were spotted by a very alert young soldier, who, while escorting the dogs on the first floor of the cow shed, saw the hiding terrorist's head movement through a small crack in the wooden floor of the first floor. The young soldier must be commended for his presence of mind because when he saw the terrorist move his head, he did not raise any alarm because doing so would have resulted in the terrorists firing through the wooden planks, which would have definitely caused harm to him and his buddy.

'Thereafter began a firefight and we were able to neutralize two Pakistani terrorists by evening Finally, when Zorawar arrived, and I was expecting a pat on the back for a job well done (which I did get, though a little later), his phone rang just then, and I could hear the caller congratulating him for a successful operation. Then came the bombshell for me, as I heard Tiny Sir saying, 'Oh no, no, this was just a side operation, my main swarming operation is going on somewhere else.' For that one moment, mera Bhagwan se vishwaas hi uth gaya tha (I lost faith in God for that one moment)! I was like, "What a man, yaar, I put my life at stake and was nearly killed, and he's not even considering me as 'main course' but just a starter." That was Tiny Sir at his operational best!

'However, I realized later that the insistence by Zorawar to maintain the cordon and keep an eye on the house emanated from the fact that these two terrorists had been caught in an ambush a few days ago but were *able to escape by taking cover in the thick foliage of the jungle. Both these terrorists had been injured in that firefight and so had one of our jawans. Tiny Sir had vowed to get them within a fortnight and had tasked his sources to track all the local nursing assistants, who would be summoned for treatment of these injured terrorists. Hence, while he was busy in a major swarming operation in the forests of Rajwar, this small side operation fell into my lap.'*

16

Jammu and Kashmir: A Geo-Historical Perspective and the Context of Articles 370 and 35A

I was the Corps Commander in Kashmir on 5 August 2019, when the Indian Government initiated important steps to administratively reorganize the state of Jammu and Kashmir into two union territories and abrogate Articles 370 and 35A of the Indian Constitution. Before I proceed further to delineate how the Team Security Forces and the civil administration of the newly formed union territory of Jammu and Kashmir, in absolute and close coordination with the Union Government, helped implement this decision of the government with zero civilian casualties at the hands of the security forces, and with absolutely no loss or damage to government or private property, it is important to describe the geo-historical perspective of Jammu and Kashmir. In addition, there is a need to list the whats, whys and ifs of Articles 370 and 35A for the readers to enable them to understand and establish for themselves a fact-based narrative for demystifying the half-truths and disinformation that have been emanating with regard to Jammu and Kashmir.

Geographical, Cultural and Demographic Perspectives

The state of Jammu and Kashmir (J & K), as it existed on 15 August 1947 under the rule of the then Maharajah of J & K, had a geographical area comprising Gilgit Baltistan, Shaksgam Valley, Ladakh, Kashmir, Jammu region and Pakistan-occupied Jammu and Kashmir, with the Kashmir Valley per se forming only approximately 7.7 per cent of the total area. Hence, the narrative that the Kashmir Valley is the centre point of Jammu and Kashmir is a little flawed and needs to be understood in the correct perspective.

A glance at the history of India, and indeed of the world, is clearly indicative of the fact that Kashmir has always been an integral part of India. It has actually been an abode for the sages and *rishi*s since the Vedic period. In recent times, the area has been ruled by various dynasties. This has had a profound impact on the social, cultural and religious evolution of the state. Kashmir's cultural heritage has amalgamated Hindu, Buddhist, Sikh and Muslim philosophies, which have created a composite culture for it, based on the values of humanism and tolerance—commonly referred to as 'Kashmiriyat'.

The demographic character of the erstwhile state of J & K has been fairly diverse in that while the Kashmir Valley is predominantly inhabited by Sunni Muslims, the Jammu region has a majority Hindu population. The union territory of Ladakh has a significant mix of Shia Muslims and Buddhists. Other religious denominations such as Sikhs and Christians, though negligible in terms of numbers, form an important component of the very vibrant and colourful canvas of J & K. However, the exodus of Kashmiri Pandits from the Kashmir Valley has impacted the demographic profile of the region. As per the 2011 Census, nearly 62 per cent of the population of the then state of Jammu and Kashmir was under the age of thirty years, but this figure is likely to have shot up to approximately 66 per cent or so by now. This would mean that nearly two-thirds of the population in J & K was born after 1989, and has grown up under the shadow of the gun! Their psyches and lives have been impacted by the violent events of nearly three decades. This aspect needs to be kept in mind while dealing with the youth of Kashmir.

Despite suffering years of violence engineered by external actors, J & K has sustained a commendable literacy rate and has a sizeable youth population, which is increasingly gravitating towards urban areas in the quest for better job opportunities and a peaceful life. The exodus of Kashmiri Pandits from Kashmir from 1989–90 onwards has left a scar on the soul of Kashmir, as it is not only the Kashmiri Pandits but also a part of the soul of Kashmiriyat that departed from Kashmir. The Kashmiri Pandits were the mainstay of the education system in Kashmir right from being primary schoolteachers to lecturers and professors in colleges or universities. The education system in Kashmir thus literally crumbled post the exodus of the Kashmiri Pandits, which was further accentuated when Pakistan-backed terrorists burnt down all the school buildings made of wooden structures, especially in the remote areas in those days. This double blow to the education system has adversely impacted the young Kashmiri students, who are otherwise very intelligent and aware, but find it difficult to compete and succeed in clearing the competitive exams for admission to higher education colleges and universities in other parts of India and abroad.

Historical Perspective

The princely state of Jammu and Kashmir came into being under the suzerainty of the British Indian Empire following the signing of the Treaty of Amritsar between Maharaja Gulab Singh and the British on 16 March 1846 after the First Anglo–Sikh War. Gulab Singh stayed neutral when the British fought against the Sikh Army of Maharaja Ranjit Singh. Gulab Singh was succeeded by his son, Ranbir Singh, followed by Pratap Singh and Hari Singh, the fourth ruler, who became the king of the state of Jammu and Kashmir on 23 September 1925, and remained its sovereign head until 12 November 1952.

It is pertinent to mention here that Hari Singh was the ruler when India gained Independence and later, when he signed the Instrument of Accession. Kashmir was the microcosm of everything that India signifies, especially its 'unity in diversity'. On the eve of Independence, Pakistan was confident that the state of Jammu and Kashmir would automatically accede to it. However, when it did not see that happening, it grew impatient and decided to annex it by force. Pakistan infiltrated tribesmen from its forward areas under the leadership of the Pakistani military officers into the state of Jammu and Kashmir. Although the people of Jammu and Kashmir resisted the invasion, they were no match for this invading force comprising the Pakistan Army regulars who were equipped with modern weapons. The plunder of Baramulla bears testimony to the cruelty, ruthlessness and atrocities committed by this invading force. It would be imperative to highlight the cold-blooded murders of a young British couple, Tom Dykes, an Army officer, and his wife, Biddy, and the rape and murder of the nuns at St Joseph's Catholic Mission and Hospital at Baramulla in October 1947.

Thereafter, the Maharaja of Jammu and Kashmir decided to accede to the Union of India on 26 October 1947 by signing the instrument of accession in favour of the Union of India and became a part of India. The instrument of accession in this case was the same as the instruments of accession signed by all the other princely states, and was unconditional and irrevocable.

The United Nations Resolution on Kashmir

An entire generation of Pakistanis have been brought up on a diet of mischievous accounts of the provisions of UN Resolution Number 47 of 1948, concerning the state of J & K. First and foremost, the UN Resolution never contested the accession of the princely state of Jammu and Kashmir to India. The Resolution only spoke of three actions, all of which were conditional and sequential. The first necessary condition was the absolute and unqualified withdrawal of Pakistani troops, tribesmen and Pakistani nationals from the area. On satisfactory confirmation of the fulfilment of the first condition by the UN, the Indian troops were to withdraw, leaving behind sufficient elements as necessary to maintain the security of the state. Only on having fulfilled these conditions was the state to hold a plebiscite. The UN Resolution did not recognize or grant any role to Pakistan in the conduct of the plebiscite.

The moot point in this context is that given the simplicity of the resolution and Pakistan's misplaced notion of the two-nation theory, Pakistan has not fulfilled the first essential condition of the resolution till date. This self-inflicted wound, in the form of a convoluted, contrived and cultivated storyline of the UN Resolution, exposes the deceit perpetuated by Pakistani decision-makers since its creation, and is now an albatross around their neck. In any case, the context of the Resolution has changed in the present, and all the issues between India and Pakistan now have to be dealt with bilaterally between the two nations in the spirit of the Shimla Agreement of 1972.

A. Restoration of peace and order

1. The Government of Pakistan should undertake to use its best endeavours :

(a) To secure the withdrawal from the State of Jammu and Kashmir of tribesmen and Pakistani nationals not normally resident therein who have entered the State for the purpose of fighting, and to prevent any intrusion into the State of such elements and any furnishing of material aid to those fighting in the State ;

2. The Government of India should :

(a) When it is established to the satisfaction of the Commission set up in accordance with the Council's resolution 39 (1948) that the tribesmen are withdrawing and that arrangements for the cessation of the fighting have become effective. put into operation in consultation with the Commission a plan for withdrawing their own forces from Jammu and Kashmir and reducing them progressively to the minimum strength required for the support of the civil power in the maintenance of law and order ;

B Plebiscite

6. The Government of India should undertake to ensure that the Government of the State invite the major political groups to designate responsible representatives to share equitably and fully in the conduct of the administration at the ministerial level while the plebiscite is being prepared and carried out.

United Nations Resolution number 47 of 1948

Articles 370 and 35A—Genesis

Before discussing the abrogation of Articles 370 and 35A, and its effects, it is important to understand the basics of both these Articles, which most of the people in Kashmir themselves were not aware of, before 5 August 2019. Article 370, incorporated into the Constitution in 1954, grants an autonomous status to Jammu and Kashmir, which provides special rights and privileges to the citizens of the state. A very important aspect that needs to be clearly understood is that both these constitutional provisions, that is, Articles 370 and 35A, were applicable to all the subjects of the erstwhile state of Jammu and Kashmir, irrespective of their religious faiths, and were not applicable only to a particular religion or a particular section of society. These were constitutional provisions and had nothing to do with any religion or a specific area of the state.

The instrument of accession of the state of Jammu and Kashmir into the Union of India was signed on 26 October 1947. As on that day, Article 370 was neither a part of the instrument of accession nor was any pre-condition mentioned about it in the instrument. It was thought of, for the first time, as part of the draft Constitution of India which was placed before the Constituent Assembly on 17 Oct 1949; almost two years after the signing of the instrument of accession of J & K into the Union of India. Post the debate on the issue, the Article was co-opted into Part 21 of the Indian Constitution, which deals with *temporary and transitional* provisions of the Constitution. Article 370 basically spotlighted the provisions of the Indian Constitution that were not applicable to the state of Jammu and Kashmir. Since then, many amendments to the Indian Constitution that were brought in for the welfare and benefit of the citizens of India were made applicable all over India but not implemented in the state of Jammu and Kashmir.

Article 35A defines the permanent residents of Jammu and Kashmir. It, however, infringed upon the basic rights of women, denying a woman inheritance rights to ancestral property if she married a man who was not a subject of the state of Jammu and

Kashmir, whereas no such restriction was there for the men from Jammu and Kashmir marrying a girl from outside the state. It facilitated the unrestrained violation of the fundamental rights of scheduled castes (SCs)/scheduled tribes (STs), who have resided in the state for generations. Refugees, who came from the erstwhile West Pakistan into Jammu and Kashmir at the time of Partition in 1947, were not given state citizenship for seventy-two years till Articles 370 and 35A were in force. These West Pakistan refugees voted for the first time in the District Development Council Election held in 2020, after the abrogation of Article 35A on 5 August 2019.

ARTICLE 370 OF THE INDIAN CONSTITUTION

* A temporary provision
* Grants special status to Jammu and Kashmir.
* Under Part 21 of the Constitution of India, which deals with "Temporary, Transitional and Special provisions", the State of Jammu and Kashmir has been accorded special status under Article 370.

Article 370—main aspects

Abrogation of Articles 370 and 35A—Why Was It Needed?

On 5 August 2019, the Government of India issued a Presidential Order superseding the 1954 order and making all the provisions of the Indian Constitution applicable to Jammu and Kashmir. The order was based on the resolution passed in both the Houses of India's Parliament, with a two-thirds majority. This emerged as a landmark event in the history of Jammu and Kashmir, though it evoked mixed emotions in India, while drawing a contemptuous reaction from Pakistan. Since the abrogation, Pakistan has commenced unjustified and fake propaganda to spread its own narrative before both the international audience as well as the people of Pakistan.

Articles 370 and 35A, which were temporary and transient in nature, and aimed at the integration of the state of Jammu and Kashmir, had actually resulted in just the opposite outcome. It created various classes of people; disempowered important sets of the population, particularly women; and prevented the creation of any base for sustainable educational, economic and industrial opportunities. In the interest of the people of Jammu and Kashmir and their well-being, and for the fulfilment of their legitimate aspirations, it was imperative to afford them the same opportunities that were available to their counterparts in the rest of the country, and for that to happen, Articles 370 and 35A had to go!

Administrative Re-organization of Jammu and Kashmir

The decision of the Government of India relating to the administrative re-organization of the state of Jammu and Kashmir is a matter internal to India, and has taken place on different occasions in the past as well, including the trifurcation of the border state of Punjab into Punjab, Haryana and Himachal Pradesh, and the bifurcation of another border state of Uttar Pradesh into Uttar Pradesh and Uttarakhand, among others. This particular process does not, in any way, impinge upon the boundaries of the state of Jammu and Kashmir, or the international border or the Line of Control, and is, therefore, an in-house administrative exercise, with no impact on any other country.

Insofar as the administrative re-organization is concerned, it implies that the erstwhile state of Jammu and Kashmir has been bifurcated into two union territories; one of them is the union territory of Jammu and Kashmir, which will have its own legislative assembly and its own chief minister, and the other is the union territory of Ladakh, which will have an elected council. Further, the abrogation of these articles has been undertaken with due diligence through a democratic and legislative process, which involved the introduction of the bills into both Houses of Parliament, which were voted upon. The bills received explicit support in both Houses and became an act and came into effect after the assent of the Honourable President of India, The question that may be asked is: What does the abrogation of Articles 370 and 35A, and the administrative re-organization of the state entail in terms of making a difference in the lives of the people of Jammu and Kashmir vis-à-vis the earlier times? It really means that the people would have the opportunity to benefit from the provision of accountable governance, social justice, economic development of the region, empowerment of women and the marginalized communities, and the application of many other proactive and positive legislations promulgated by the Government of India, which hitherto did not apply to the erstwhile state of Jammu and Kashmir because of the provisions of these articles. Hence, the verbiage coming out of Pakistan on a daily basis is not as much about the abrogation of the articles as it is about the imminent prosperity of the people of Jammu and Kashmir, which will expose Pakistani fabrication and make it irrelevant to the narrative.

Socio-economic Impact

Terrorism started in Jammu and Kashmir around 1989–90, and that was also the time when the Indian economy opened up to the world in a big way. The economic benefits and the resultant job opportunities that accrued because of the liberalized economic policies could not be harnessed by the state of Jammu and Kashmir because of restrictions on property ownership imposed by Article 35A and the non-conducive environment for carrying out business due to terrorism that prevented the establishment of industry in many sectors where multinational corporations (MNCs) were making major investments all over India. Even the existing industrial sector suffered because most of the hi-tech engineers from other states working in various industries in the state left in the 1990s due to fear for their lives. The lack of industry and other major business opportunities led to a reduction of job opportunities for the youth of the state. This, coupled with the falling standards of education after the exodus of Kashmiri Pandits and the onset of terrorism, as discussed above, created a major socio-economic adversity, pushing the youth of Kashmir towards the morass of an uncertain future. This was also instrumental in creating a situation whereby young Kashmiri boys started becoming cannon fodder for terrorist organizations controlled, funded, equipped and run from Pakistan, who were looking to recruit young men from the state into their ranks.

There is another very important aspect that has resulted in gradually compromising certain sections of the lower bureaucracy in Jammu and Kashmir, especially Kashmir, over the last three decades of terrorism. Terrorists and separatists have practically boycotted all the elections held in the state. This boycott call forced the common Kashmiri to stay away from the polling booths and only a handful of the votes were cast, which ensured victory for the winning candidates who will subsequently be forming the government or otherwise. As a result of this, some political parties, not wanting to be seemingly harsh towards the separatists, did not take proactive steps to deny supporters of the separatists' entry into the government departments at the lowest levels. These officials in the various government departments have now reached the middle levels of the lower bureaucracy, that is, the functional levels dealing with the public at the grassroots level. In spite of the best efforts of the political dispensation and top bureaucracy, the sympathizers of separatists at the functional level of bank managers, headmasters, *patwari*s or station house officers, for example, are a major cause of concern for the smooth functioning of the administration.

Another social aspect of Kashmiri society that has manifested itself in the rank and file of terrorist *tanzeem*s (organizations) is the existence of a hierarchy of the caste system. The higher castes like Beigh, Mirza and Syed, comprising the Andrabi, Bukhari, Mufti, Geelani and Qadri castes, to mention a few, will rarely be found at the cannon fodder level of terrorist ranks but are invariably at the controlling level of the terrorism or separatist movement—for example, Syed Salahuddin, who is currently located in Muzaffarabad in Pakistan-occupied Kashmir and leads the Pakistan-backed United Jihad Council, which is the umbrella head of all Pakistan-backed terrorist organizations in the Kashmir Valley, or the late Syed Ali Shah Gilani, who used to head the All Party Hurriyat Conference, respectively. On the other hand, surnames like Ahangar, Chopan, Dar, Dhobi, Ganie, Gojree, Khanday, Lone, Paddar, Sheikh, Sofi, Wagay, Wani or Zargar are the ones that make the headlines for getting killed in various encounters with the security forces every other day. Adil Dar, the car suicide bomber who blew himself up in Lethpora, Pulwama, on 14 February 2019, was also from the Dar caste. Interestingly, the prefix or suffix of 'Sheikh' is very intriguing. Kashmiri sociologist Bashir Ahmed Dabla writes in his book, *Directory of Caste in Kashmir*, the title of 'Sheikh' when prefixed means the person belongs to a higher caste, for example, 'Sheikh' Mohammad Abdullah. However, if 'Sheikh' is suffixed to a name as a surname or caste, it means that the person belongs to a very underprivileged community of Kashmiri Muslims.

Overall, therefore, the state suffered socially and economically due to the provision of these two articles and the terrorism perpetuated by Pakistan for over three decades now.

17

Chinar Corps Commander: Baptism by Fire—Dirge at Pulwama

Command of Chinar Corps—*Que Sera Sera*

Having served most of my life in the most prestigious and 'always in combat' formation of the Indian Army, and voluntarily each time, it was my dream to command 15 Corps when I got approved for the rank of lieutenant general in December 2017 in the Command and Staff Stream. Being approved in this stream meant that I had been found suitable to command a formation, Corps and above, as also that I could be a staff officer at any headquarters. Only eleven officers had been approved for the rank of lieutenant general in this stream among all the officers commissioned in 1983 (the March, June, September or December commissions) from NDA, IMA, ACC or OTA into the General cadre (Infantry, Armoured Corps, Mechanized Infantry) or the Combat Arms, who could later opt for the General cadre.

Three officers had been approved for the 'Staff only' stream. I got promoted to the rank of lieutenant general on 1 October 2018 and assumed the appointment of Director General, Perspective Planning (DG PP), at the Army Headquarters. It is pertinent to mention here that an officer gets promoted in his own seniority as a legal provision, but an appointment for the command of a formation can be made in any sequence. Notwithstanding, the seniority rule is normally followed there as well unless for operational reasons or some extraordinary administrative constraints.

This chapter takes me back to my epochal tenure as Chinar Corps Commander, which was not only eventful in itself but also coincided with two momentous events in the history of the country, viz., the dastardly attack on the CRPF convoy in Pulwama in February 2019, and the abrogation of Articles 370 and 35A in Kashmir in August 2019. Going back in time a bit, even the manner in which I ended up at Chinar Corps, like most events in my life, seems providential, something that was 'meant to be'. The foundation for my appointment as Chinar Corps Commander was laid by my promotion to the rank of lieutenant general. I was positioned at around number eight or nine in the order of seniority awaiting the appointment as corps commander, and lieutenant generals senior to me by six months or more were also waiting for their turn to command a corps.

The time for reckoning came towards mid-December 2018, during a late evening meeting with the then Chief of the Army Staff, General Bipin Rawat, in his office. After we finished with the work at hand, without mincing any words, he came straight to the point, asking me, 'Tiny, when are you picking up the command of a corps?' I told him, 'Sir, I'm waiting. As per the order of seniority, I am in the eighth or ninth position. So, the appointment might happen sometime in October 2019 or so.' The logic for my argument was that once an officer becomes a corps commander in any of the fourteen corps in the Indian Army, his appointment is usually not changed for at least one year. Therefore, as per a mathematical calculation, I was due for tenanting the appointment of corps commander only by October 2019 if the appointments followed the seniority. General Rawat then asked me, 'Are you willing to go to 15 Corps?' My instant response without batting an eyelid was, 'Yes, sir'. And pat came his concurrence, as he told me, **'Okay, go to 15 Corps, and do a good job.'** These exact ten words are etched in my memory forever now, as they symbolized the faith reposed in me by none other than my chief himself. If it had not happened, I would probably have gone to some other corps instead of 15 Corps in Srinagar, and someone else would have been the Chinar Corps commander, but I suppose, with all modesty, that General Bipin Rawat picked me up for that role because of my earlier experience in 15 Corps.

The command of 15 Corps is considered the most prestigious in the Indian Army as it is the only corps that is actively involved in very intense operations on both the Line of Control as well as in the hinterland on a daily basis. And, as a soldier, there can be nothing better than being posted in an operational area where active operations keep taking place. Thus, my posting order to join 15 Corps as a General Officer Commanding was issued within the next few days, with instructions for me to take over the 15 Corps on 9 February 2019. However, as the weather delayed the move of the outgoing corps commander, I practically took over the reins of Chinar Corps on 10 February 2019. It was not even 100 hours and I had barely completed the process of taking over charge of 15 Corps when the infamous Pulwama incident occurred on 14 February 2019.

Ghastly Attack at Pulwama and Its Fallout

A lot has been written and said about the Pulwama incident, but I will touch upon a few less-known aspects related to it. To give a background of this incident, a suicide bomber drove an explosive-laden car into a Central Reserve Police Force (CRPF) convoy that was moving along the Srinagar highway, and as the car reached close to the convoy, the vehicle was blown up by the suicide bomber. I received information of the attack within the first few minutes of its occurrence, and immediately called up the then

Inspector General of the CRPF, Mr Zulfiquar Hasan, to check with him the details of the incident. Some damage had obviously been inflicted on the convoy by the bomber but we did not immediately know the magnitude of the damage or the extent of the casualties and fatalities.

I immediately alerted the Army helicopter units and pushed all the available helicopters into service for casualty evacuation, simultaneously also warning the 92 Base Hospital, which is the Army hospital in the Badami Bagh Cantonment, about the casualties that were expected to reach the hospital any time. All the doctors at the hospital were also instructed to report for duty immediately and be prepared to handle the casualties and injured persons who would be requiring immediate treatment. The real-time response to such an incident is reflected in a synergy between the various forces concerned. This suo moto response by me without awaiting the official requisition is a hallmark of the highly coordinated manner in which all the security forces, intelligence agencies and the civil administration in Jammu and Kashmir operate.

Intelligence Agencies: The Faceless Heroes

An important point that I wish to emphasize here has to do with the fact that some among the general public and a few political speakers in the country have called the Pulwama episode an intelligence failure. Intelligence is a very complex and sensitive subject, which entails detailed coordination among different operating agencies at various levels. The word 'intelligence' by itself implies the collection, synthesis, sifting and sorting of the information gathered by the intelligence functionaries and then corroborating it, and finally coming to the conclusion as to whether the information thus far obtained or available is reliable enough or still has certain voids. We keep intercepting intelligence inputs and start collating and building on the inputs gathered from all the agencies, to create what we call an 'intelligence picture'. Then, the appropriate agencies are tasked to further obtain specific information to fill the 'intelligence voids', as it is called. The complete procedure is once again reviewed and it is only after this that 'information' turns into 'intelligence'. Even at this stage, it is either an 'actionable intelligence' aka 'red hot' intelligence, which needs to be acted upon immediately or it would act as a background intelligence; such intelligence is used for further developing or monitoring. The operation, based on such intelligence, is sprung or launched at the most appropriate time when the dividends are likely to be maximum. It is thus a highly technical and systematic process.

It needs to be understood in the correct perspective that, say, out of 100 incidents ostensibly planned by terrorists, timely collection and interpretation of intelligence inputs ensures that ninety-nine are not allowed to happen, signifying a 99 per cent success rate for the intelligence agencies in their operations. Since those incidents are averted completely, we rarely or never talk about them but that should not be allowed to take away from the success of the intelligence agencies. It is to prevent the enemy from realizing how we neutralized their potential threat that we do not publicize the successful intelligence operations, and therefore preclude any chances of their learning about our capabilities, especially technical and human assets, for them to amend their tactics and cover their vulnerabilities.

On rare occasions, we do announce openly if we have neutralized an enemy threat, but in such cases, we do not share the full details, such as the names and affiliations of the perpetrators, the source of our information and whether we had come across a physical leak or got a technical interception. This is the reason why information about most successful intelligence operations is not in the public domain.

As regards Pulwama, though, I would say that though this highly unfortunate incident should have been pre-empted, I would still label it as one of those rare incidents that the intelligence agencies could not counter in time. However, this does not mean that the intelligence agencies are not doing a commendable job. For them, it is a perpetual cat-and-mouse game, as the terrorists keep employing different methods and evolving new techniques. We too need to continuously overhaul our intelligence techniques to stay one step ahead of them. I am sharing all these details to highlight how unjustified was the subsequent criticism of the intelligence agencies in social media and other forums after the Pulwama tragedy.

Another Pulwama Averted

In fact, most of the readers may not be aware that another similar suicide attack had been planned, which was intercepted and neutralized on 24 February 2019, just ten days after Pulwama, wherein a potential suicide bomber terrorist had already made a video showcasing explosives and other weaponry to indicate plans of a second Pulwama-like operation. However, when Intelligence and other agencies intercepted information about the plans of this operation, the security forces moved in instantly to neutralize the module urgently.

After the Pulwama incident, intelligence agencies, the Jammu and Kashmir Police (JKP) and Army further intensified their intelligence-generation operations and were able to successfully infiltrate the network of the proscribed terrorist organization Jaish-e-Mohammed (JeM) in South Kashmir. The operation at Pinglan Village on 17 February 2019, wherein the main perpetrators of the Pulwama IED blast, including Pakistani terrorist Kamran @ Ghazi, were eliminated within 100 hours of the incident, had galvanized the security forces to eliminate the perpetrators at the earliest and not allow any more such incidents. In this endeavour, all the agencies relentlessly pursued all the intelligence inputs of the terrorist movements and were successful in generating hard actionable intelligence regarding the presence of JeM terrorists in Turigam Village planning another Pulwama-like suicide attack. Deputy Superintendent of Police, Kulgam, Shri Aman Kumar Thakur, immediately shared this input with the local Army's Rashtriya Rifles (RR) unit and a joint operation was launched on the night of 24 February 2019. I vividly remember all the details as the operation was very sensitive and we had to neutralize this module post-haste lest they execute another suicide attack. We, therefore, could not afford to fail in this operation, under any circumstances. Acting with stealth, speed and surprise, the joint team was successful in trapping three JeM terrorists inside the cordon. Soon a contact was established, and a heavy exchange of fire ensued.

Deputy SP Aman Kumar Thakur, a very brave officer, was personally leading his team from the front in coordination with the Army's RR unit. During the operation, he saw that Sepoy Baldev Ram of 34 RR was hit by terrorist fire, which left the sepoy bleeding profusely. With utter disregard for his personal safety and well-being, Thakur evacuated Sepoy Baldev Ram to a safe location. However, in doing so, he was hit by a terrorist firing from a concealed location. Despite his injuries, Deputy SP Aman Kumar Thakur, displaying rare courage and steely determination, evacuated the injured soldier and subsequently closed in on the terrorist. Thereafter, he engaged the terrorist accurately from close range and eliminated him in a fierce gunfight. The slain terrorist was later identified as Noman of the JeM, a resident of Pakistan. Deputy SP Aman Kumar Thakur received multiple bullet wounds during this battle at close quarters with the terrorists and later succumbed to his injuries. He was awarded the Shaurya Chakra (posthumously) by the Honourable President for his unparalleled gallantry. This operation saw some very determined and motivated sons of Mother India with steely nerves and raw courage fighting for *Naam, Namak, Nishan*, as per an Army adage, and averting another Pulwama-like tragedy.

During the intense firefight in this operation, JCO Naib Subedar Sombir of 34 RR, exhibiting unmatched courage beyond the call of duty, cordoned off the target house along with his buddy, covering the most likely escape route of the terrorists. As anticipated by the JCO, one of the terrorists attempted to break the cordon by firing indiscriminately and lobbing grenades on them, which resulted in grievous injuries to his buddy. Seeing his buddy in danger and not caring about his own personal safety, Sombir seized the initiative and engaged the terrorist. In a close-quarters battle, he killed the Pakistani terrorist, later identified as Osama, a Category A++ terrorist of JeM. During this extremely courageous act, Naib Subedar Sombir received grievous gunshot wounds, due to which he made the supreme sacrifice. These acts of valour by the combined Army and Police teams led to the neutralization of three hardcore JeM terrorists, including two Pakistani terrorists, along with the recovery of a huge quantity of weapons and explosives, and a major terrorist strike was averted in time. In this operation, three other soldiers were also critically injured and they were evacuated to the 92 Base Hospital in Srinagar, where all of them eventually recovered well. Naib Subedar Sombir was awarded the Shaurya Chakra by the Honourable President for his indomitable spirit and valour.

If these terrorists had not been neutralized ten days after Pulwama, it would have been a huge disaster. Meanwhile, another incident of a similar terrorist strike was averted in Banihal a few months later, again because of the alertness of the intelligence agencies and their coordination with the security forces. In this case too, all the people involved in the planned attack were caught from their respective places in real time due to the alertness and perfect coordination among the security forces and intelligence agencies.

'Team Security Forces' Hunt down Ghazi of Pulwama

Coming back to the Pulwama incident of 14 February 2019, it was actually a turning point for the nation. Such a large and radical terrorist operation, coming after a gap of many years, symbolized a major challenge for the intelligence and security agencies. This kind of a car bomb suicide attack had not happened in Kashmir for a long time, as the last time that such an attack had taken place was way back in April 2000, at the Badami Bagh Cantonment Gate in Srinagar. In the recent past, such attacks had happened in Syria, Afghanistan, Kuwait, Iraq and Libya, among other places, but not in India.

After the incident and post management of the casualties and the injured, a meeting of all the security forces and intelligence agencies was held, which was attended by all the high officials of the Army, Police, CRPF, intelligence agencies and the civil administration. One of the points that emerged from this meeting was that all the events or discrepancies that had led to the Pulwama incident would emerge in the subsequent investigation and the immediate main aim of the Team Security Forces, which included the Army, J & K Police (JKP), CRPF, intelligence agencies and civil administration, should be to first target the terrorists responsible for Pulwama without indulging in any blame game, leaving the task of identifying the masterminds and behind-the-scenes perpetrators of the incident to the investigating agencies. I remember my ADC, Captain Sandeep Singh, asking me while we were on our way for this meeting, 'Sir, what will happen now?' My curt response was, **'We will get the bastards.'** Our immediate focus and emphasis, therefore, was on neutralizing the terrorists' module through a synergized effort among all the security forces and intelligence agencies. And we went all out in that effort, meeting numerous times over the next forty-eight hours, sharing the information pieces obtained by various agencies and putting together an intelligence picture. Our efforts bore results and finally, we were able to successfully pinpoint the exact location of the module on the evening of 17 February, that is, within seventy-two hours of the incident. That is when we launched the counter-terrorism operation to eliminate this module of JeM. The intelligence and operational situation was being handled at multiple levels but in a highly synergized manner. The intelligence gathering through technical means and human assets was being assisted by the security forces launching relentless operations at all the suspected hideouts of the terrorists in South Kashmir over the next three days with a view to unhinge the terrorists and prevent them from reorganizing and hiding at one place. It was essential for the intelligence agencies that the terrorists make a move and communicate with each other, as the lack of any movement or communication on their part would reduce the chances of the terrorists' hideout being identified by technical or human intelligence means. On receipt of specific intelligence from the JKP, a swift joint operation was launched by 55 RR, JKP and CRPF in the Pinglan Village of Pulwama district. Pinglan is a very dense built-up area having more than sixty houses (some with cowsheds), and narrow lanes with limited accessibility, where any movement without being noticed was difficult. Some of the houses were multi-storeyed and very close to each other, giving ample opportunity to the hiding terrorists to shift from one house to another even during the firefight.

Kar Chale Hum Fida Jaan o Tan Sathiyo

The security forces had to act with utmost speed, as they were aware that the terrorists may have been planning to shift their base yet again during the night. The CO and officers of 55 RR, including Major Vibhuti Shankar Dhoundiyal, knew the area well and they, along with the JKP officers, made a quick plan of approaching the village from multiple directions, using circuitous routes to avoid detection. Without compromising the element of surprise, they completed the cordon of the target house by around midnight of 17/18 February 2019. Post the cordon, the forces, led by Major Dhoundiyal, commenced a focused search of the target area. Without going into the operational details, here I would like to briefly narrate the most valorous act of Major Dhoundiyal, who led his men from the front. Since his posting in the 55 RR Battalion, Major Vibhuti Shankar Dhoundiyal had exhibited unparalleled valour and exceptional leadership qualities while leading five successful operations, resulting in the elimination of five hardcore terrorists in the past. During the search on the fateful day, when the major and his buddy were searching a suspected cowshed, the hiding terrorists opened indiscriminate fire on them, which was immediately and effectively retaliated by the duo. In this exchange of fire, Major Dhoundiyal received multiple gunshot wounds. Despite being grievously injured, the intrepid officer maintained his tactical composure and retaliated with ferocity. He crawled close to the cowshed under fire and continued to rain effective fire on the hiding terrorists. The terrorists were thus forced to move out of the cowshed firing indiscriminately. The officer, despite his injuries and blood loss, brought down effective fire on the fleeing terrorists and neutralized one of them before they could escape into the nearby house. However, by now, grievously injured, he finally fell down and despite being administered the best medical care, he could not be revived.

During the course of the operation, apart from Major Dhoundiyal, Havaldar Sheo Ram, Sepoy Hari Singh, Sepoy Ajay Kumar and Head Constable Abdul Rashid of the JKP laid down their lives. This sacrifice by the young officer and these men, though causing us immense mental trauma, inspired and galvanized the team, which eventually succeeded in neutralizing three hardcore JeM terrorists, including two Pakistani terrorists, one of them being the main mastermind of the Pulwama blast, Kamran @ Ghazi, along with the recovery of a huge cache of war-like stores. I remember paying homage to the bravehearts the next day and I must confess here that the most difficult part of a commander's duty is to salute one's brothers in arms one last time.

Paying homage to the Pinglan bravehearts, Srinagar, 19 February 2019

The initial reversal and the loss of Major Dhoundiyal and his men of 55 Rashtriya Rifles did not deter the team, and the unit, without losing its morale, pressed on with the operation, which continued for another eighteen hours. Brigadier Harbir Singh, the sector commander of this RR force, was on leave at the time of the Pulwama incident. The moment he came to know of the launch of this intelligence-based counter-terrorist operation, he voluntarily cut short his leave, returning to resume his duties. He directly drove to the encounter site straight from the airport, taking control of the situation and leading his men from the front. He and DIG Amit Kumar of the J & K Police were on the spot, leading their boys from the front, and both were injured. The senior military and police officers, leading their men in operations from the front, speaks volumes of the ethos and commitment of the security forces in counter-terrorism operations. The operation ended successfully on the evening of 18 February, when all the terrorists had been neutralized, albeit at a heavy cost in terms of the lives of the security forces men. This question about the number of our casualties was raised in the subsequent press conference held on 19 February 2019, to which my reply was that we did not want to use excessive force that could have resulted in civilian casualties or collateral damage, and we **'took it on our chin'**.

Why Do Indian Army Officers Lead from the Front?

On other occasions, too, I have been asked this question many a time, especially by my civilian friends, as to why the Indian Army suffers such a high percentage of officers' casualties, be it during Operation Pawan in Sri Lanka or counter-terrorism operations in J & K, or in other operational areas. My basic understanding of and explanation for this stems from what Subedar Major Nand Ram of my unit told me unambiguously on my first day in the Army, and that was '*Officer Hamesha Aage* (the officer always leads from the front).' However, as I progressed in my Army service, I realized the more pragmatic reasons for this simple advice. The most important aspect and consideration of any military operation is to ensure minimum losses of own men and resources while achieving success in the operation at the earliest. It is here that the commander's control from the scene of action is extremely critical, because he is the one who has the maximum inputs and information about the target prior to the launch of the operation and the subsequent evolving intelligence picture during the operation.

During the operation, all the means of communication with higher headquarters or his own controlling headquarters are available with the commander, which makes him the most suitable person for modifying the plan or asking for reinforcements, or any other initiative as per the evolving operational situation. An NCO or a JCO who may be part of or commanding one of the many teams in that particular operation, on the other hand, would not have access to these inputs and would be following the commander's instructions to make the overall operation a success. In case the commander is not present right at the place of action, the passage of the situation report may get delayed and the full picture may never be available to the commander sitting away from the operational area. Hence, it is critical for the commander of the team to always lead from the front, enabling him to take timely and well-informed decisions that help save lives. Any signs of weakness or capriciousness on the part of the commander could thus prove costly for the operation. Simultaneously, it is important to remember that the Indian Army never retreats. We might modify the plan, or seek reinforcements, or even wait and bide our time in an operation, but we never retreat and the commander always leads from the front.

The Colour of the Uniform is Not Important

The persistence of the security forces to complete this operation in the face of all odds was also evident from the fact that, despite suffering casualties right at the beginning, they stayed put and did not abandon the operation, eventually achieving the objective. If they had let down their guard or suffered a loss of morale after the initial casualties, the terrorists might have escaped. In this operation, Head Constable Abdul Rashid from the J & K Police, who belonged to Karnah in Tangdhar bowl, also laid down his life and was awarded the Kirti Chakra (posthumously). I met his wife and brother-in-law during the investiture ceremony, when they had come to receive the posthumous award from the Honourable President of India. When my wife and I spoke with the wife of Head Constable Abdul Rashid and I narrated to her how bravely her husband had fought the terrorists, she expressed surprise that even though I was from the Army and her husband was a policeman, I knew everything about him, including the name of his village, and also the circumstances in which he had made that supreme sacrifice. This also proves that when we are conducting an operation, all the members of the team are like brothers in arms, and we do not differentiate between the colours of our uniforms. Every soldier, every constable on the ground, is a member of the security forces, and it is based on this concept of brotherhood under fire that I coined the term '**Team Security Forces**'.

Honesty before the Nation—'*Kitne Ghazi Aaye, Kitne Ghazi Gaye*'

Coming back to Pulwama, after our operation against the module that had planned the Pulwama attack, we eliminated the main mastermind of the Pulwama blast, a Pakistani terrorist called Kamran, a commander of the JeM terrorist outfit, whose code name was Ghazi (hence my statement, '*Kitne Ghazi Aaye . . .*', which is invoked later). 'Ghazi' used to be a preferred code name for the Pakistani terrorists and many terrorists with this code name have been killed by security forces in the past, including one 'Ghazi Baba' killed by the BSF in 2003 in Kashmir.

We had a press conference the day after the Pinglan operation was concluded. There is a small history behind that famous press conference. Since I had taken over the 15 Corps just four days prior to the Pulwama incident, I was scheduled to visit the Line of Control. I was suddenly informed about the press conference and had to return to base. The IG JKP Mr Swayam Pani, IPS; IG of the CRPF, Mr Zulfiquar Hasan, IPS and GOC Victor Force Major General (later Lieutenant General) Johnson Mathew were also present at that press conference. While I was sitting in my office along with the other officers mentioned above, waiting for the mediapersons to assemble and set up their equipment, my staff handed me a one-page press note, with the suggestion that I read out that press note, while its copies would be distributed among all the mediapersons present at the conference. I asked if there would be any questions and was told that there would be no question-answer session. I also asked if the press conference would be aired live and was once again told, 'No, sir, it's not live. You just have to read out this press note in front of the journalists and then walk away.' My reply was, 'I'm not attending this press conference like this. I want it to be live. I will speak whatever I have to speak. I'm not taking this one-page press note. I will take as many questions as they want to ask, be they from the international or the national media, because if we do not take questions, no one will ever know the reality and the message we will be sending out is that we have something to hide or cover up.'

So having this interactive press conference was an on-the-spot decision. Subsequently, the messages I received from various quarters proved that the whole nation appreciated the efforts of the Team Security Forces. A lot of questions were asked in this press conference of 19 February 2019, details of which are still available on many Internet platforms. I recall that the press conference continued for well over forty minutes, with our initial comments being not more than four to five minutes and the questions by the journalists accounting for the balance of the time. Ever since the Pulwama incident four days prior, the media had been sensationalizing the name 'Ghazi' as the main mastermind of the attack, and therefore, among the many other questions that were asked, one question that came towards the end of the press conference was whether 'Ghazi' had been killed or not. And that is when I made my seminal statement, which has since become famous, *'Kitne Ghazi aaye, kitne Ghazi gaye . . . Parwah nahin*, **we are there, don't worry**.'

Another question that was asked in the press conference had to do with the Taliban in Afghanistan and the likelihood of Taliban fighters coming to Kashmir for fighting. Although the resurgence of the Taliban in Afghanistan took place on 15 August 2021, this press conference was held two and a half years earlier, on 19 February 2019, My response to the question about the potential resurgence of the Taliban in Afghanistan and its possible impact on Kashmir was, 'A lot has been written and said about the situation in Afghanistan and its impact on Kashmir, but coming down to the Kashmir Valley, we are very clear that **anyone who enters the Kashmir Valley will not go back alive** in whichever way. Our focus is very clear on counter-terrorism operations.'

92 Base Hospital—a Lifesaver That Challenges Death

Any discussion of terrorist operations and their violent fallout would be incomplete without a mention of the stellar role played by the 92 Base Hospital, the military hospital located inside the Badami Bagh Cantonment in Srinagar. This hospital is staffed by doctors in all the important specialities relating to the management of trauma and war injuries. It is staffed with more doctors from the specialities of surgery and anaesthesiology, basically because a lot of patients come here with injuries such as gunshot wounds or wounds caused by explosives, as these are typical injuries suffered by security forces personnel, especially in Kashmir. This hospital is one of the finest hospitals in the country, and the best doctors are posted there. During any operation conducted by the security forces, the doctors, nurses and the entire staff at the hospital are always on 'Stand To' or full alert so as to not waste even a single second in attending to the incoming casualty. At times, when a critically injured soldier requiring urgent care is being flown in by a helicopter, the medical team receives it at the helipad itself and the treatment commences right then and there.

Even the J & K Police and CRPF casualties prefer to be evacuated to the 92 Base Hospital instead of the civil hospitals in Kashmir. There is a very strong belief among all the police personnel and soldiers that if they reach the 92 Base Hospital breathing, they will survive. This hospital has the golden reputation of saving the maximum number of casualties, provided they are brought alive. The doctors, nurses and the entire support staff are so committed that there is no concept of being 'on duty' or being 'off duty'. They have jackets of various colours depending on the rank and speciality, which are placed in a particular room called the 'Trauma Centre' in the hospital where casualties are brought in first. The moment there is news of an incident wherein some casualties are expected, all the doctors and nurses get information via a central alarm system and all of them rush to the Trauma Centre of the hospital. Regardless of whether they are wearing a uniform, civil dress, jeans and T-shirts, or whatever, they just slip on their jackets over their dresses, which depict their ranks and specialization, and get down to the job at hand in the most professional manner. I have personally seen all the staff, including the doctors and the nurses, rushing to the hospital within five to seven minutes and getting into the operation theatre in the first ten minutes of receiving news of the arrival of a casualty at the hospital.

When an ambulance reaches the hospital with a casualty, the ambulance gate is opened and a stretcher is immediately placed against it. The hospital has a commendable concept of a 'six-people team', which includes an anaesthesiologist, a surgeon, a radiologist and others, all of whom are present at the gate of the ambulance, ready to receive the patient. They are so well-prepared that they do not waste any time even while bringing the casualty from the ambulance to the Trauma Centre and thereafter, to the operation table as needed. They immediately start working on the patient, assessing the injuries, and carrying out check-ups even while evacuating him from the ambulance. The X-rays and even emergency CT scan is done at this Trauma Centre as required, and the casualty is then immediately ferried to the operation theatre where the team comprising multiple surgeons, anaesthesiologists and other staff are already waiting to carry out the required intervention or surgery. The entire exercise of transporting the casualty from the ambulance to the operation theatre and carrying out all the checks and tests does not take more than ten minutes. And this protocol is implemented 24/7/365 days a year.

Here, I want to specifically mention a very interesting anecdote, which was narrated to me by Swayam Pani, IPS, IGP Kashmir, at the time when Pulwama occurred. He said that when he was a newly commissioned young SP in Kashmir, like all military cantonn ents, proper checking used to take place at the entry gates of Badami 3agh Cantonment too as a security drill, following which the entry passes were issued. Entry into the hospital was allowed only on showing the security pass and anyone coming without a pass was not allowed to enter the cantonment area. Swayam Pani told me that as young police officers, they always carried their security passes to the 92 Base Hospital in their pockets so that if they were hit by a bullet or a grenade, there would be no wastage of time in trying to get a new pass made at the gate. All the police officers used to carry this pass so that they could reach the 92 Base Hospital at the earliest, in the belief that 'Ek baar Badami Bagh hospital pahunch gaye to bach jayenge (If we reach the Badami Bagh hospital alive, we will survive)'. My salute to all the lifesavers at the 92 Base Hospital!

With Commandant, 92 Base Hospital and all the doctors in front of 92 Base Hospital Building, Srinagar, 2019

With Commandant, 92 Base Hospital and Military Nursing Service officers on 94th MNS Raising Day, Srinagar, 1 October 2019

18

The Abrogation of Articles 370 and 35A: Build-up

Balakot: A History of Animosity against India

Since the Pulwama incident was a major tragedy and setback for the nation, there was no way that India could take it lying down. Thus, the Government of India, in conjunction with all three defence forces—the Army, Navy and Air Force, along with the intelligence agencies—drafted a plan to hit back, selecting Balakot as the target, which is situated in actual Pakistan, and not in Pakistan-occupied Kashmir. It has a history of assault and antagonism against India. It was also the site of a major strike during the Sikh War. I quote an excerpt from a Haroon Khalid article published on 6 March 2019 in Pakistani daily *Dawn.com*:

> Barelvi's religio-political movement needs to be located in its time.
> In the 19th century, Muslim political power was on the wane as

Punjab had fallen to the Sikhs, while the British were slowly spreading through India. Seeing the demise of Muslim power as a result of their lack of religiosity, Barelvi wanted to reassert this political power, which is what brought him to the western boundary of Punjab. Here, in a predominantly Muslim region, he wanted to lead an uprising against local Sikh overlords and eventually make his way into Punjab. A few historians have pointed out that after the Sikhs in Punjab, he wanted to challenge the British. However, he had grossly misread the situation. The local tribal communities 'betrayed him' to the Sikh ruler. He eventually lost his life in the Battle of Balakot in 1831, hundreds of kilometres away from his home, and his movement was brutally crushed by the Sikhs. His philosophy and jihad, though, continued to inspire those who sought the purity of religion.

It is not merely a coincidence that on 26 February 2019, when Indian Air Force fighter aircrafts bombarded Balakot in surgical air strikes, the Indian Air Force Chief was Air Chief Marshal B.S. Dhanoa. Since it is located in Pakistan territory, India's air strikes on Balakot were thus a concrete means of conveying a very strong message that India would not hesitate to retaliate right inside Pakistan (and not restrict itself to just PoK), if Pakistan indulged in any mischief of launching a terrorist attack on India's soil.

On the night of 26–27 February 2019, Indian Air Force fighter jets entered PoK from Kashmir, flew over the air space of PoK and proceeded to hit targets inside Pakistan. They attacked a major terrorist camp and installation at Balakot and successfully completed their mission over the Pakistani air space, returning home without suffering any harm.

Pakistan, however, retaliated the next day in the Jammu sector. The famous incident of Group Captain Abhinandan Varthaman, an Indian Air Force fighter pilot who was held captive in Pakistan for sixty hours after his aircraft was shot down in an aerial dogfight, also occurred on the same day. Eventually, however, the Pakistani air strike in the Jammu sector was thwarted, with the Pakistan Air Force suffering disproportionate casualties. The famous statement—well-articulated in 'COAS Bajwa's legs were shaking' in *Hindustan Times* (on 29 October 2020), in the Pakistan Parliament by Ayaz Sadiq, Pakistan Muslim League-Nawaz leader: 'I remember Shah Mahmood Qureshi was in the meeting which Imran Khan had refused to attend and the Chief of the Army Staff General Bajwa came into the room, his legs were shaking and he was perspiring. Foreign Minister said for God's sake let Abhinandan go, India's about to attack Pakistan at 9 p.m.'—is now part of history and, of course, inked in the pages of Pakistani Parliamentary records. Group Captain Abhinandan Varthaman returned home unharmed as Pakistan had to release him in the face of tremendous diplomatic pressure and ignominy at its involvement in the Pulwama incident.

'You Pick up a Gun, You are Dead'

'You pick up a gun, you are dead unless you surrender'—this was not merely a statement made in the press conference of 19 May 2019 but was also followed through in actions on the ground. Many young Kashmiri boys who had joined terrorist outfits were given a chance to 'return' (I hate to use the word 'surrender'; I prefer the word 'return') to their mothers and families under 'Operation Maa' (details of which are discussed later in this book), which was very successfully executed by the security forces. More than fifty local youth who had joined the terrorists' tanzeems did 'return' and made a new beginning in life. Notwithstanding humanitarian initiatives like Operation Maa, after the main perpetrators of the Pulwama blast were eliminated within 100 hours of the attack, security forces continued to target the terrorist leadership in the Valley in a highly concerted and synergized manner. Consequently, during the first five months of 2019, up to 31 May 2019, security forces had gunned down 101 terrorists, including twenty-five foreign terrorists as against fifty-seven and seventy terrorists, respectively, who were eliminated during the corresponding periods in 2017 and 2018. Around the same time, that is on 23–24 May 2019, a highly significant incident occurred, which bolstered our preparedness and boosted our confidence in terms of maintaining peace and efficiently tackling any terrorist attack in the days to come. This had to do with the neutralization of the notorious terrorist Zakir Musa, who was in the league of Burhan Wani, and like the latter, was also associated with the dreaded terror outfit, the Ansar Ghazwat-ul-Hind. Our security team had been relentlessly tracking Musa (incidentally 'Musa' means 'mouse' in Gurkhali) for quite some time and finally managed to run him down following a fierce night-long encounter in Dadsara Village in Tral bowl hiding inside a wheat drum. This was really hot news and was widely covered by all the TV channels. His killing, in fact, aroused such intense media interest that press persons kept calling me repeatedly through 23–24 May to inquire about Musa's fate.

On our part, however, Musa's killing was not important, as anyone who has picked up a gun has to get killed one day at the hands of the security forces. More than Musa's killing; we were concerned about the maintenance of peace in the Valley in the aftermath of the killing. With the entire security team working in synchronization with each other, I was in constant touch with the DGP and IGP, Kashmir, and the civil administration throughout the night, as we coordinated all the aspects of maintaining law and order down to the absolute last detail, to avert any repercussion or disturbance, such as stone-pelting, arson, damage to public or private property or loss of innocent lives following Musa's death. Our apprehensions were not unjustified as memories of the violent reactions that had engulfed Kashmir following the death of Burhan Wani at the hands of security forces in 2016 were still fresh in our minds, and this time, we tied up all the loose ends noticed during the agitation of 2016.

The top brass among the Team Security Forces, including the Army, Police, CRPF, intelligence agencies and civil administration, was thus huddled in an intensive and cohesive planning exercise throughout that night to ensure a clinically synergized operation akin to the one we had launched to hunt down and neutralize the perpetrators of the Pulwama attack three months ago. Our efforts paid dividends as we were not only able to complete the operation of neutralizing Musa like clockwork but also, much to our belief and visualization, when Musa was finally killed on the morning of

234

24 May, a few people attended his funeral that afternoon, which remained absolutely peaceful, despite our decision to refrain from imposing any restrictions on people wishing to attend it. Indeed, the situation was in complete contrast to what was witnessed three years ago, and we silently patted our backs for this was no mean accomplishment.

After the funeral, I, along with the DGP, Mr Dilbagh Singh, undertook an aerial survey of the surrounding areas in a helicopter, covering the entire volatile and vulnerable belt, including Shopian, Anantnag, Pulwama, Bandipore and Kupwara, as also the heavily terrorist-infested region of Tral, the hometown of Musa and also the place where he was killed. As we flew over the exact location of Musa's house, funeral place and the site of the encounter leading to his killing, we could not help but be reassured at the absolute and much-desired peace that had prevailed in the entire region, signifying a stark deviation from the past when such incidents had led to incensed reactions from the general public. This time though, not a single speck of disturbance was visible to us; clearly indicating that the professional and minute planning that had gone into the 'detailing' had paid off. It also augured well for the future, as the entire episode of Musa's killing could be likened to a dress rehearsal for the much more serious test that we would inevitably face in the next two and half months. And we could say with absolute authenticity and credibility that the situation was fully under our control.

Speculation Runs Rife throughout Kashmir

The interim period between Musa's killing and the government's decision to abrogate Articles 370 and 35A around the months of June and July 2019 was marked by intense speculation about the National Democratic Alliance (NDA) Government's next move on Kashmir, especially because it had left no doubt about its intention to abrogate these articles in its election manifesto prior to the May 2019 elections. When the NDA Government assumed power at the Centre for the second time after the polls, the speculation magnified, with questions being raised as to whether both articles or either of them would be abrogated, and what would be the fate of the state of J & K, that is, would it continue to remain a single state or would it be bifurcated or trifurcated into two or three states, or would it be converted into a union territory—such chatter dominated social media and the press and was a hot topic of debate in public conversation across the country.

In the midst of all this debate and discussion, an infamous statement made in 2017 by a former chief minister of Jammu and Kashmir that **'If Article 35A is tinkered with, there would be no one in Kashmir to hold tricolour'** was being circulated again. Similarly, incendiary statements were also made by leaders of another major political party in Kashmir. Hence, a lot of heat and dust was replete in the political landscape of Kashmir, and the volatility was slowly but surely building up. To top it all, Home Minister Mr Amit Shah decided to make a crucial two-day visit to Kashmir around the end of June, ostensibly to take stock of the situation. The timing of his visit was, in fact, particularly strategic, as the Sri Amarnath Ji Yatra was scheduled to begin on July 1. The primary stated objectives of Mr Shah's visit were to review the security and other arrangements for the Sri Amarnath Ji Yatra, as well as to interact with some key Panchayat leaders, some political leaders and the grassroots functionaries of the Bharatiya Janata Party in Kashmir. However, there was a deep undercurrent to the visit, which conveyed the impression that a lot was simmering below the surface, waiting to explode at an opportune moment, and that moment was not far!

Article 370—'To Be or Not to Be' Was Never the Question

The high point of Mr Amit Shah's visit, already being touted as a precursor to a dramatic announcement, was the occurrence of two high-level meetings in Srinagar on 26 June 2019, which were attended by a veritable who's who of the state administration and security personnel, including the Honourable Governor of Jammu and Kashmir, security adviser to the Governor, the DGP, senior police officials, members of the intelligence agencies, the chief secretary and officers of the civil administration, CRPF and BSF, and, of course, the General Officer Commanding in Chief of the Army's Northern Command and the General Officer Commanding of 15 Corps, that is, me—in effect, the entire star cast of the state security team. Post his review of the security situation, the home minister expressed his subtle appreciation of the way the law and order and security were being handled in Kashmir, especially spotlighting the notable synergy between the police forces, intelligence agencies and the Army, to maintain law and order in the state.

With the political temperature rising and fuelling further speculation about what was to come, the above meeting was followed by another late evening meeting of very select high-level attendees lasting towards the middle of the night, aimed at a more detailed review of the security situation and the possible ramifications of the future government actions, if any. With his schedule chock-a-block with appointments, the next morning, the home minister was slated to meet the family of a police officer, who had made the supreme sacrifice in a terrorist encounter, followed by a few individual engagements before flying back to Delhi.

In this backdrop, I was taken by complete surprise when I received a call in the middle of the night at about 2 a.m., informing me of a breakfast meeting with the home minister at 7 a.m. This information had barely registered when I got another call an hour later, wherein I was asked my choice of food dishes for breakfast. Still in a stupor, I replied that there was no need to tailor the menu to my taste as I would have whatever the others would be served at the meeting. And then dropped the final bombshell—I was told that I would be the only one attending that breakfast meeting as it was intended to be a one-on-one duologue between the home minister and me.

As I arrived for the meeting punctually at 7 a.m. sharp, Mr Amit Shah was ready for the day's events and what followed was an hour of intense discussion. A lot of sensitive issues and key points were on the table for discussion apart from the delectable food that included aloo parathas and the famous Gujarati dish dhokla during our tête-à-tête. I will not divulge here the exact details discussed for obvious reasons but it will suffice to say that the issues flagged by Mr Shah included the current law and order situation, the potential for it to deteriorate immediately after any declaration by the government, repercussions of the latter on the Line of Control, and the pros and cons from the perspective of an anticipated Pakistani reaction to the path-breaking declaration that was now certain to follow. Ultimately, the home minister was seeking my inputs on the likely situation before and after the government action, as well as assurances that the Team Security Forces would be able to handle any situation that may arise in the state post the abrogation (which, it was by now clear to me, was in the offing).

I must point out, and with absolutely objectivity and great professional inputs, that the home minister was in absolute control and fully conversant with the meeting agenda and knew without a doubt the level and extent of the information he was seeking, including some very intrinsic and key issues related to the Army and its operations, directly or indirectly concerning the situation in the Valley, and implications of the heightened infiltration or any other reaction by Pakistan for the Army on the Line of Control post the abrogation. He had obviously done extensive research and homework before organizing this meeting with me and also had his ear to the ground, and was extremely intuitive about the finer details of every issue being discussed. Further, he also touched upon the flashpoints and the possible events that could occur and, more importantly, how we would handle these eventualities. The fact that my experiences during my previous tenures in Kashmir also came up for discussion during that meeting indicated the depth of our discussion in time and space. At one point, when I was asked my frank and personal view, my immediate response was '*Agar itihas likhna hai toh kisi ko itihas banana padega* (We can write history only if we make history.)' His parting words at the conclusion of the meeting, as if doing a final check of my resolve or confidence were, 'What is the guarantee that things will remain peaceful?' And my honest and confident reply was, 'I, on my part, give you my personal assurance that the peace will not be disturbed in any way.' My confidence was based on the recent experience of the Team Security Forces in handling the events prior to and post Zakir Musa's death, with the entire security outfit acting as a close-knit team to prevent any untoward incident in any part of Kashmir. I must say that the home minister's knowledge and in-depth assessment of the situation, including the likely fallouts, was exceptional as he had not only covered all bases but was ready with counter-plans for every possible eventuality and contingency. The rest, as they say, is history (*itihas*). History was in the making and here I am writing about it (*Itihas banaya ja raha tha aur main aaj uske bare mein likh raha hun*). My words were coming true. I am honour-bound to say no more.

After this meeting, when I reached home, my wife, who had also been awake the whole night due to the multiple telephone calls I was receiving, asked me, 'How was the meeting with the home minister?' My instant response to her query was, '*Bees yuvraj mil kar bhi iss bande ka muqabla nahin kar sakte* (Even twenty crown princes together will not be able to match up to this person).' And I was talking in terms of his decision-making prowess, analytical ability and absolute preparedness to handle any situation with guts and gumption.

Prepping up for Maintaining Peace Post the Abrogation

Thereafter, the home minister returned to Delhi, and we got down to making security arrangements for the Sri Amarnath Ji Yatra, which was scheduled to commence within the next four days, that is, on 1 July. The next important event, which took place on 8 July, was the anniversary of the death of the former Hizbul Mujahideen terrorist Burhan Wani, and maintaining peace on that day was an inexorable challenge for us, in view of the chaos and violence that had followed the actual death of Burhan Wani in 2016. Since the Sri Amarnath Ji Yatra was in progress, I received a message through staff channels a day before Wani's death anniversary, on 7 July, that all movements of the convoys of the security forces and the vehicular movement for the yatra would be suspended for a day on 8 July to prevent any possible terrorist-initiated incident on this day. When my staff conveyed this message to me, my candid and unambivalent response was that none of these activities, neither the Army convoy movement nor the movement of vehicles of the Sri Amarnath Ji Yatris, would be suspended for even a minute, leave alone a day, notwithstanding the anticipation of any untoward incident, as the security forces were fully prepared to take any terrorist action head-on.

My declaration must have raised a few hackles and must have been discussed with some trepidation by the local police, among others, as soon thereafter, I received a call from the senior police officers urging me to revisit my decision. Their suggestion was in absolute good faith and stemmed from the fact that all such activities were suspended every year on the anniversary of the elimination of Burhan Wani to prevent any public outrage or unrest and damage to public property like buses and vehicles, and risk to people's lives, especially the yatris, and that we should follow this precedent this year too. I was, however, adamant about my decision and determined to deviate from the norm this year. While the police and civil administration had their genuine concerns about the maintenance of law and order, my intent stemmed from the information I had based on my discussions with the home minister, narrated above. On my part, I was insisting on ensuring the normal conduct of all activities as this would be another dry run of preparing for the actual challenge of ensuring peace and normality as and when the abrogation took place, which was most likely in the not-too-distant future. Moreover, in case anything untoward (though highly unlikely) occurred on 8 July, it would enable us to tie up all the loose ends well in time and strengthen our security grid even more stringently on the ground before the abrogation actually happened.

Since almost everyone in the police and civil administration were not in the know of the things to come, they were a little unenthusiastic and sceptical about my plan, and decided to escalate the issue, referring it to Delhi and informing the latter that they were in favour of suspending the yatra but the Army was in favour of continuing with it. Being fully aware of the security grid and its effectiveness in meeting any challenge, the unambiguous response from Delhi was that the yatra should continue. Delhi and I were obviously on the same page.

Thus, the yatra continued on 8 July as usual, with the traditional fervour of Mahadev's blessings with more than a thousand-odd vehicles of yatris plying that day, and so did the movement of the security forces' convoys. I can say with some pride and satisfaction that not a single violent or unpleasant incident occurred on the day. This enhanced our confidence that the security forces' drills, coordination and synergy were working, and we could face any challenge, no matter how grim, to deal with any potential antagonistic situation. Thus, our plan was not merely to ensure peace on the day of the abrogation, but to prepare a longer-term strategy, including devising counter-terrorist mind games to be able to pre-empt any risk and maintain peace. We, the Team Security Forces, were, in effect, building on our assets and our resources in an absolutely synergized manner so that nothing would go wrong on the purported day. It is pertinent to mention here that only a select few in the security apparatus and administration knew of the things to come. I, on my part, can say that though we were gearing up to deal with any situation, no one under my command in the Chinar Corps was made aware of it and that's the reason even Pakistan was taken by total surprise, and so were some potential troublemakers within the country.

In the meantime, towards the end of July, a very authentic Intelligence input was received about an impending attack on the yatra by terrorists. Initially, since we were keen to refrain from creating any panic, we did subtle checks and searches, but the intelligence kept building up and a lot of 'chatter' continued to be intercepted by the intelligence agencies that a major terrorist attack or multiple strikes on the yatris were imminent. Subsequently, after our intensive search operations, on the morning of 2 August, the search parties found some portents of the potential attack along the route of the yatra, including a few prepared improvised explosive devices (IEDs), an M-24 American automatic rifle, and most importantly, a Pakistan Ordnance Factory-manufactured Claymore mine with the markings of a Pakistani ordnance factory, including the catalogue part number and manufacturing date. Such a Claymore mine is usually victim-activated by a booby-trapped trip wire, which would throw up hundreds of small steel balls and splinters in an arc of 60 degrees in the direction of the victim up to a distance of 100 metres or more depending upon the type of mine, causing intense damage and injury to people within this arc. We, therefore, immediately organized a press conference after recovering the IEDs, rifle and Claymore mine, wherein the DGP and I informed the media of our recoveries, with the weapon and actual mine having been airlifted from the place of recovery and displayed live before the mediapersons at the press conference.

Since we had the complete data as to the number of yatris at each specific point and the halting and staging areas along the route of the yatra, we had ensured that all security arrangements were in place to deal with any unusual or perilous incident, including a possible aerial rescue of the yatris using helicopters. As a precautionary measure, the government decided to call off the yatra just an hour after our press conference. Our next challenge, however, was to ensure the safe exit of all the yatris, including both domestic and foreign tourists. Fortunately, none of this was needed as the situation remained absolutely peaceful and under control in spite of certain unfounded remarks made by certain politicians.

Selfies with yatris, 1 July 2019

Sri Amarnath Ji Pratham Pooja at the holy cave with the
Honourable Governor, 1 July 2019

The Beauty of the Amarnath Yatra 2019

Here is an important characteristic related to the Amarnath Yatra of
2019, which primarily is an annual pilgrimage, undertaken by people
who profess the Hindu faith. Although people from other religions
and a lot of foreigners also traverse this yatra, mainly for the divine
experience, the yatra is predominantly associated with the Hindu
religion. As mentioned earlier, I myself have paid obeisance at the
holy cave on fifty-nine occasions.

Intriguingly and quite aptly for the canvas of India, in 2019,
the people in the top hierarchy who were connected with ensuring
security and maintenance of peace during the yatra that year,
in addition to many other officers at different levels, included
the following—Lieutenant General Ranbir Singh, Northern
Army Commander; Lieutenant General K.J.S. Dhillon, Corps
Commander (that is, me); Major General Johnson Mathews,
General Officer Commanding Victor Force; Brigadier S.A. Usman,
the brigade commander in charge of the security of the yatra;

Mr Dilbagh Singh, DGP, J & K Police; Mr Muneer Ahmad Khan, additional DGP law and order; Mr Zulfiquar Hasan, additional DGP CRPF; Mr Baseer Ahmad Khan, the divisional commissioner; and Mr Ravideep Singh Sahi, IGP, CRPF of Kashmir Zone. Four of them were Sikhs, four of them, Muslims, and one of them belonged to the Christian faith. This is a true indicator of the unity in diversity that characterizes India and aptly showcases India as a *guldasta* or a bouquet of flowers of different fragrances. This was also the team that ensured peace during the entire year of 2019.

Security arrangements being checked at Baltal; left to right: Brigadier S.A. Usman, Lt Gen. Ranbir Singh, Maj. Gen. Johnson Mathew, Lt Gen. K.J.S. Dhillon

Saluting Maneka

Another incident related to the Amarnath Yatra occurred on 1 July 2019, when I had gone to the holy cave for performing the *Pratham Puja* (First Prayer), accompanied by the then Honourable Governor of J & K, Mr Satyapal Malik. This Pratham Puja is performed as a ritual by the Governor and the corps commander in addition to others on the first day of the yatra every year. Since I had reached a little early and was checking the security arrangements and meeting personnel from various forces, I came across a dog, which stood on its hind legs in front of me. When I asked the handler what this dog was doing, he told me that Maneka (as the dog was named) was saluting me. Deeply impressed by Maneka's antics, and as per Army tradition, every salute must be returned with a crisp salute, I went down on my knees and saluted Maneka back. Meanwhile, my ADC, Captain Sandeep Singh clicked a picture of me saluting the dog, and soon thereafter this photograph went viral on social media. So much so that a US magazine contacted me, requesting permission to publish this photograph in the context of an article on wildlife or nature, and asking for the name that should be credited for taking the picture—I gave them the name of Sandeep Singh. This episode indicates how in the Army, we treat every life with deep respect. There are special rations authorized for dogs and ponies in the Army and they are also subjected to special training, have individual handlers and are housed in comfortable, heated rooms in winter.

Saluting Maneka at Sri Amarnath Ji cave, 1 July 2019

An Intricate Logistics Exercise

Meanwhile, apart from its political implications, the abrogation also necessitated detailed logistical planning at several levels. As a corps commander who had such a large force of troops deployed on the Line of Control, which would be laden with snow in December, I was absolutely responsible for organizing the storage of rations for these troops for winter, which starts when the snow melts and continues till the snowfall at higher reaches, which is around October or November, that is, the period which exactly coincided with the abrogation. Ironically, I was the senior-most Army officer in Kashmir when the abrogation was declared, and no one else in my corps had the slightest prior inkling of it, not even my General Officers Commanding or the staff at Corps Headquarters. As a contingency measure, I undertook an exercise to complete the stocking of rations for the forward areas much in advance to ensure its completion by 31 July, so that it would not be affected by any potential disruptions of vehicular movements subsequent to the abrogation, due to incidents of stone-pelting or mob violence. However, I conducted this entire exercise by mobilizing our vehicles and resources without arousing any suspicion among my staff or outsiders about the future plan. In fact, when the announcement of the abrogation was actually made after being ratified in both Houses of Parliament on 5 August, both my Brigadier, Army Service Corps and the Sub Area Commander, who are responsible for the stocking of rations, came to me and told me that the logistics exercise was a blessing in disguise, little knowing that it was actually a planned and deliberate operation to forestall any eventuality that would adversely affect the stocking of rations post the abrogation.

Maintaining the secrecy of the impending government decision, as and when it would be, was the main pre-condition without compromising on the preparations. Chinar House (official residence of the Chinar Corps Commander inside Badami Bagh Cantonment) was thus considered to be the most secure place where all those who 'knew it' used to assemble and discuss minor details, to the last bit, threadbare. Not even a shred of paper went out of the four walls of Chinar House and, as they say, the rest is history. Full of confidence that we could handle the situation peacefully due to all the experiences of the recent past and the preparations that went into it, we were at the cusp of being part of history and all set for the big day now.

19

Implementation of Abrogation: Peace Ensured

A Date That Would Be Part of History

On 5 August 2019, the Government of India abrogated Articles 370 and 35A of the Indian Constitution by an act of Parliament passed by a majority vote and duly assented by the Honourable President of India. Details of these have been covered in an earlier chapter and extensively commented upon by many in the media. I would, therefore, only restrict myself to the actions of the Team that are not known to the public at large but which made it succeed. The entire 'cast' of the Team Security Forces met in the evening, and thereafter we would meet every evening, at times even twice a day, to take stock of the developing situation. National Security Adviser Mr Ajit Doval also arrived in Srinagar on the evening of 5 August, and stayed there for about a fortnight, personally chairing all the daily meetings of our Team Security Forces. The senior and eminent officials who attended these meetings included the Chinar Corps Commander, Security Adviser to the Governor, Chief Secretary,

DGP, Additional DGP law and order, Inspector Generals of police, CRPF and BSF, heads of the intelligence agencies, Divisional Commissioner and the Principal Secretary, Home. The agenda at these meetings was both to assess the situation on the ground in the past twelve to twenty-four hours as also to plan and coordinate actions among all agencies for the future. We would also conduct a 'war-gaming' exercise and brainstorming to anticipate what could go wrong and how we would counter it. At these meetings, all the attendees also shared feedback from their individual sources about every aspect including that which may or may not have fallen within the domain of their department's activity or jurisdiction. For instance, whenever I received some inputs through Army channels, I would share micro-level information such as a particular medical shop not opening or an ATM running dry of cash, and this was immediately taken care of by the divisional commissioner on the very same day. Our regular meetings were highly effective and enabled instant implementation of any critical suggestion or feedback made by anyone based on their experience or information.

Non-negotiable Aims to Maintain Peace

We as Team Security Forces had laid down two aims for ourselves. One was that a 'nation's law' had been passed in both Houses of Parliament, signed by the President of India, and we had to do everything in our power to ensure its implementation. The second aim was to ensure that while implementing this writ of the government, there should be no loss of life or damage to property anywhere in Kashmir. And I can say that there was no loss of innocent life due to the security forces' actions and the three-month period post the abrogation was probably the most peaceful in the history of Kashmir over the last three decades in terms of the loss of human lives or damage to public or private property.

Compassion and 'Cricket' Win the Day

Here, I would like to recount an interesting anecdote pertaining to the day of the abrogation, that is, 5 August 2019. Readers may be aware of the fact that the former captain of the Indian cricket team and India's famous sports star Mahendra Singh Dhoni is a Territorial Army officer of the rank of lieutenant colonel. He had come to Kashmir for a normal training schedule with his battalion, which was deployed in Chinar Corps at that time. Taking a break from his training, he had met me in my office in the morning of 5 August 2019 and that same evening, he was slated to visit my residence for dinner, wherein I had also invited a few more officers and ladies with an avid interest in cricket, who were keen to meet Dhoni, the cricketer par excellence. We were all covertly busy with the preparations for dealing with the situation post the abrogation but had to carry out all these routine activities overtly, as it was necessary to show normality and not let the inimical elements gauge our intentions. In the Army we call this 'Surprise and Deception', and I daresay we achieved it to the hilt of military precision.

Meanwhile, the announcement of the abrogation of Articles 370 and 35A on 5 August 2019 by the Government of India had led to a mountain of work for me, and I was extremely busy figuring out our future plan of action, which could now get stymied if things were not controlled in time. Hence, despite being the host for the dinner party at my home that evening, I returned home as late as 11.30 p.m. because of my work-related preoccupations, whereas all the guests, including Dhoni himself, had reached much before me.

In the meantime, in order to deny the use of high-speed Internet to the terrorists and the Pakistani propaganda machinery, and to ensure the safety of the installations and people, all the mobile services were temporarily suspended in Kashmir. In the midst of all this confusion, my son called me on one of the Army lines informing me that the sister of one of his friends, Divya, who was a PhD student in a hostel in Kashmir University, needed to be evacuated from her hostel. Based on all the details about Divya shared by my son, I instructed one of my teams to visit the university, locate her, ferry her to the airport and arrange a ticket on a flight that would take her home, unharmed and safe. However, though my team managed to locate Divya, and even accompanied her to the airport, unfortunately, she was not able to get a ticket for the flight.

Thereafter, while I was busy in official meetings, my ADC, Captain Sandeep Singh, whom I had deputed to help evacuate Divya, gatecrashed my meeting, informing me that the girl had not succeeded in getting on to a flight and was extremely apprehensive and worried about her fate. I told Captain Sandeep to ask her what she wanted to do now that she could not catch a flight—she had the option of either coming to the Srinagar Army cantonment and spending the night there, or going back to her hostel till she could actually get an airline ticket for her journey back home. Incidentally, being a Kashmir University student, she was deeply influenced by exaggerated propaganda about the 'intransigent and unfriendly' behaviour of Army personnel in Kashmir. She, therefore, was reluctant to come to the Army cantonment but at the same time, absolutely unwilling to go back to the hostel. Finally, she hesitatingly agreed to come to the cantonment and Captain Sandeep arranged a room for her for the night next to the house of a commanding officer who was staying there with his family, including his mother and wife. But she was intensely disturbed and on edge, and broke down. This news of her relentless sobbing was also conveyed to me while I was in an important meeting where we were discussing the modalities of dealing with a crisis-like situation at hand, and here was an actual humanitarian crisis involving a young girl student caught in the imbroglio, who was extremely scared to stay in the hostel and equally scared to come to the cantonment.

As I put on my compassionate cap and tried to view the situation from this girl's perspective, an idea suddenly occurred to me, which would possibly help to tide over the situation. I urged Sandeep to request her to join us for dinner at my residence, where she may have been able to overcome her fear in the company of other ladies and, more importantly, get to meet Dhoni. So, she was escorted to my place for dinner and sure enough, this ingenious idea did the trick so well that by the time I reached home at around 11.30 p.m., Divya had not only been pacified but was quite upbeat, taking 'selfies' with Dhoni and thoroughly enjoying herself at the party. This incident clearly shows that the Army also has a humane face, and Army personnel can show tremendous gentleness and compassion when required just as effectively as they can show their tough side in a war-like situation. I, for instance, had all the reasons to say that I was too busy to deal with one individual who had been caught unawares in the city in the midst of a volatile environment, but I opted to adopt a humane approach and do my best to tackle the sensitive situation with empathy and solicitude, almost treating Divya like a daughter and trying to act the way a father would have done had his own child inadvertently found herself in a difficult situation. I can also vouch for the fact that numerous other security forces personnel and civil administration staff would have been helping people in Kashmir in a similar manner that night to deal with the emerging situation, helping them safely return to their homes. Divya continues to be in contact till date and I even received an invitation to attend her brother's marriage. What an honour.

An important aspect of being an effective senior leader is never to lose your composure and humour even in the face of the worst adversity or tense situations. Notwithstanding the various operational contingencies burdening my mind space, my conversation with my guests was as normal as any other day. A snapshot of Mahendra Singh Dhoni's remarks in the visitors' book at Chinar House is appended here.

Indian cricketer Mahendra Singh Dhoni's remarks in the
Chinar House visitors' book after the dinner on 5 August 2019,
the day Article 370 was abrogated

With Mahendra Singh Dhoni, the Indian cricketer, at Chinar House
on 5 August 2019, with Divya in the background

Precluding False Propaganda

As an aside, I must mention here that the authorities had to shut
down the Internet to preclude any mischief or sharing of misleading
or contrived information on the social media—for instance, there
was a possibility that some mischievous elements could pass
around a video depicting violence in, say, Palestine or Syria or
some other country, as that occurring in Kashmir and provoke and
agitate youngsters by spreading misinformation. The high-speed
Internet was thus curtailed to prevent downloading and sharing
of propaganda videos, and spreading of fake news. However,
landlines were restored after a few days. Even 2G internet was
restored, thereby facilitating all important and routine activities like
uploading of application forms and depositing fees for admission

by students, Internet banking and booking of airline tickets and hotel reservations, among others. Kiosks were also set up in the district and *tehsil* offices, police stations and the airport, among other important access points to enable people to conveniently carry out their online transactions.

The negative and false propaganda that everything had been shut down and that normal life in Kashmir had been completely crippled was being spread by Pakistan.

I can say with absolute conviction and honesty that all necessary facilities like hospitals, dispensaries, medical stores, grocery stores, ATMs and government offices were fully functional. The canard about an indefinite 'lockdown' was also absolutely incorrect, as no 'lockdown' had been imposed anywhere in Kashmir. Out of all the police stations jurisdictions through the length and breadth of the then state of Jammu and Kashmir, CrPC 144, restricting the assembly and movement of more than four people at one location, was imposed in the initial days only in limited areas, which housed certain sensitive installations. Even in these areas, people were free to move around in smaller numbers and perform their day-to-day outdoor chores. All food provisions, groceries and daily necessities were freely available and people had the liberty to shop for them as and when required. The word 'lockdown', as legally tenable, was a misnomer and was not a reality in post-abrogation Kashmir. In fact, Pakistani proxies and terrorists tried to impose a 'lockdown' by killing the local Kashmiri shop owners who opened their shops to earn their livelihood and also by killing truck drivers and labourers, and burning down apple orchards and trucks that were transporting the apple produce from Kashmir.

My Encounters for Peace: Humanitarian and Philanthropic Initiatives

During this period, all the security forces and civil administration undertook several humanitarian and social initiatives at their respective levels, in addition to the existing government schemes, to help connect with the people in Kashmir, especially in the far-flung areas, to resolve their problems and make life easier for them. Some of the initiatives that were undertaken by the Army are delineated in detail below.

Operation Maa

The guiding principle of this initiative was to involve mothers in the campaign to prevent young men from succumbing to the temptation of joining the terrorists' ranks, especially those who were unemployed or discontented, and therefore easy targets for being lured into the terrorists' fold. Taking a cue from the Holy Koran, which says, 'Do good and serve your Mother, then your Mother and then your Mother, and then your father', I made a direct appeal to mothers to prevent their children from being misguided by inimical forces. This was reported in the media as well. On 19 November 2019, the *Economic Times* brought out a story: 'Operation "Maa" by Army in J & K yields results; around fifty local militants return to families'. My message to the mothers was simple: 'Today's stone-pelter is tomorrow's terrorist, so save your children from being killed.' This struck a chord with the mothers in particular, and the *awaam* (common public), in general.

Our analysis of the situation over the last one and a half years highlighted the short shelf life of a local terrorist—7 per cent of the local youngsters who picked up a weapon were getting killed in the first ten days of their joining the terrorists' tanzeems, and 9 per cent inclusive of this 7 per cent were getting killed in the first thirty days, 17 per cent in the first three months, 36 per cent in the first six months, and about 64 per cent were getting killed in the first one year. This implied that if three boys had joined the terrorists' organizations, two of them or two-thirds of them were likely to get eliminated in the first one year alone. Further, 83 per cent of the boys who had joined terrorists' organizations had a history of having indulged in stone-pelting. This message was conveyed with facts and figures to the mothers, and also widely disseminated publicly. It gradually started appealing to mothers, who realized that if they were sending their sons for stone-pelting to earn a paltry Rs 500, the boys were literally being moulded into becoming future terrorists, who could get killed either within the first seven days or at the latest, within a year. Thus, in a way, we were subtly affixing the responsibility of curtailing the recruitment of young boys as terrorists on themselves, by clearly informing them of the perils of allowing their children to indulge in incidents of stone-pelting, which would eventually lead them up the garden path to certain death.

I realized from my experience that Kashmiri boys listen to their mothers much more than to their fathers. Hence, the genesis of 'Operation Maa' lay in my understanding of this societal and family dynamic in Kashmir. During my previous tenures as a captain, major or commanding officer and brigade commander in Kashmir, on the elimination of a local terrorist, we invariably found a letter in his pocket, which had been written either by him to his mother or by his mother to him. It was thus very clear to me that the boys in Kashmir have an extremely strong bond with their mothers, which was what we were trying to exploit to achieve our goal of preventing the entry of young, impressionable boys in their formative years, into the league of terrorism. Operation Maa, which was initiated in this backdrop, resulted in the 'return' of at least fifty boys who had joined terrorists' organizations—I consciously use the word 'return' instead of 'surrender' because I realized that these boys had been led astray. The families of these boys were given absolute assurance that their identities would be kept confidential, as also that no legal case would be filed against them, and they would be relocated to some other place in India for work if they so wanted.

The government had devised a very admirable package as part of its 'surrender' policy. But more than that, the security forces and the civil administration would have helped them in whatever way possible. If found suitable in terms of qualifications and a physical test, they could have been recruited in the Territorial Army—the government has certain units of the TA called 'Territorial Army Home and Hearth', in which the boys are recruited from local areas. This and recruitment to the post of special police officer in the Jammu and Kashmir Police were other options for these young men, who could be described as 'fence-sitters'. Operation Maa can actually be equated to a holistic approach for motivating these young boys away from the fence that would misguide them towards terrorism back into the mainstream of a respectable future life. Thus, the multiple options and reasons offered to the youngsters to stay away from terrorism enabled the huge success of Operation Maa.

As I mentioned earlier, more than fifty boys returned to the fold of their families. Interestingly, at times, many of the encounters were stopped halfway through, and the parents and friends of these boys living in their villages were called to come and convince them to absolve violence. In such cases, the anti-terrorist operation would be suspended for about two or three hours, and when the family members or friends of these recently recruited terrorists came to the site where the operation was in progress, they would be given loudspeakers and encouraged to interact with the boys face-to-face or through a telephone call. There have also been instances when the mobile recharge of the terrorists had run out, and we stepped in to get their mobile phones recharged so that they could speak to their mothers or any other family member or neighbour or friend. At times, the boys have also 'returned' during an actual encounter. That was the sum total of the peace that we ensured during the immediate period before and after the abrogation on 5 August 2019. It, therefore, did not happen all of a sudden, and a lot of effort and preparation had gone into it to ensure its effective implementation.

The Anguish of Being a Terrorist's Mother

A lot is usually said about the loss of civilian lives and about the people killed by terrorists, but it is also pertinent to understand the agony caused to the mother when her son ends up becoming a terrorist. This is because there is very little reporting of the agony and loss suffered by the family of a slain terrorist, with the mother usually bearing the brunt of this anguish. We always condone the statement that terrorists causing damage to life and property should be eliminated, but do we ever stop to think of the mother who has been shattered by the untimely and brutal death of her son, who had been led astray by a cruel system of radicalization propagated and planted in Kashmir by Pakistan, which ends up converting an innocent boy into a feared terrorist, a system that has been thriving on false narrative? If he had not been lured into terrorism, this boy would have been able to acquire a decent education in a professional or academic institution, he would have been able to engage in some service or private business, and would have been staying with his family, close to his mother. Instead, he lost his life in the prime of youth and the mother lost her child because of the scourge of terrorism in Kashmir. This pain of being a terrorist's mother is rarely documented and barely understood. As one who conceived Operation Maa, with the mother at the centre of this initiative, I have deep compassion and concern for the Maa of a terrorist or a potential terrorist, which is why I conceptualized this campaign to help alleviate or forestall her suffering.

A statement by me was quoted in the same article in the *Economic Times* referred to above, 'There are some vultures across the border who want to target these young boys. We have successfully managed to keep their identity under wraps as I know some would be attending college, some helping their father in fields or some earning daily bread for their families. I wish them good luck.'

Khairiyat Patrol

As the name suggests ('Khairiyat' translating as well-being or welfare), the Khairiyat Patrol comprised a group of security personnel who visited the far-flung areas for their routine area domination or reconnaissance, in order to help resolve any problems faced by people not having access to normal services due to inclement weather and hostile terrain. A typical Khairiyat Patrol is led by an officer or JCO and in addition to combat soldiers, invariably has a doctor or a nursing assistant, and is equipped with medicines. These patrols also used to carry white-listed mobile phones for people to make free calls within and outside India when mobile services were temporarily suspended immediately after the abrogation. In addition, at times, the Khairiyat Patrols also carried generators in their vehicles to enable people to charge their mobile phones and other devices in areas with poor access to electricity, power and communication facilities.

As part of the Khairiyat Patrol initiative, we also organized regular liaison conferences at the level of the company commanders, which helped in amicably resolving some long-standing small 'irritants'.

Humsaya Hain Hum

I coined the phrase 'Humsaya Hain Hum' (we are neighbours) to reiterate that we were co-inhabitants in a common land, and had to live peacefully and congenially with each other. This initiative is really close to my heart as I have never lived in my village as much as I have lived in Kashmir. The people of Kashmir are thus my true co-passengers in the journey of life, and I realized that everything needed to be done to make this journey meaningful and positive, especially for people who had suffered prolonged violence and misery, often for no fault of theirs.

Every Army post on the Line of Control and in the hinterland thus acted as the nodes of the Humsaya concept. Humsaya, symbolizing the values of humanitarianism and peaceful co-existence, would thus come to people's help anywhere and everywhere, especially those living in the harshest climatic and topographical regions and in a state of deprivation. We encouraged people to approach the Army posts for assistance at any time of the day or night, where we would provide every type of help, including the use of military aircraft to evacuate or transport people in an emergency, such as for carrying patients to hospital or a medical facility. In an emergency, the use of an army helicopter to pick up civilian patients from remote areas in Kashmir and bring them for medical attention to the nearest hospital was part of the concept of 'Humsaya Hain Hum'. Additional doctors and medical supplies were organized to aid the public in far-flung areas, symbolizing the true spirit of the Army as a peacetime ally and a wartime protector.

Humsaya Hain Hum

I remember an incident that happened on 14 January 2020, a day before Army Day, that is, 15 January, wherein one routine Khairiyat patrol in the remote areas of Baramulla was informed about a pregnant lady, Mrs Shamima, who had started having labour pains and required urgent hospitalization. As all the roads were blocked due to heavy snow, the patrol leader immediately contacted the base and requested a helicopter evacuation for the lady. However, though the helicopter took off for the destination, it could not land there because of inclement weather and poor visibility, and they had to call for an ambulance instead. But this effort, too, seemed in vain. The post commander, therefore, immediately summoned about 100-odd soldiers along with thirty villagers, who beat the snow along the route manually to enable the ambulance to move on the snow-laden road up to the halfway point, with the jawans physically pushing the ambulance. In the meantime, the expectant mother was literally carried on a charpoy perched on the shoulders of jawans for four hours to the halfway point from where she was shifted into the ambulance and taken to a hospital in Baramulla, where she delivered a healthy child. This incident attracted lots of media attention and the Honourable Prime Minister retweeted the quote the next day, which was Army Day, that is, 15 January 2020.

 **Narendra Modi** ✔
@narendramodi

Our Army is known for its valour and professionalism. It is also respected for its humanitarian spirit. Whenever people have needed help, our Army has risen to the occasion and done everything possible!

Proud of our Army.

I pray for the good health of Shamima and her child.

🦌 **Chinar Corps** 🌲 **- Indian Army** ✔ · 14/01/20
#HumsaayaHainHum 🪖🌲
During heavy snowfall, an expecting mother Mrs Shamima, required emergency hospitalisation. For 4 hours over 100 Army persons & 30 civilians walked with her on stretcher through heavy snow. Baby born in hospital, both mother & child doing fine. #VRWithU4U

Tweet your reply

The concept '*Humsaya Hain Hum*' was particularly effective in the mountainous areas in the upper reaches of Kashmir, which have very sparse footfalls, and are largely occupied by the marginalized classes, including the scheduled castes, Bakharwals, Pahadis and Gujjars, who stay on the foothills and close to the Line of Control (LoC), and remote and far-flung areas in the Valley. Since most of the Army units on the LoC as well as in the counter-terrorist grid are deployed in these areas where the terrain is very difficult and life is extremely tough, it has been offering all support to the locals (*Humsaya*) people, including conducting free tuition classes for the children of Bakharwals (nomads who come to the higher reaches with their families during summers to graze their livestock). In fact, in most of these areas, Army posts are the only approachable means of succour and support for these population groups. This is where the concept of '*Humsaya Hain Hum*' comes in, as we live together with people residing in those areas.

Taleem se Taraqqi

This concept implied that only imbibing proper education (*taleem*) can help one progress (*taraqqi*) in life, and ensure success and prosperity for the family. This initiative was intended to offer the larger community opportunities to flourish by imbibing education, as those who are deprived of education are bound to become easy targets for the jihadis and terrorists seeking to recruit youngsters in their ranks, eventually losing their lives in encounters with the security forces.

All these initiatives continued unabated during the entire post-abrogation period, hand in hand with other humanitarian and professional campaigns taken by various social groups. While some of these initiatives were routine, several others were add-ons during the abrogation period to make life easier and more productive for the local people. These initiatives had multiple objectives and outcomes—they helped in maintaining peace, while also fostering confidence in the locals that their lives were important and the Army would go a long way towards enriching and protecting these lives.

Army Goodwill Schools

As part of 'Project *Sadbhawana*' meaning 'goodwill', the Army runs twenty-eight Army Goodwill Schools all over the Kashmir Valley with up to 10,000 students at any one time. In these schools, the faculty of more than 500 and support staff of approximately 200 are all local Kashmiris and so are the students. These schools have never shut down, even during the *hartal* calls given by the separatists in the years gone by, and the students were provided uninterrupted quality education. As a result, the students of Army Goodwill Schools are always working towards a brighter future and never got attracted towards terrorism. As per the available information, no student of Army Goodwill Schools has joined the rank and file of terrorism in the recent past.

'Super 30' and 'Super 50'

At some stage, the Army realized that only imparting good education at the school level was probably not adequate and the students had to be guided and motivated for the next step of getting admission into eminent professional colleges. This initiative, entailing the selection of students to prepare them for competitive examinations, was implemented throughout J & K by the Army, who would create groups of thirty or fifty children who had just completed high school for partaking of higher education. These children were provided with free boarding and lodging, free coaching and stationery, and every kind of assistance towards preparing them and even applying for competitive examinations for entry into medical and engineering colleges.

These initiatives also continued uninterrupted during the post-abrogation period. We offered the students who were part of the 'Super 30' or 'Super 50' groups the option of returning home after the abrogation in case they apprehended some unrest, but not a single student from these groups left for home, and all of them continued their routine studies and coaching throughout this period. Even the local instructors or coaches continued to visit the coaching centres regularly, and the results of that year's batch were highly encouraging—almost 90 per cent of the students got placements in very eminent professional colleges.

I would like to specifically make a mention of the teachers of the Army Goodwill Schools and Super 30 and 50 who take into their hands young and formative children, work on them creatively, craft and curate intelligent thinking minds that would productively and efficiently contribute to society. '*Mitti toh mitti hai, lekin kumhaar usko jab hath lagata hai toh woh hi mitti bartan, khilona ya bhagwan ki murti ban jaati hai. Warna woh mitti kisi raste mein dhul ki tarah padi rehti* (Mud is mud, it only gets transformed when the potter diligently works with it, ending up creating beautiful yet utilitarian

Interacting with Super 30 medical students at Srinagar, 2019

pots, toys and even sculptures of gods. Otherwise, the same mud would remain merely dirt on some track).'

Dividends of Peace

The various initiatives and strategies adopted to curtail terrorism in Kashmir, especially in the backdrop of the abrogation of Articles 370 and 35A, had a common thread—deploying a spirit of compassion and cooperation while dealing with the local Kashmiris, and selfless service and diligence to duty, on the part of the Team Security Forces. We were determined to convey the message that the security forces are partners in the development process of the country and the union territory, and the Team Security Forces therefore had to walk the talk.

Throughout this challenging period, the most significant aspect that characterized the functioning of the security forces was the complete absence of 'credit-taking'. No agency took any credit for the maintenance of peace or for ensuring the implementation of law and order—what we attained or could not achieve was a collective success or a collective failure. As mentioned earlier, it is also heartening to note that not a single innocent civilian casualty happened after 5 August due to the actions of the security forces. All the casualties that took place were the result of terrorists killing civilians. Although terrorism had declined substantially during this period, civilians were being threatened by terrorists and told not to open up their shops, not to move around—they were trying to impose a local curfew, to give an impression of unrest and discontent in Kashmir. The common local Kashmiris do not support any violence and disturbance and are keen to have a lasting peace.

The perfect synergy among the Team Security Forces proved effective not only in maintaining peace during the pre- and post-abrogation period but also in eliminating the top terrorist leaders and their cadres by putting terrorist groups under tremendous pressure, ultimately causing fragmentation and disarray in their ranks. There were also reported instances wherein terrorists refused to lead a particular tanzeem, for fear of being eliminated, even after being directed by their masters from across the Line of Control. Thus, an appropriate mix of human resources and technology coalesced to effectively prevent infiltration along the Line of Control, and to create fissures within the rank and file of terrorists' organizations in Kashmir. Here, I would like to mention the primary finding of an analysis we conducted to determine how and why the period following the abrogation was peaceful. The perpetration of emotive and volatile incidents like Pulwama and the abrogation should technically have led to an increase in the recruitment of young boys by terrorists to join their ranks. On the contrary, however, in 2019, the recruitment by terrorists actually reduced as compared to the preceding and following years. As per an article by Snehesh Alex Philip in *The Print* dated 28 February 2022, quoting the official data, the number of young men from across Kashmir who had joined the ranks of terrorists year-wise was 210 in 2018, 117 in 2019, 178 in 2020, and 142 in 2021.

'Lockdown'—As the World Saw It

Another indicator of peace that prevailed was when a delegation of twenty-seven Members of the European Parliament (MEPs) arrived in Kashmir on a two-day visit from 29 October 2019, two days before the union territory of Jammu and Kashmir came into existence on 31 October 2019, to assess the ground reality first-hand post the abrogation of Articles 370 and 35A, in the backdrop of the very vicious Pakistani narrative and propaganda of 'lockdown'. Then, on 9–10 January 2020, another fifteen-member delegation of foreign diplomats (ambassadors and high commissioners), including representatives from the US (Kenneth Juster, then ambassador to India was part of the delegation), Bangladesh, Vietnam, Norway, Maldives, South Korea, Morocco, Niger, Nigeria, Argentina, the Philippines, Fiji, Uzbekistan, Peru and Togo, visited Kashmir. Subsequently, on 12–13 February 2020, the third twenty-five-member delegation of foreign diplomats, including envoys from Germany, Canada, France, New Zealand, Mexico, Italy, Afghanistan, Austria, Uzbekistan, Poland and some envoys of the European Union (EU), visited Kashmir. All the delegates drove through the city of Srinagar, met the mediapersons, politicians and civil society representatives from various fields, and were briefed about the prevailing situation by the Army and civil officials. This was widely covered in the media.

With Kenneth Juster, US ambassador to India, February 2020

With the foreign delegation; US Ambassador to India Kenneth Juster in front row

Walter Linder, Germany's ambassador to India who was part of the third delegation, while speaking to the *Hindustan Times* after his visit said: 'On the way from the airport to the hotel, we got our first little glimpse of what's out there. The shops were open, things seemed normal. **We didn't see a "lockdown".**' On being asked 'What were your critical questions?', his response was, 'How they feel about the current situation, about Article 370 being abrogated, what they think of the previous governments in J & K, what their main worries are, and so on. And we questioned the authorities too; for instance, the army corps commander, Lt Gen. K.J.S. Dhillon, who is an impressive person, told us about incursions and terrorist attacks along the Line of Control (LoC).' One can refer to his interview which appeared in the *Hindustan Times* on 15 February 2020 ('Each of us had an opportunity to ask our most critical questions': German envoy on J-K visit').

Walter Linder, Germany's ambassador to India's report in the
Hindustan Times

I would like to say that the maintenance of peace post the abrogation saved innocent lives and that is the most important thing for me as a human and an officer; and the government. I attribute this to the successful implementation of various humanitarian initiatives mentioned earlier in this chapter, with special reference to Operation Maa, which had a major positive impact in curbing terrorism along with the required security and preventive measures we adopted to preclude violence and terror in Jammu and Kashmir in the wake of a significantly unprecedented development such as the abrogation of Articles 370 and 35A.

Some people compliment me even today that the situation post-abrogation was handled very well but it is important to highlight that the situation did not pass off peacefully on its own; there was lots of foresight, planning, preparation, coordination and hard work that went into it to make it a huge success. All the incidents that I have narrated above and in the previous chapters were thus actually building up to the abrogation and how we successfully handled its aftermath peacefully. I would fail in my duties if I do not make a mention of the brave Army soldiers, JKP and CRPF constables and civil administration staff who worked day in and day out through rains and snow to ensure that peace prevailed on the streets of Kashmir and the countryside. And believe me, I have not even recounted a fraction of the preparatory activities that were undertaken by every stakeholder at all levels to ensure peace and security. **And 'WE' did it.**

20

'When You Go Home, Tell Them of Us. And Say, for Your Tomorrow, We Gave Our Today'

Chinar Corps . . . Chinar Leaf and Battle Axe Formation

15 Corps, or Chinar Corps as it is popularly known, is one of the fourteen corps of the Indian Army responsible for operations along the Line of Control and Valley floor in Kashmir. The Chinar Corps has carved a niche for itself in the annals of history, and readers would be curious to know more about its history and the valour of brave men and women who had the rare honour of serving with the Chinar Corps in combat in various battles, wars and counter-terrorism operations.

The Chinar Corps, as it is known today, was initially formed as HQ 15 Corps at Port Said in Egypt on 12 January 1916 during World War I. It moved to France on 22 April 1916, where it participated in the famous battles of Somme and Ypres. The corps was demobilized after World War I. During World War II, it was raised again at Calcutta (now Kolkata) on 20 March 1942. The corps became operational in the Arakan and earned its spurs in the Burma campaign as part of the 14th Army. It was disbanded at the end of the war on 10 February 1947.

Meanwhile, in Jammu and Kashmir, the state forces and the 161 Infantry Brigade were amalgamated to form the J & K Force after the signing of the instrument of accession, in October 1947. The HQ 21 Communication Zone Sub Area was raised at Badami Bagh Cantonment. Subsequently, the Srinagar Division and the Jammu Division were raised in J & K; 21 Communication Zone Sub Area was upgraded and renamed '21 Communication Zone' in June 1952. It incorporated the Chinar leaf from the erstwhile Srinagar Division and the battle axe from the Jammu Division and created a formation sign, which was a combination of the two—a battle axe superimposed on a Chinar leaf. On 4 January 1955, the HQ 15 Corps was raised again at Udhampur and it adopted the formation sign of 21 Communication Zone, which was disbanded. When the HQ Northern Command was raised at Udhampur, HQ 15 Corps moved to Srinagar on 1 May 1972.

15 Corps has participated in all the operations since then. HQ Jammu and Kashmir Force and later the Jammu and Kashmir Corps valiantly fought against the Pakistan Army-led *Kabayali* infiltrators in 1947, including the battles of Badgam and Shalateng fought to open the Srinagar–Baramulla axis, and successfully recaptured the border towns of Uri and Tangdhar.

In 1962, the Himalayan Division was raised and assigned to the Order of Battle (ORBAT) of 15 Corps to defend the Ladakh region. The formation's steadfast defence during the historic battles of Rezang La and Sirijap stalled the Chinese in Ladakh and inflicted severe casualties. Major Shaitan Singh of the 13 Kumaon Regiment was awarded the Param Vir Chakra (posthumously) in this battle.

In the 1965 operations, the 15 Corps launched courageous operations to the north and south of the Pir Panjal range, culminating in the capture of the strategic Hajipir Pass in the Uri sector and the Tithwal Bridge in the Tangdhar sector.

In 1971, operations in the Shyok Valley, Partapur, Kargil, Lipa Valley and Tangdhar sectors resulted in the capture of some strategic areas. In April 1984, defying inhospitable terrain and inclement weather, 15 Corps occupied what is today's highest battlefield on earth, that is, the vital passes on Siachen Glacier, offering a strategic advantage to India vis-à-vis Pakistan.

Since 1989–90, as a result of the diabolical proxy war initiated by Pakistan in Kashmir, 15 Corps has again risen to the challenge by conducting sub-conventional operations for countering the growing secessionist movement. The Rashtriya Rifles (RR) Counter Insurgency Forces, Victor and Kilo (popularly known as Victor Force and Kilo Force) were raised under 15 Corps for carrying out counter-terrorism operations. The Chinar Corps, in synergy with other security forces, has ensured peace and stability in the Kashmir Valley through sustained counter-infiltration and counter-terrorism operations.

In May 1999, the Indian Army launched 'Operation Vijay' to neutralize enemy intrusions in Kargil, following the ill-conceived military misadventure by the regular soldiers of Pakistan. During this battle, the troops of 15 Corps fought gallantly in the Drass, Mushkoh, Kargil and Batalik sectors. After the Kargil War, 15 Corps was split into two on 1 September 1999, that is, 14 Corps with its headquarters at Leh and 15 Corps, with its headquarters at the Badami Bagh Cantonment in Srinagar as hithertofore.

The history of 15 Corps is inextricably interwoven with the post-Independence history of Jammu and Kashmir. Besides guarding the frontiers during several conflicts and ongoing eyeball-to-eyeball confrontations along the Line of Control, 15 Corps has contributed immensely in terms of maintaining stability and peace, and promoting prosperity in the state/union territory, though at a very heavy cost. A total of 3218 Indian Army officers, JCOs and jawans serving in the Chinar Corps have made the supreme sacrifice since 1989 (these figures do not include the sacrifices made in the Jammu region south of the Pir Panjal range in the neighbouring corps) till the middle of year 2022.

With prayers on my lips, gratitude and pride in my heart, I salute the supreme sacrifice of all these bravehearts. The sacrifices made in the line of duty by Chinar Corps personnel have been acknowledged and the numbers of these bravehearts who have been bestowed with gallantry awards till Republic Day 2022 are delineated in the following table:

PRE-INDEPENDENCE	
Victoria Cross	4
Distinguished Service Order	1
Military Cross	4
Total	**9**
POST-INDEPENDENCE	
Param Vir Chakra	13
Ashok Chakra	25
Param Vishisht Seva Medal	9
Maha Vir Chakra	103
Kirti Chakra	90
Uttam Yudh Seva Medal	30
Ati Vishisht Seva Medal	65
Vir Chakra	503
Shaurya Chakra	502
Yudh Seva Medal	118
Sena Medal	3476
Vishisht Seva Medal	223
Mentioned in Dispatches	601
Total	**5758**

Many of these sacrifices were made during my tenure as the Chinar Corps Commander and the awards were also bestowed during this period. I am not mentioning all the individual names of my Army colleagues, including the absolutely professional General Officers Commanding, highly committed Infantry Brigade and Rashtriya Rifles sector commanders, and the cutting-edge commanding officers, with their excellent teams of young officers and brave soldiers, staff officers at the Chinar Corps headquarters, Sub-Area and other headquarters, as also their contribution during my tenure as Chinar Corps Commander, especially after the Pulwama blast and the abrogation of Articles 370 and 35A, but their invaluable contributions are well acknowledged and highly appreciated.

Jammu and Kashmir Police—a Force That Evolved to Be the Best

The Jammu and Kashmir Police, having always fought shoulder to shoulder with the Indian Army in the service of the nation, have, over the years, evolved from a normal 'Thana Police' into one of the most professional counter-terrorism police forces in the world.

The naysayers and critics apprehended some sort of dissent among the rank and file of the J & K Police post 5 August 2019, yet the leadership of the force, especially the officers at the helm at that juncture, never had any such apprehensions. I vividly remember their complete faith and trust in the constabulary, including the special police officers (SPOs), temporary 'hire and fire' cops, expecting them not to create any trouble, and their confidence in their men proved to be absolutely justified. The entire force stood together to ensure the best interest for the side of the nation, and consequently, we saw the most peaceful transition for J & K as it was integrated into the national mainstream. In fact, the synergy and togetherness exhibited by all the forces, especially with the Indian Army during those historic times, was at an all-time high.

With hundreds of cops and officers of the police and CRPF making the supreme sacrifice and many more injured in counter-terrorism operations and battling rioters in the streets over the years, the resolve of each and every member of these forces to safeguard and support the cause of the country is worth appreciating. The Jammu and Kashmir Police have been fighting Pakistan-sponsored terrorists over three decades, and have made the supreme sacrifice of 1600 of its personnel (1086 regular and

514 SPOs) in the entire erstwhile state of Jammu and Kashmir till the middle of the year 2022. I salute their supreme sacrifices in the line of duty, which have also been recognized with the JKP personnel having been awarded 1518 Gallantry Medals (the President's Police Medal for Gallantry/Police Medal for Gallantry), 1666 Sher-e-Kashmir Medals for Gallantry (renamed as the Jammu and Kashmir Medal for Gallantry), one Ashok Chakra (posthumously), two Kirti Chakras (posthumously) and eighteen Shaurya Chakras (of which fourteen were awarded posthumously) till Republic Day 2022. In addition, the JKP personnel have been awarded 672 President's Police Medals for Meritorious Service (from 1990–2022), seventy-nine Distinguished Service Medals (from 1990–2022), 164 Jammu and Kashmir Police Medals for Meritorious Service (from 2003–22) and 592 Parakram Medals (from 2001–22).

The RR units of the Indian Army and special operation group (SOG) of the J & K Police, jointly operating in the hinterland along with the CRPF, have achieved tremendous success in counter-terrorism operations. The coordination and synergy among the police and Army have benefited both the forces, with the police picking up the operational nitty-gritties and learning from the strengths of the Army, and the Army, on its part, also benefiting greatly by absorbing the intimate local and institutional knowledge of the police. The synergized operations among various forces, with no exhibition of 'one-upmanship', have been the single biggest winning factor in our success against Pakistan's proxy war.

I must ascribe due credit to the J & K Police leadership over the decades that has encouraged and motivated the local police in capacity-building, including imparting training in counter-terrorism skills and equipping them with the latest state-of-the-art weapons and equipment.

The success of the security forces resulted in the dismantling of the organized structures of the proscribed terrorist tanzeems like the Hizbul Mujahideen, Lashkar-e-Taiba, Jaish-e-Mohammed and Ansar Ghazwat-ul-Hind (AGUH), so much so that no one is now willing to take over the leadership of these tanzeems. The remnants like lone wolves and small terrorist gangs, devoid of any coherent structure, are being dealt with effectively and shall eventually cease to exist, thereby ushering in complete normality. The challenge which, however, remains is to deal with the ideological and logistical framework that has been sustaining and nurturing terrorism rather than the minions carrying small arms and creating some minor ruffles. Yet Pakistan's designs to proliferate small weapons into every nook and corner of the Kashmir Valley, and the Chenab and Pir Panjal regions of Jammu, may emerge as a serious challenge in future. Our aim of achieving total normality, wherein all sections and sects of society can live in peace and harmony, faces impediments as often a lumpen drug addict is provided with a pistol and asked to target some unarmed innocent civilians with the aim of instilling fear among the public. Our efforts to bring them back into the mainstream and wean them away from the Pakistani machinations should continue. And in this sphere, the Army, J & K Police, CRPF, intelligence agencies and civil administration are cohesively playing a critical role, but there is a definite need to upgrade our energies in the mission.

CRPF—'Never Say Die' Spirit Force

As mentioned at various places in this book, the Team Security Forces have played a crucial role at every juncture during various counter-terrorism and internal security operations. Hit by one of the most dastardly tragedies in Pulwama, the CRPF lost forty of their bravehearts on 14 February 2019, but even in that desert of despair and tragedy, there was an oasis of hope and encouragement, as the CRPF men did not lose morale. They bravely carried on their mission of protecting the homeland under all circumstances, and under the leadership of Mr Zulfiquar Hasan, then IGP, CRPF, participated with vigour in various operations even immediately after Pulwama. This included the operation in Pinglan, referred to in an earlier chapter, and subsequently the one on 24 February 2019, wherein we averted another Pulwama, also referred to earlier. The officers and men of the CRPF have thus represented a critical component of the Team Security Forces conducting those operations to successfully eliminate terrorists, and deserve all accolades for their professionalism and bravery.

Team Security Forces

Here I would like to make special mention of the **Team Security Forces** that worked like a punch during the most challenging times after the Pulwama incident and the abrogation of Articles 370 and 35A.

Mr K. Vijay Kumar, a retired IPS officer of the 1975 batch, was the adviser (security) to the Honourable Governor of Jammu and Kashmir during the Pulwama incident and the abrogation of Articles 370 and 35A. Mr K. Vijay Kumar had earlier served in the Kashmir Valley as the Inspector General of BSF during the period 1998–2001, when the border guarding force was actively involved in counter-terrorism operations. He had also earlier served as the chief of the special task force of Tamil Nadu, credited with the elimination of the dreaded sandalwood smuggler Veerappan in October 2004 during Operation Cocoon. He was appointed director general of the world's largest paramilitary force, the CRPF, in 2010. He, therefore, had extensive experience of counter-Naxal and terrorist operations in the Valley and other areas. The presence of Mr K. Vijay Kumar at the helm was a motivating factor for the entire Team and his vast experience in dealing with such situations ensured the smooth and cordial functioning of all members of the security and civil administration apparatus. His guidance, motivation and encouragement to officers and jawans of all the security forces in J & K were a source of inspiration.

Mr B.V.R. Subrahmanyam, IAS, Chief Secretary, J & K (presently chairman and managing director, India Trade Promotion Organization after retiring as commerce secretary in the Government of India), a 1987-batch Chhattisgarh cadre IAS officer, with a management degree from the London Business School, had been instrumental in combating insurgency in Chhattisgarh in the 2010s. He also previously served in the Prime

Minister's Office (PMO) under two prime ministers. In view of his specialized experience and leadership, it was an absolute honour professionally to have him as the senior-most and exceptionally professional bureaucrat in Kashmir during those challenging times. A team man to the core, he was a natural facilitator in the smooth functioning of the Team Security Forces and the civil administration. One of Mr Subrahmanyam's qualities that I admired the most was that he never wasted any time in the exchange of routine pleasantries and got down to the task at hand straight away. A thorough professional, he knew his job well and more importantly, how to do it.

Mr Shaleen Kabra, IAS, Principal Secretary, Home, a 1992 AGMUT cadre officer, a graduate in mechanical engineering from IIT Delhi and an MBA (part-time) from the Faculty of Management Studies, Delhi. He was the district magistrate of Kargil during the Kargil War and a year prior to that when intense shelling was the norm. He has also worked as director in the PMO for two years. He successfully conducted Panchayat and Municipal elections in 2018, the first democratic exercise since April 2017 when elections had to be cancelled in Kashmir due to violence. Although they were due in 2016, the Panchayat elections were postponed repeatedly and could be held only after Governor's Rule was promulgated. With such an illustrious career background, he was a one-man system when it came to legal scrutiny or administrative backing for any action for peaceful implementation of the abrogation of Articles 370 and 35A. A man with a perpetual smile, and that showed very much in the manner he did his otherwise very stressful job. He motivated others with his sheer presence.

Mr Dilbagh Singh, IPS, DGP J & K, a 1987 batch officer, who was the main pillar of the Team Security Forces and commanded his force by leading from the front. He was constantly on the move, visiting his officers and men in the most active areas. During all such visits, he would make it a point to interact with the Army and RR officers in the area, most of whom he knew personally by name. He started his career as a trainee officer and later became additional superintendent of police Kupwara just at the onset of terrorism in J & K. He survived two deadly ambushes and attacks on his life in Lolab (where I served as the company commander later in 1999–2000) and Natnussa Kupwara in 1991. His vast experience in counter-terrorism operations includes his stints as SP Doda and Baramulla and DIG, South Kashmir Range, Jammu Range and North Kashmir Range. He is a recipient of the Distinguished Service Medal and Meritorious Service conferred by the Honourable President of India, Gallantry and Bar to Gallantry Medal, Sher-e-Kashmir Medal for Gallantry and for Meritorious Service, and State Medal for Outstanding Service. An exceptional colleague, I would love to work with him any time, any place and any day again.

Mr Muneer Ahmad Khan, IPS, Additional DGP law and order, a state police officer of the 1984 batch, is a daredevil with vast experience in counter-terrorism operations ever since its onset in Jammu and Kashmir. He was inducted into the IPS with effect from 1994. I have personally worked very closely with 'Khan Saheb' in my earlier stints, including as RR sector commander in Handwara and Brigadier General Staff (BGS) in Corps Headquarters responsible for operations and coordination with the Police and Central Armed Police Forces (CAPF), among other duties, when he was DIG Police, North Kashmir. As DIG, he has the unique distinction of commanding all three police ranges of the Kashmir Valley. He was promoted and appointed additional DG law and order, and security in 2018. Although he was due to retire in June 2019, he is the only IPS officer in the history of J & K Police to get a one-year extension in service. He contributed immensely during the events of 5 August 2019 and towards the maintenance of peace in the Valley after that. He is a recipient of the President's Medals for Distinguished Service, Meritorious Service and Gallantry, besides having been awarded the Chief of the Army Staff Commendation Card.

Mr Zulfiquar Hasan, a 1988 IPS officer of the West Bengal cadre, was the IG CRPF in the Kashmir Operations Sector during the Pulwama incident of February 2019. During his posting in Kashmir, he handled many challenging situations, including the aftermath of the agitation of 2016, after the killing of the terrorist Burhan Wani, and joint counter-terrorism operations during the period 2017–19. As a very important member of the Team, he handled the scenario post the abrogation of Articles 370 and 35A with great sensitivity. He is a very meticulous officer who would work out every single detail and address it in the most professional manner, ensuring near-zero violence and absolutely no collateral damage during the agitations, which were subsequently brought to nought by the combined and synergized efforts of security forces, intelligence agencies and the civil administration. His experience in counter-Naxal and terrorist operations includes his appointments as Inspector General (operations), CRPF in Chhattisgarh during 2012–13; Inspector General, operations directorate, CRPF during 2013–16; Inspector General, Kashmir operations sector, CRPF during 2016–19; and additional DG, CRPF J & K Zone during 2019–20, which came in very handy in dealing with the challenges thrown up by the Pulwama incident and the abrogation. He is an officer gifted with the exceptional skills of senior police management, especially in anti-Maoist operations in Chhattisgarh and counter-insurgency/counter-terrorism operations in Kashmir. He is a recipient of the UN Peace Medal 2004 (twice); Police Medal for Meritorious Service, 2006; Police (Special Duty) Medal, 2017; 'First Bar', 2019; President's Police Medal for Distinguished Service, 2013; Police Antrik Suraksha Seva Police Padak, 2019; and the Home Minister's Ati Utkrishta Seva Medal, 2021. He was subsequently appointed special DG Operations, 2020–22 and is presently serving as Director General of the Bureau of Civil Aviation Security (BCAS).

Mr Swayam Pani, IPS, IGP Kashmir, a 2000 erstwhile J & K cadre (now AGMUT) officer, who served extensively in various parts of Kashmir as SP, SSP, DIG and finally IGP, was responsible for counter-terrorism police operations as well as routine policing duties in the entire Kashmir Valley. He had an in-depth knowledge of the terrain and local population, especially in South Kashmir, the hotbed of terrorism then and even now. He upgraded the technical intelligence acquisition means to a level wherein everyone started depending upon it heavily, and in the bargain, the age-old human intelligence started getting neglected, the need and importance of which had to be specifically impressed upon the junior commanders. His professional dynamism, selfless commitment and inspiring leadership, especially during the post-Pulwama operations, and maintenance of peace after 5 August 2019 will always find a recognized and acknowledged mention in all professional forums with a sense of utmost élan and approbation.

Mr Vijay Kumar, IPS, additional DGP (IGP Kashmir during 2019–22), a 1997 batch IPS officer of the erstwhile J & K cadre, has experience in handling both terrorism in Kashmir and Maoism in Chhattisgarh. He has served as SP, Awantipora, Kulgam and Kupwara, and DIG, South Kashmir. He has also served as IG, CoBRA (Commando Battalion for Resolute Action) and Operation in CRPF in the Government of India. He is presently serving as IGP, Kashmir, since December 2019. He has been awarded the Police Gallantry Medals by the Honourable President of India three times and the J & K Police Gallantry Medals by the Governor of J & K twice. The Election Commission of India has awarded him the prestigious National Award for conducting Assembly elections in nine states in the year 2018, and the award was conferred by the Honourable President of India. He was awarded the Police Medal for Meritorious Service by the Honourable President of India in 2013 and the Jammu and Kashmir Police Medal for Meritorious Service by the Honourable Lieutenant Governor of Jammu and Kashmir in 2021. He is also a recipient of the Chief of the Army Staff Commendation Card, General Officer Commanding-in-Chief Northern Command Commendation Cards and Commendation Discs by the DG CRPF and DGP J & K. An absolutely committed officer, he has given a new dimension to the hard intelligence-based counter-terrorism operations in the Valley.

Mr Ravideep Singh Sahi, IG CRPF, Srinagar Sector, a CRPF officer of the 1986 batch, was responsible for the Central

Kashmir district, covering Srinagar, Budgam and Ganderbal, including the security at the Srinagar International Airport. The security forces in the Srinagar Sector handled the anti-terrorism and law and order challenges in a professional manner and kept Srinagar city safe, ensuring that no civilian suffered during the highly volatile law and order situations before and after the abrogation of Articles 370 and 35A. The CRPF men on ground, along with the JKP, kept the sensitive area of downtown, the hub of the law and order disturbance and terrorist activities, under control. The principle of operational excellence in the anti-terrorism operations and the use of minimum effective force for handling the law and order situation day in and day out remained the guiding and motivating force for CRPF officers and jawans on the ground. Thus, the period after the abrogation of Articles 370 and 35A was managed peacefully, with no civilian casualties. The excellent coordination with the Indian Army and its leadership role in anti-militancy operations helped the Team Security Forces to overcome security challenges in an effective manner. He is a recipient of the President's Police Medal for Distinguished Service, 2018; the Police Medal for Gallantry, 2017; the Ati Utkrisht Seva Padak, 2019; the Governor's Appreciation Letter, 2017 and 2018; and the Commendation Disc of the DG, CRPF, in 2017 and 2018, among many other awards.

I may not have mentioned here each and every outstanding Police, CRPF or civil administration officer of the Team working at the ground level 24/7, who made huge contributions in the maintenance of peace in the Kashmir Valley, but some other names that deserve special mention are Rajesh Kumar, IPS, IG CRPF; Suleman Choudhary, IPS, DIG, North Kashmir; Vidhi Kumar Birdi, IPS, DIG, Central Kashmir; Amit Kumar, IPS, former DIG, South Kashmir, who got injured in the operation post-Pulwama which I have mentioned in an earlier chapter; Atul Kumar Goel, IPS, DIG, South Kashmir, a highly tech-savvy officer, who single-handedly enhanced analysis of technical intelligence and acquisition techniques; and last but not least, Imtiyaz Hussain, senior superintendent of police, whose personal outreach towards the youth at the social level worked wonders in bringing many of them back into the mainstream.

Tulla of Zojila

In the midst of all the security-related issues, there are some incredible human stories happening all around us and during one's Army service, one gets an opportunity to serve in various parts of the country and also travel abroad. One often meets some ordinary people doing extraordinary work in their respective fields, though their work remains unknown and unsung at times. I recall one such story of exceptional devotion to duty and exhibition of human intelligence and mental faculties in the face of extreme challenges posed by hostile weather and treacherous terrain. The protagonist of this tale is Mr Anayatullah, popularly known as 'Tulla of Zojila'. Just to reiterate, Zojila Pass, which is situated at a height of 11,649 feet on the Srinagar–Leh highway, lies along the Great Himalayan Range and remains inaccessible to traffic during the winter months as it lies buried under mounds of snow often stretching up to 50 feet in height at places.

Tulla is a specially abled, hearing and speech-impaired bulldozer driver, working with Project BEACON of Border Roads Organization (BRO), which is responsible for the construction, maintenance and improvement of all the important roads in the Kashmir Valley. During the snow clearance operations carried out at the Zojila Pass every year, Tulla drives the leading bulldozer and makes the first alignment by cutting through the heavy snow at places where the road is not visible at all. Since he is unable to hear any instructions, he works with his instincts to move the bulldozer on the mountainous pass buried under the heavy snow and avalanches that constitute a regular phenomenon on the roads at those altitudes throughout the winter months. Tulla hails from Nilgarath Village of Sonamarg and has been working with the BRO for the last thirty-odd years.

I met Tulla in April 2019 when, as the Chinar Corps Commander, I had travelled to Zojila Pass on the very day that it was thrown open to traffic. Impressed with his selfless dedication and utmost commitment to the job assigned to him, I immediately presented him with a cash award and subsequently he was also awarded the Northern Command Army Commander's Commendation Card by Lieutenant General Ranbir Singh, General Officer Commanding-in-Chief of the Northern Command.

I also tweeted about Tulla from my Twitter handle and that tweet went viral with lots of people wanting to help Mr Anayatullah financially. Further, I shared details of his bank account with some of my close friends so that they could make monetary contributions to help him. Anayatullah is a known name now and it is not uncommon for travellers on the Srinagar–Leh highway to halt at the BRO Sonamarg camp for a selfie with the famous 'Tulla of Zojila'!

With Tulla of Zojila aka Anayatullah on top of the Zojila Pass,
April 2019

21

General Bipin Rawat: The Soldier and the Man as I Knew Him

The Soldier

I am writing about General Bipin Rawat in my autobiography not because I served with him or because he was my Chief and subsequently India's first Chief of the Defence Staff (CDS) and I worked directly under him, but because I want to apprise the readers as to what a great leader and visionary India lost in that unfortunate helicopter accident on 8 December 2021.

The first time I personally met General Bipin Rawat was when he was commanding the Rashtriya Rifles Sector in North Kashmir, responsible for operations in Sopore and the surrounding areas. He always came across as a very down-to-earth mission-oriented leader who had a knack for working congenially, both with his subordinates and his peers, incentivizing them to give their best by reposing full faith in them. He always issued absolutely calm, clear and concise instructions and thereafter rarely intervened in the functioning of his commanders or staff officers, allowing them full autonomy to perform the assigned task in their own style, if they adhered to his one key mandate—to work in full coordination and cooperation with each other as part of a cohesive team working towards achieving the organizational goals. However, in his dictionary, there was no place for wilful transgressions. He was a thorough professional both in his dealings with others and in the mandate he set for himself.

General Bipin Rawat's purported omniscience was the stuff of legend as he believed in acquiring a deep knowledge of every subject. A very innocuous looking statement made by his staff in front of him could be discussed threadbare or effortlessly countered by him, supported with cogent logic and hard facts. That is why one could never get away by providing any half-baked information to him and had to prepare thoroughly before giving him any briefing or attending a meeting with him. He also had a photographic memory. I have personally observed him during various discussions vividly recalling details of events that occurred more than two or three decades ago. He would recollect the graphic details of those incidents as though they had happened just yesterday.

Most intriguingly, apart from his memory of past events, he had a razor-sharp vision of the future too. He could paint an extremely lucid picture of what the Defence Forces would look like in the next twenty years and provide all the inputs that were needed to make them future-ready. I had an insider's view of this vision of General Rawat as when he was the Chief of the Army Staff, I was the Director General, Perspective Planning, responsible for making long-term perspective plans, before I took over command of the 15 Corps. While preparing these long-term perspective plans, I used to interact regularly with General Rawat and observed his extremely well-orchestrated vision of the future and crystallized perception of the realities of the present.

A very critical attribute of a senior commander's professional acumen is his decision-making ability. A correct decision taken at the right time by the commander will have a long-term impact because numerous staff officers and commanders below him are waiting to implement various aspects of that decision in synchronization with many other stakeholders. General Rawat's pragmatic philosophy, therefore, was that in today's era of rapid technological developments and ever-evolving dynamism in the entire spectrum of warfighting, any delay in taking critical decisions would have a pernicious and cascading effect on the nation's war preparedness to counter the contingencies already knocking on our doors. His style of functioning was thus characterized by simultaneity and cohesive coordination to execute and implement the decision taken.

The Man

General Rawat's personal lifestyle was extremely simple. He was a thoroughly practical soldier, with his ear to the ground and a deep desire to strike a personal bond with his entire team, right up to the last man in the hierarchy. He would very often end up dancing with his troops at the regimental functions. Coming as he did from the Gorkha Regiment, he would sing Gurkhali songs at regimental and unit 'bada khanas' (celebratory community meals) and happily mingle with the men. He was a great proponent of the infusion of high-end, state-of-the-art technology in the defence forces and, at the same time, strongly believed that a jawan will always be the fiercest war-fighting machine of the Indian Army, given the harsh terrain along our borders.

At heart, however, he was literally a son of the soil, a real grassroots person, who worked hands-on in every situation, always in the forefront, leading his men, egging them on to give their best, even in the most difficult areas and most difficult situations.

The Family Man

The other face of this hardcore professional was that of a compassionate and committed family man, a fact that was repeatedly evident to me whenever we met him with his wife, Mrs Madhulika Rawat, and their two daughters. Just like the General, Mrs Rawat too would interact unselfconsciously with the families of jawans and officers. General Rawat's father was posted in Army headquarters as Lieutenant General and was staying in the same house that I was occupying during my last tenure prior to superannuation. Their elder daughter played on the beautiful lawns of this house as a child when he was posted in a field area and Mrs Rawat was staying here with her in-laws. He was a family man to the last. Mrs Rawat was always by his side, even on the fateful day of 8 December 2021, when the helicopter crash took them away from us.

Now that he is no longer in our midst, I am reminded of a small anecdote pertaining to the period when I was the Director General of the Defence Intelligence Agency and he was the CDS, and I used to interact very closely with him on all matters of Intelligence as I was reporting directly to him. One Sunday morning, I received a sealed package from the CDS delivered by a military courier. This instantly raised my antenna as a sealed packet sent by the CDS, especially on a Sunday, usually does not augur well. As I was opening the packet, my mind was already racing, envisioning different kinds of intelligence inputs that he had probably received and was sharing with me in that courier packet, expecting me to work on the intelligence input and take it further. However, as I opened the package, much to my surprise, I found a very elegant printed gents' silk shirt inside it. Puzzled at this unexpected present, I looked at the shirt suspiciously and then assumed that the CDS had inadvertently sent it to the wrong address and it was actually meant for someone else. But then I came across a handwritten note in the package—his preference for writing notes by hand was, in fact, one of his special and endearing qualities. The note said, 'Dear Tiny, I got this shirt while I was in Indonesia and it is the traditional dress of that country. But it is a little loose for me and does not fit me well. However, I think it will definitely fit you.' I still have that shirt as a token of remembrance of General Rawat.

Having engaged very closely with General Rawat both professionally and socially, I can say that I never observed even a whiff of superciliousness or patronizing behaviour towards his officers or men on his part. On a more personal and social front, whenever we landed up at his house, we were witness to the couple's exuberant hospitality; the warmth exuded by him and his wife on such occasions is deeply ingrained in our memory. They rarely offered their guests 'a seven-star' meal, but their personal involvement in making all guests feel at home and their incomparable hospitality was invariably way beyond even all the stars in the sky, let alone only seven of them.

Adieu General

The date of his death, 8 December 2021, in a helicopter crash near Coonoor in the Nilgiris district of Tamil Nadu, will forever be etched in my memory as one of the toughest days in my life. Just one day prior to the fateful crash, that is, on the evening of 7 December 2021, I had met him and we were engaged in an hour-long discussion, which also involved Brigadier L.S. Lidder and Lieutenant Colonel Harjinder Singh, two of his staff officers who also lost their lives in that crash. We exchanged some critical information, and the next morning I received a message from him that he would resume the discussion on his return from Wellington, which was never to be.

Sometime on that afternoon, I received a telephone call from a TV journalist wanting to confirm the tragic news. As the news of the crash started drifting in, I immediately visited his home with my wife, where his younger daughter was alone at that time as his elder daughter is married and settled in Mumbai. My wife and I stayed with their daughter for about four hours till their friends and family members started arriving. Those were the most difficult four hours of my life that I can ever recall. While there was a lot of speculation as the news was still not confirmed, his daughter kept asking us for an update. I have faced a lot of tough and tense situations in my life, numerous combats, assaults and near-death experiences, but those four hours that we spent with their younger daughter, gripped in a period of uncertainty and yet a foreboding of their death, were indescribably difficult for me and my wife, both because of our emotions stemming from our deep personal bond and also an intense sadness at the untimely and sudden loss of such a fine gentleman and a graceful lady.

In the death of General Bipin Rawat, the nation and the defence forces have lost a commander of the highest credentials and a visionary who had plans with far-reaching benefits for the country's defence forces, which will hopefully be implemented in the coming days and years. We will realize the true worth of his contribution only after the implementation of these plans. I salute the General for all that he has done for the defence forces and the Army, and for his friendly professional bond and guidance, memories of which will stay with me till the last.

Au revoir, my General!
Jai Hind!

With General Bipin Rawat during one of his visits to the Kashmir Valley as the Chief of the Army Staff, 2019

22

Future Possibilities and Envisioned Strategies

The ISI's Intent

To understand the future possibilities and envisaged strategies in Kashmir, it is important to understand how Pakistan and the ISI are going to play their cards in Kashmir. To envisage future possibilities entailed within the gambit of a proxy war by the Pakistan Army, which is, in my opinion, not a professional army and the ISI in Kashmir, the canvas would include the pursuit of the following actions:

- Orchestration of a trigger event or exploit an event to get the masses on the streets so that a vicious cycle of violence could be set into motion as seen after the killing of Burhan Wani. The aim being to keep the Kashmir pot boiling and remain in international headlines.
- Impetus to foment infiltration through multiple routes like the Line of Control, international boundary or via a third country.

- Sustenance of financial networks to infuse funds for anti-India entities to enable them to initiate inimical actions as chalked out in their overall design for conducting a proxy war against India.
- Strive to push in maximum war-like stores into Kashmir, again either through the Line of Control, the international border, or procured through under-the-radar criminal illegal arms-making networks within India or through a third country.
- Continue to use 'religion' as a tool to exacerbate the metrics of 'polarization', 'alienation' and 'radicalization' of the youth in Kashmir. This thread continues to remain a prime driver for luring formative young minds into this agenda, inciting them to pick up arms and join the terrorist ranks, as per the time and geographical targets set by the ISI. The socio-economic impact of more than three decades of terrorism on Kashmiri society discussed in earlier chapters is adding to their efforts.
- Further all actions to corrupt the Kashmiri mind space, especially that of the youth, in consonance with its agenda, covering the domains of social media and vernacular print media, distribution of literature (both electronic and print) and drug addiction.
- Keep the ecosystem of disruption functional despite the imposition of a ban on the Jamaat-e-Islami (JeI) by the Indian Government or the increased raids by the National Investigation Agency (NIA) on related entities.
- Periodic planned targeting of minorities congruent to their disruptive and violent agenda to achieve the desired effect.
- Disrupt the political process, as and when it is getting stabilized with development taking place, through financial, ideological, coercive or kinetic means.

Our Counter Strategy

In order to respond to Pakistan and the ISI's policy of creating a complex and disruptive ecosystem in Kashmir, our strategy ought to entail all facets of '*Saam*' (persuade), '*Daam*' (purchase), '*Dand*' (punish) and '*Bhed*' (exploiting the secrets), as spelt out by Kautilya.

Concomitant with this strategy, our approach must thus encompass seeking the advice and engagement (*Saam)* of key segments of the population and opinion-makers, including the mothers as in the case of Operation Maa, offering better avenues (*Daam*) for providing improved education and employment avenues, punishing the anti-nationals (*Dand*), and last but not least, creating fissures (*Bhed*) in the policy aimed at embroiling the youth in inimical and terrorist activities.

Without going into greater detail of many long-term plans and long gestation period actions required at various levels of governance to counter Pakistan's strategy, a few tenets that need to be addressed immediately on priority are enunciated below.

- *Saam*
  Outreach to the Common Man: An all-encompassing programme entailing 'outreach to the common man' needs to be undertaken to bridge the divide between the masses on one hand, and the state, district, block and panchayat level on the other hand. This bond has been almost completely missing for many years due to the prevalence of corruption, high-handedness, political meddling and candidates who have been sponsored by members of the JeI and separatists securing appointments at lower levels of state administration in view of the nexus between the politicians and them. There is also a need to create e-governance portals facilitating online redressal and submission of the relevant documents, as has been initiated in some other states. Meanwhile, the 'Back to the Village' programme initiated by the government of the newly constituted union territory is a step in the right direction and must be pursued with vigour.

  Drug De-addiction: The scale of drug addiction in Kashmir has assumed alarming proportions, with a reasonable number of youngsters in the union territory estimated to be victims of this addiction. What is a matter of great concern is that the bulk of these addicts are in the age group of eighteen to thirty-five years, and even more alarmingly, a large number of cases are also being reported among children in their early teens. Since the addicts need money to finance their addiction, they try to source the funds by indulging in anti-social and anti-national activities like stone-pelting, lone wolf attacks (isolated terrorist strikes using pistols or grenades), or working as 'over ground workers' at the behest of terrorists ready to lure them into their fold. Some of the young addicts, with a background of systemic ideological infusion, also pick up arms and become jihadis. This necessitates the creation of a robust institutional approach involving multiple agencies to maximize outreach for offering psychological counselling, organization of seminars and outreach events to spread awareness about the ill effects of addiction, especially in schools and colleges, setting up medical camps and de-addiction centres and offering the vulnerable youngsters opportunities for employment through skill development and identification of alternate avenues for employment generation, to prevent youth in their formative years from falling into the trap of drug addiction.

De-radicalization: One of the most critical initiatives for achieving normality in Kashmir is the de-radicalization of impressionable youth and dissociating religion from radical beliefs. This is imperative in view of the large-scale radicalization of youth that has already taken place in Kashmir. This is, however, a sensitive exercise as attempts at de-radicalization should not be interpreted as 'questioning of the youth's faith (religion)'. Further, the identification of targeted youths for this exercise is also a challenge due to both the context and scale of the narrative. A 'whole of the nation approach' thus needs to be adopted to address this malaise in right earnest, entailing the use of various tools, such as physical outreach mechanisms, online help portals, peer reform groups and community reform committees, supplemented by incentivized policy packages offered by the government. Models and best practices that have worked in other states in the past may be analysed for replication as applicable in the context and background of Kashmir. The civil administration, Indian Army and other security forces are doing their bit in this area and have undertaken various contact programmes. One such programme called 'Sahi Raasta', covering various aspects like psychological mapping, skill identification, counselling, organizing religious perspective sessions, interface with eminent and learned speakers and avenues of recreation, was conducted recently with good success. All these measures collectively signify a small yet vital step towards outreach that could ultimately help in de-radicalization of the affected youth.

Development: Apart from outreach aimed at the youth who are being targeted by terrorists as potential recruits, it is also imperative to provide an impetus for development. Due to the scourge of terrorism that affected all aspects of normal life in the Kashmir Valley, it missed the opportunity of participating in the post-economic liberalization and concomitant development that the rest of India benefited from in the 1990s. Post the abrogation of Articles 370 and 35A, however, there is hope for reviving the aspirations of the Kashmiri common man to lead a normal and financially secure life, symbolized by access to improved civic amenities and enhanced job opportunities. A mega developmental boost is the need of the hour in Kashmir, which can be achieved through various constructive measures such as attracting both foreign investment as well as investment by Indian business houses, implementation of projects for technological advancement and development of civic amenities, including better road infrastructure, water and sanitation facilities, and municipal development projects. The first step in this exercise has been the allocation of funds to block presidents, which has enabled them to initiate such welfare projects at the grassroots level.

* *Daam*

Improve the Education System: Since education directly helps in shaping the minds of youth, who comprise the most crucial segment of the population in Kashmir, the education system needs to be improved and upscaled on a priority basis. First, the institutions that are imparting religious education to children need to be scrutinized to assess their management, sources of funding, content of the curriculum and activities propagated among students, and the conduct and ideological and political leanings of the teachers/religious figures who impart learning in these institutions. The aim of this exercise should be that education should improve their chances of admission in a good college and enhance employability of the students after their schooling. In addition, all the schools run by the Jamaat-e-Islami (JeI) should also be subjected to a similar audit. The other key initiatives in the sphere of education include institutionalizing of pursuits to educate the teachers, skill development and enhancement of learning to enable the children to confidently appear for all-India competitive examinations. The goal should be to facilitate the integration of the Kashmiri students and youth into the national mainstream and provide them better chances of acquiring higher education in reputed institutions.

Revival of the Political Process: The revival of the political process in Kashmir necessitates clarity in defining the boundaries of political space in Kashmir vis-à-vis national interests. The political ecosystem of Kashmir also needs to be infused with fresh, educated talent rather than the persistence of relying on the existing dynastic families that have hitherto occupied centre stage in Kashmir, often leading to the submergence of the state's developmental interests and infringement of the country's national interests. While it is important to determine the timing of the elections, this process must be well thought out and not implemented in haste, giving the new and emerging political parties sufficient time to establish a connect with their electorate. The first metric of progression towards that would be progress in the governance canvas of Kashmir, for eliminating partisan pursuits and corruption, a system that allows the hobnobbing of many political elements, who often do not think in the best interest of the country.

- *Dand*

Uproot All Malignant Entities: It is necessary to take strict action against all those who work against the national interest and block their access to funds and deny them the space to further their inimical agendas. The JeI has already been banned since February 2019. In addition, entities like the Dukhtaran-e-Millat and JKLF have been banned. It is high time that other entities propagating anti-national agendas too meet the same fate, as they have been the most obtrusive separatist face of the proxy war being waged by Pakistan and the ISI.

Eliminate Terror-Funding Networks: The network through which illegal funds are used and transferred to feed the disruptive ecosystem in Kashmir includes Kashmiri NRIs (who send remuneration back home to the off-the-radar entities), businessmen (under and over-invoicing of cross-LoC trade), NGOs, trusts, religious institutions, including religious educational institutions and the separatists' network for the internal collections of donations and contributions. These networks need to be exposed and thwarted, followed by legal action. Various trusts and NGOs operating in Jammu and Kashmir have long been known to be conduits for these pursuits.

Evaluate and take adequate action against those in administration, who work against the interests of India: A provision exists under Sub-clause (c) to Clause 2 of Article 311 of our Constitution, wherein the services of an individual whose continuation in service is prejudicial to the security of the state can be terminated. There is a need to realize that the inimical network of the Jamaitees has infiltrated all strata of Kashmiri society to promote and further their inimical agenda. These need to be weeded out by invoking the Constitutional provisions. A small beginning to this effect has already been made, which needs to be continued, and indeed escalated while intricately examining each such case of anti-nationalism.

Invoking the Law: Various legal provisions exist for robust enforcement of the law in Kashmir, the important ones among these are the Unlawful Activities Prevention Act (UAPA), the J & K Public Safety Act (J & K PSA), the Prevention of Destruction of Public Property Act (PDPPA) and the Prevention of Money Laundering Act (PMLA), along with the NIA Act. These provisions can, however, be effective only in the absence of political interference in the functioning of the police, and the courts are allowed to independently pursue adjudication of cases to their provisioned conclusion in an expedited manner. This remains a challenge, mandating certain police reforms to negate unnecessary political interference.

Response-Preparedness: This implies preparedness for putting in place a system that helps secure India's national interests by preventing violence and terrorist activities. Although a well-knit and functional system (at times ad hoc) does exist, this response-preparedness must entail the following measures:

- Formulation of a Joint Doctrine for counter-terrorism operations for all security forces.
- Refining the Joint Counter Agitation Strategy, which is in consonance with the prevalent and evolving security environment.
- Institutionalizing a Joint Response Coordination Centre at the district level.
- Pursuit of intelligence to enable intelligence-based surgical operations against potential terrorist activities. Prevention is better than cure.
- Continuous provision of advanced equipment to all the security and intelligence agencies to help them mitigate casualties and collateral damage.
- Establishing a coherent, transparent and efficient redressal system to process and address public grievances efficiently and in a time-bound manner.

297

Security Forces' Footprint: It is also imperative to constantly audit the scale of the footprint of security forces that is required to maintain peace in Kashmir. Currently, the metric being used for this assessment is the number of terrorists operating in the Valley. These metrics need to be reviewed periodically both in terms of the scale of the terrorists' activities as well as the addition of other possible parameters that could compromise peace in the Valley. The possible parameters in this regard could be the administration footprint apart from that of the security forces, the scale of development activities being undertaken in the Valley, the absence of untoward incidents, the impact of administrative and legal measures for maintaining peace, the revival of the transparent and honest political process, and other steps aimed at achieving positive transformation of the youth. A focus on these activities will also help reduce the overall footprint of the security forces in the Kashmir Valley, including the hinterland, thereby hastening the process of normalization.

- *Bhed*

  Secure the Mind Space of Youngsters: The bulk of the youth in the college-going age group (eighteen to twenty-four years) have witnessed the large-scale protests that took place during the years of 2008, 2010 and 2016, and have been adversely affected by killings as part of the unending vicious cycle of violence among their kith and kin. These experiences have bitterly scarred the mind space of youngsters constantly exposed to an anti-India narrative while simultaneously being targeted by the ISI and other Pakistani agencies for radicalization and recruitment among the ranks of the terrorists. Therefore, robust measures are needed for monitoring social media dissemination and the activities of individuals and organizations suspected to be indulging in anti-national pursuits.

The enumerated measures are not enough in themselves but are the barest minimum that needs to be implemented on priority.

23

God's Favourite Child

Someone very dear to me, who is well-versed with my life's story, recently told me, 'You are God's favourite child!' I am not sure if that's true, but I can say with absolute certainty that the three-year-old boy of nearly six decades ago would not have been writing this book without God's blessings. So, with all the humility at my disposal, I would like to say a big heartfelt 'Thank You' to all my friends, peers, superiors, subordinates and relatives, who made me what I am today, 'THE KJS DHILLON' as someone on Twitter said the other day.

This book is for young boys and girls aspiring to be part of the Indian Army family, to give them an idea of what lies ahead if they choose this way of life. I want to motivate these young people to always think highly of themselves, to walk ahead with the determination to succeed, to unleash the warrior within themselves and face life with the courage and confidence to bring their aspirations to fruition. By narrating my life story, I want to motivate my readers to treat challenges as opportunities and to realize that there are no easy battles ever won. The guiding principles for achieving a life well lived are to make people feel important, admire their efforts more than their achievements, celebrate friends, nurture and honour relationships, and most important, be there when you are expected to. As a leader, to protect what is under your watch is not only your duty but an honour code that you have to live up to, so that you can inspire posterity to follow in your footsteps and to remember you with deference and respect. Men and women are born to die one day; only a few live in the legends; be that 'one'.

An Ode to a 'Not-So-Old Man' by the 'Men-to-Be'

Getting the opportunity to command a battalion is the ultimate test and 'high' for any military professional's career. I cannot help but end this book with a first-hand account of some events that occurred during my command tenure, witnessed by the person who bore the maximum brunt of my position at that time and now happily narrates tales of the incoming fire, as he saw it from the vantage point of the persons at the target end. Then a young lieutenant, later a captain, and now a colonel, Manish Sanga, my adjutant during my command of the battalion, is an exceptional professional, an excellent sportsman and a natural storyteller. Here, I end the book and quote what he has to say in his own words:

> Often we come across a loosely used phrase 'Men will be men'. While the phrase evokes diverse emotions, it's important to understand what kind of men would men be? In the fraternity of olive greens, there are too many men trying to be better men, because the balance men in society look at them as portraying the 'Best Men'.
>
> In the Army, a commanding officer (CO) has to be certainly the best man and that's the responsibility and weight a newly appointed CO lugs along when he is given the honour to command a battalion. Imagine the number of eyes whose perceptions and expectations have to be set right when one takes over the reins. Tiny Dhillon walks into the scene as the

eleventh CO of the battalion, in Kashmir, in the middle of Operation Parakaram, with the immediate task of steering the paltan during an imminent-looking war, which seemed likely as a fallout of the Parliament attack and the Kaluchak incident. Let me put things into perspective: the motivation in the Army and more so in an infantry battalion is drawn from a physically fit and impressive leader, in simple words, a 'Man who is more of a Man'. The new CO came up to the stage with a towering personality, a perfect soldierly bearing, and the flair of a 'TIGER', but would he pass the test of leading the best men into battle, his past record notwithstanding?

'Tiny Sir', the new CO, took over the command of the battalion in the salubrious climes of the pristine valley with snow-clad peaks, somewhere in Kashmir wherein sightseeing was only a by-product of some bigger challenges at hand. The prying eyes of the entire battalion were evaluating, judging and forming their opinion on all the TINY steps being taken by the not-so-TINY man at the helm of affairs. As he trickled into the intricate biological system of the unit, he was generally witnessed moving around stern-faced, laden with big operational responsibilities, along with the welfare and administration of close to a thousand human beings. Duly trained for withstanding various combat stresses, these individuals were still humans . . . with families . . . responsibilities . . . a:d mainly emotions, which at times couldn't be handled with mere logic. It would be absolutely honest to state that a smile on his face was as rare a phenomenon as a rainbow . . . Ohhh! When would it rain?

The operational flair and professional competence of this man is not being dwelled upon as his legendary status of today already reeks of it. Suffice it to say that he quickly established himself in the various profsssional echelons of a highly challenging operational environment, leading the unit from the front.

In a field area, it is a regular practice for all officers to dine together in the makeshift officers' mess. The rule was in vogue that if the CO closes his plate, the balance officers had to follow suit. Is there an issue here? What if the CO is on a diet? What if he is struck with some 'senior officer depression syndrome'? What if he just feels like having only one chapatti? Now by the time chapattis are delivered to the young officers (YOs) (delayed due to serving as per seniority), the dreaded clink of the CO closing his plate is heard. Here comes the new Boss, the same stage is set, the same drills are about to be followed. This time, the radars of the YOs could not register that unnerving clink from the far and famous end. 'Lieutenant Sahab ko chapatti pehle do.' 'Badhai ho!' ('Serve the chapatti to the Lieutenant first.' 'Congratulations!') to the doting Moms, who have a tough competitor here in the much-dreaded man in the Kashmir Valley.

Time has passed by with the much-in-control CO moving the battalion to the arid spaces of a small but not-so-remote town in Rajasthan. The station, though a modified field area, was ripe with a lot of station activities like sports, mess functions, welfare events/meets and so on. It was also a breeding ground for anecdotes and stories as these events had their unique flavours, with this uniqueness infused in them due to the presence of the YOs around.

The unit excelled in all sports activities and had carved a name for itself in the sphere of sports. Once a basketball match of the junior commissioned officers (JCOs) with a neighbouring infantry battalion was underway and incidentally, the CO was away as he had to attend a conference at the higher headquarters located at a distant place. The third quarter of the match was in progress and our team was apparently lagging behind. The best and most inspiring moves by the YOs in their cheerleader avatars were not inspiring enough, nor were the continuous rants of the battalion war cries by the troops. The 'josh' of our JCOs was somehow not revving up the team and at stake was the battalion's record-winning streak. Subedar Major of the paltan could not wait to see the end and sensing a certain defeat, walked away in despair towards the end of the third quarter.

At the beginning of the fourth quarter, we suddenly witnessed the famous Gypsy with the old man joining us at the venue, still in his uniform itself. The Good Lord must be aware of the flushed look full of ire on his face (ostensibly caused by brow-beating by his bosses or the appalling performance of JCOs on the scoreboard), as we could only gauge a space perfectly set for popping corns. 'Match haar gaye to phir paltan mein entry nahi milegi (If you lose the match, you will not be able to enter the battalion)' was the stern and potentially dangerous line that emanated from the CO where he was standing on the edge of the court. Red signifies *danger, and rightly so, and for sure, the superlative wisdom garnered by our JCOs with age didn't miss it at all. Voila! How could it be? A lost match was won. Subsequently, the cheer or motivation caused by that one simple line from the CO was potent enough to put the illusionary tricks of David Blaine to shame. Apple charges a hefty amount for its fast battery chargers; human battery charger . . . Any takers for the human battery charger that suddenly appeared in our team?*

Another incident which merits narration here is of a time when the parents of a young lieutenant were visiting their newly married son. With it being a typically hot and dry location, the officer made all arrangements to make his parents comfortable. However, with the limited resources at his disposal, and with his household being a typically young one, he could not ensure access to a lot of basic facilities. But the unexpected and unannounced delivery of a few curtains, a refrigerator and a desert cooler at his door pushed the officer into a delirium. It was subsequently found that the coveted items had been sent from the CO's house as a gesture of welfare and as an anticipated welcome for the young officer's parents. The parents came and stayed comfortably, happily admiring the clout of their son. After they left, the officer was painted more deeply in the olive colour of the Army! A brutally honest but financially frugal CO was difficult to deal with and impossible to convince when it came to the financial management of the unit. In his crusade to find the most viable and best transparent deals for the unit, he took the pains of sending teams comprising individuals of mixed ranks for purchasing even small items like stationery, or contacted tens of dealers and cities for procuring sports items.

One fine day we (the enabled YOs by then) decided to give a rough time to the CO (as we wanted to change the equation) wherein we decided to call on him (raid) for drinks at the odd hour of midnight. The complete bunch of YOs (already a few drinks down) was received by a groggy CO, who would probably have been half an hour into his sleep. The only remorse we had was that, in the process, we also troubled the first lady. A couple of drinks flowed, and I being the senior-most member of the raiding party, signalled a practised code for all the YOs to leave in order to end the agony of the CO. However, I, as a naïve YO, was not experienced enough to have envisaged an anticlimax. Take two—the tables had been turned.

The CO was now as fresh as a flower while all of us were groggy-eyed *(almost bordering on tears)*. 'Where is the hurry, the night is still young and so are we. *Aaye apni marzi se the, jaaoge meri marzi se (You decided when to come, I will decide when you go)*'—this diktat was delivered in such a smooth and practised tone that even the bravest of hearts among us started craving for bulletproof vests. What followed were drinks and the old man's tales of his RR days, in a disproportionate combo of sometimes five stories to a drink. The sun too had woken up from its sleep but this not-so-'old man' was not willing to give up his narration. 'Don't miss the PT parade, I will be there' was the last and most lethal weapon unleashed by him.

Kaleidoscopic glimpses of events rush past as I fast-forward time and recollect the departing moments of the CO, as he relinquished command. In some ghettoes, there was happiness, in some a little sorrow, and in a majority of them, a feeling of emptiness as a tough CO, who was a known disciplinarian, was all set to become a part of the 'Rogues' Gallery'. As a tradition, a portrait of the CO was placed in the Rogues' Gallery along with his league of predecessors. Not wanting to waste regimental money on his photograph, he clicked a few at his residence with his buddy doing the honours behind the lens. It was office time and the CO called for his adjutant (that's me) for giving an opinion regarding the most adorable self of himself that he managed to produce as a print. 'Young man, how is this? Fits the frame?' Now having been under the direct mentoring of the CO, the time was ripe for me to showcase him the product of his teachings, as I prepared myself for a professional disagreement. 'Sir, you have been such a tough CO throughout your command and now you wish to announce your departure with this adorable smiley picture of yours as a legacy. NO, it doesn't fit the frame,' was my honest reply. 'It takes a lot of heart for a young captain saheb to tell his CO what you just did, and this is what I appreciate in you, young man' came the famous 'no mincing of words' reply from Tiny Sir. So another picture was chosen and the prestigious gallery now has a portrait of Tiny Dhillon with such a stern look that he would surely be giving uneasy times to the gentlemen whose portraits hang beside his. **Who knows, he might have been thinking of the 'Ghazis' when the picture was clicked!**

The list of incidents is so long that just one chapter is not adequate to recount all of them. As I jog down memory lane, reminiscences *of all the incidents come cascading in the limited horizons of my mind and heart. It can, however, be said in conclusion that it was definitely a unique honour and privilege for us YOs to have walked our formative years in the Army, under the able stewardship and mentoring of a CO who groomed, curetted and helped us mature in a way that conformed to the rich culture, traditions and camaraderie of this great Indian Army. The repository of incidents and anecdotes which came as freebies to us was part of the multidimensional personality called 'Tiny Dhillon'.*

*I have walked enough with Tiny Sir in the jungles of Kashmir and dunes of Rajasthan, and thus I must end my story with the famous lines of Odysseus in the movie Troy (2004), 'If they ever tell my story let them say that I walked with giants. Men rise and fall like the winter wheat, but these names will never die. **Let them say I lived in the time of Hector, tamer of horses. Let them say I lived in the time of Achilles.***'*

Trying out a new weapon, Finland, 2012

Acknowledgements

'*Shukrana*' and '*Waheguru mehr*' are the evocative words that express my deep sense of gratitude and acknowledgement for the blessings of God, for it is only that which helped me relentlessly perform my duty towards the nation without fear or favour, with utmost professional integrity and diligence, a duty that I would willingly and happily fulfil again if ever the need arises.

I begin the acknowledgements for my book with a bow in reverence and an utmost feeling of pride and gratitude for all the bravehearts among my colleagues and peers who made the supreme sacrifice in the service of the nation. With prayers on my lips and pride in my heart, I salute them with a swollen chest and a promise that their sacrifices will motivate future generations in the years to come.

My first thanks, of course, goes to my wife of more than thirty-five years, Nita, and our son and daughter, who wholeheartedly supported this endeavour even at the cost of deferring the foreign sojourn post my retirement that we had planned long ago. I am also eternally thankful to my family for their understanding and quiet acceptance of the challenges of an Army life that allowed me the space to fulfil my duties with motivation and gusto throughout my service life.

I also convey my profound respects to Bijee, my maternal grandmother, and Lalli Veer (my elder brother), who were the glue that cohesively bound my childhood, imparting meaning to the life of a three-year-old boy, who had lost his mother to a tragic incident and who would have been without an anchor but for their care and comfort. It is my bad luck that they left rather early to be with the gods. Thank you, Bijee and Lalli Veer!

I would like to thank my Dad, Mom, and brothers, Sukhbir and Tejveer, for being there in my life. My heartfelt gratitude also goes out to my Mamaji, Guravtar Singh Sandhu, and Mamiji, Rashpal Sandhu, who groomed me through early childhood and stood by me as an unwavering pillar of strength. In addition, I would like to acknowledge the support of my wonderful cousins with whom I have shared precious moments during my growing-up years.

I would like to make a special mention of my father-in-law, the late S. Atma Singh Bajwa, and mother-in-law, Balbir Kaur Bajwa, for always being around for my wife and me, especially during the birth of both of our children when I could not be present due to pressing professional commitments.

The first person outside my family I would like to acknowledge is Major Gaurav Arya (Retd) as the thought of writing my memoir occurred to me for the first time during an interview I had with him for the Chanakya Forum just a few days after my superannuation in February 2022. Even as I was toying with the idea of a book, things suddenly fell into place and here we were, ready with the manuscript in less than six months thereafter.

I would like to put on record my sincerest thanks to Anupma Mehta, who helped in building this book right from its exordium with her perceptive inputs, editorial craft and research-based contributions to my story. During my various sittings with her and the patience with which she heard me extrapolate the diverse and momentous incidents in my personal and professional life, she discerned the wheat from the chaff, gradually giving concrete shape to the eventful yet brutally honest tale narrated in this book.

She, in fact, personified an eager beaver who knitted it all together at a punishing pace, enabling me to meet the stringent deadline imposed by the publishers. Indeed, without her vital association, I would not have been able to realize this dream project, which I am delighted to present before my readers.

Premanka Goswami, executive editor at Penguin Random House India, inspired me to 'give my all to the promise of an engaging book', and meticulously reviewed the draft of the book while recommending many mid-course structural changes for refining the manuscript. A big thanks to you for your earnest efforts, Premanka!

Talking of my professional life, I benefited from the unstinted support of several of my respected seniors and dear colleagues both during the initial years of my service as well as subsequently when I was the Chinar Corps Commander at the helm of affairs in Kashmir during the challenging times post the Pulwama IED blast and the abrogation of Articles 370 and 35A in August 2019. Here I would like to highlight the critical role played by Brigadier Trigunesh Mukherjee, AVSM (Retd), my first commanding officer and a veritable father figure, in continuously mentoring me over the last forty years, and still counting. He taught me the professional ethos and personal values that have not only honed my career but also deeply influenced my social and personal life. Thank you, Mukho Sir!

I was also singularly fortunate to have been groomed by the best of regimental junior commissioned officers and non-commissioned officers in the Rajputana Rifles throughout my career, right from my freshman days when I joined the Army as a second lieutenant. The names that unbiddingly come to mind are those of Subedar Major Nand Ram (Retd, 4 RAJRIF) and Subedar Major Amar Singh (Retd) of 15 RAJRIF, when I was commanding the battalion. I apologize for not mentioning the names of many others who have been instrumental in making me what I am today.

Our rigorous grooming and mentoring in 4 RAJRIF ensured uncompromising adherence to duty, which I daresay, taught me to never let my colleagues down under fire. This foundation was strengthened by the persistent guidance of all my senior officers.

My tenures in the Rashtriya Rifles have been both extremely challenging and professionally rewarding. Brigadier S.D. Nair (Retd), my commanding officer in Manipur, taught me to be strong and stolid, especially under adversity. Among all the colleagues who had my back during our numerous perilous swarming operations in the Rajwar jungles of North Kashmir, I would like to mention the then Chinar Corps Commander, Lieutenant General S.A. Hasnain (Retd) and the then General Officer Commanding Kilo Force, the late Major General Ravi Thodge.

I would be amiss if I do not express my gratitude and appreciation for my colleagues in the Chinar Corps during my tenure as 15 Corps Commander. My humblest and heartfelt thanks go out first and foremost to the late General Bipin Rawat, then my Chief and subsequently CDS, for the unflinching support he offered me after the Pulwama incident and during the build-up to and following the abrogation of Articles 370 and 35A in Kashmir. His passing away has left a deep void in my life that will never be filled.

I would like to make a special mention of the ever-so-suave and an extremely thorough professional, Lieutenant General Ranbir Singh, the Northern Army Commander, whose unwavering support and advice at crucial junctures remained the single-most 'battle-winning factor' as we metaphorically call it in the Army.

Among my Army colleagues, who were there with me on the ground during those challenging times, I would like to make a special mention of Captain Sandeep Singh, my aide de camp in the Chinar Corps. Here, without taking individual names, I would like to specially acknowledge the excellent work being done on the ground by all ranks of the Army, Jammu and Kashmir Police, Central Reserve Police Force, Border Security Force, the intelligence agencies and civil administration in Kashmir for maintaining peace and law and order there under extremely trying conditions.

Some of my closest friends and mates have made my journey worthwhile and immensely fulfilling. These include Colonel Manish Sanga and Colonel Neelgagan Singh, who, despite being young officers at the time, always guided me and offered crucial advice whenever required, without bothering about seniority or professional niceties. Jimmy Bhullar alias Major Harminder Singh Bhullar (Retd) has been my all-weather friend since my youth and early career days. Jimmy is, in fact, akin to being my 'brother from another mother'.

In ending, I have to mention our third baby, my long-time companion and pet with a royal black coat, Bolt, who was unfailingly present through all the sittings with Anupma and Premanka, and who provided quiet support, sitting curled up near my chair through the late nights when I was curating my life story. Cheers, Bolt!